Managing for
Joint Venture Success

Managing for Joint Venture Success

Kathryn Rudie Harrigan
Columbia University

Foreword by
William H. Newman

Lexington Books
D.C. Heath and Company/Lexington, Massachusetts/Toronto

Library of Congress Cataloging-in-Publication Data
Harrigan, Kathryn Rudie.
  Managing for joint venture success.

  Includes index.
  1. Joint ventures—Management. 2. Joint ventures—
United States—Management. I. Title.
HD62.47.H36 1986   658.1'8   85-45417
ISBN 0-669-11617-3 (alk. paper)

Published simultaneously in Canada
Printed in the United States of America
International Standard Book Number: 0-669-11617-3
Library of Congress Catalog Card Number: 85-45417

The paper used in this publication meets the minimum requirements of American National
Standard for Information Sciences—Permanence of Paper for Printed Library Materials,
ANSI Z39.48-1984.
∞™

The last numbers on the right below indicate the number and date of printing.

10 9 8 7 6 5 4 3 2 1

95 94 93 92 91 90 89 88 87 86

Contents

Figures and Tables

Figures

Tables

Foreword

Our enterprise system is on trial. Companies are now expected to provide sustained growth in the face of global competition and social constraints. And this pressure has fomented a search for creative ways to improve our adaptability in managing business firms.

Joint ventures provide one of the hopes. By combining strengths from two or three companies, perhaps we can find new benefits from cooperation and improve productivity. The pooling of complementary strengths in a separate, new venture is the key. Through such a device it may be possible to achieve more effective use of resources, to adjust more quickly to new technology, or to gain access to large-scale economies. Indeed, during the last few years the number of domestic joint ventures has increased sharply.

This book is the first in-depth analysis of *domestic* joint ventures. It moves far beyond a listing of situations where joint ventures might be productive—and the usual antitrust strictures on where not to step. Instead, the main focus is on where and how companies can build cooperative arrangements that enable them to make advances that they *could not make alone*.

The evidence shows, however, that a joint venture is a delicate undertaking. Tender, loving care is frequently required if the potential benefits are to be realized.

This book includes the following distinctive contributions:

1. An *analytical framework* provides prospective cooperating firms with a guide to the possible benefits and pitfalls of using joint ventures. The framework indicates important considerations for each stage from first contemplating cooperation to dissolving the partnership after it ceases to serve both parties well.

2. The viability of the joint venture itself—the *newly created entity*—is of critical importance. The cooperating companies, the owners, each has its own distinct objectives; but these objectives will be served only if the new venture is provided with enough resources and enough independence to become a sound operating unit. A joint venture must be considered as a *troika*—the venture as well as its owners.

3. Problems of operating a joint venture, after it is established, require continuing involvement. This book shows that the *interactions between the venture and each owner* are sensitive. What to share, what to protect, what is fair for each owner—such questions as these are never fully answered. Who really governs is more important than the distribution of stock ownership.

4. The *passage of time* is likely to modify what each owner wants from a specific joint venture. Partly this reflects the degree of success of the venture. However, changes in the interests, the available resources, and the relative bargaining power of each owner often sharply alter what a firm seeks. Because of this inevitable shift in the viewpoints of members of the *troika,* the analytical framework includes change over time as a critical feature of joint venture management.

5. The analysis shows that joint ventures typically are an *unstable form of organization.* Even when the venture prospers, one owner is likely to buy out the interests of the other. New alignments are fashioned. Such instability does not mean that establishing the joint venture was unwise. During its life it may have served a very useful purpose. But, at least in the domestic arena, joint ventures usually are transitional arrangements.

The exploratory nature of the research for this book flushed out many other concepts and insights. After developing the analytical framework, Harrigan tested the framework in different industries. She examined background and success of 492 specific joint ventures and 392 other cooperative arrangements, and summarizes this experience in chapters 6 through 8. No other study has analyzed the individual characteristics of such a wide array of joint ventures. Moreover, much of the existing literature focuses on foreign joint ventures whereas this investigation concentrates on U.S. domestic ventures.

Because it is exploratory, this book raises more questions than it answers. Ideas for possible action abound, but no simple formulas are presented. Rather, the book is a gold mine of information and insights; managers dealing with joint venture problems must do their own digging and sorting for guidance on their specific situation.

With this book we have a quantum increase in the available knowledge about designing and managing joint ventures.

William H. Newman
Chairman, Strategy Research Center
Graduate School of Business
Columbia University

Preface

B abies are in fashion again, and many U.S. firms are rushing to find partners with whom to form joint ventures. Even skeptical managers are being swept up by the contagious belief that joint ventures and other forms of corporate marriage will solve their problems with a handshake and the stroke of a pen. Managers hope that by teaming up with partners who offer strengths which their own firms lack, the result will be a stronger competitive posture in the markets they hope to serve.

Cooperative strategies are, in fact, as difficult to sustain and nurture as are marriages. Joint ventures need as much attention and support from their parents as do babies. Yet the benefits joint ventures and other cooperative strategies provide frequently make them well worth the extra effort of learning how to cope with the complexities of shared ownership and shared decision making.

Joint ventures enable firms to undertake activities that they could not (or prefer not) to undertake alone. For decades they have been a commonplace way of doing business in such U.S. industries as offshore oil and gas exploration, petrochemicals, mining, metals processing, and electronic components. Joint ventures are required in some industries as the price of admission into non-U.S. markets. Joint ventures and other cooperative strategies now have become popular as strategy options in a wide variety of U.S. industries, such as communications services, pharmaceuticals and medical products, steel, precision controls, robotics, financial services, entertainment programming, and programming packaging, among others, where cooperation has less of a track record. Managers in many industries are recognizing that they must learn to cope with a new competitive weapon—the joint venture.

As business risks soar and competition becomes more volatile, firms are embracing joint ventures and other forms of cooperative strategy with greater frequency. These alliances are being formed in the United States, as well as in other economies where taking partners is part of the price of admission, because the requirements for successful competition have become more demanding. Joint ventures in the United States are more widespread now due to (1) the maturation of the U.S., European, and Japanese economies; (2) leaps in communications technology; (3) shorter product lives (but larger capital requirements for successful innovation); (4) globalization of industries (where competition was previously constrained to geographic boundaries); and (5) entry by new players (supported by their respective governments), among other reasons.

This analysis of joint ventures focuses on how to assess whether cooperative strategies are appropriate for a particular firm, which partners will prove to be most attractive, and how to manage the owner–venture relationship to maximize the potential of this strategy option. It offers an analytical framework that provides prospective cooperating firms with a guide to the possible benefits and pitfalls of using joint ventures as relationships evolve from the first contemplation of cooperation to the dissolution of the partnership after it ceases to serve all parties well. It offers a unique analysis of how to ensure the viability of the venture itself—the newly created entity. It suggests how to operate the joint venture over time and provides timely and unique guidance for forging, changing, terminating, and making the most of joint venture relationships.

Step-by-step, the analytical framework explores issues concerning cooperation:

The benefits (and pitfalls) of cooperation.

The advantages (and disadvantages) of some cooperative strategy alternatives.

Which synergies can be realized in joint ventures (and which expectations are not realistic).

What types of cooperative strategies have proven most useful for diverse competitive environments.

How to select potential joint-venture partners and negotiate insightful working agreements.

What trade-off between complete operating autonomy and an enforced buyer–seller relationship works best in various competitive settings.

Which "control mechanisms" best provide sponsoring firms with the feedback necessary to recognize when their joint venture needs modification without stifling the venture's initiative and viability as an operating entity.

How best to transfer knowledge, resources, and personnel between owners and venture to maximize the advantages of the cooperative strategy option.

How diverse management styles can smooth the interface between owners and between owners and their venture.

How to determine when the cooperation agreement no longer suits the conditions it was forged to remedy.

This book is unique because it exposes the reader to the diverse viewpoints of all parties to the joint venture. It offers an analysis of what has worked well in joint ventures (and what has not) and *why* some ways of cooperating are better than others in particular situations. The analytical framework offers a way to evaluate the potential for attaining various benefits of cooperation in light of each potential partner's business mix, industry, and management culture. Special insights provide information on how to manage technological joint ventures, how to diffuse information among parties to joint ventures, and how to recognize when terms sponsoring firms insist on will prove to be debilitating to the venture's potential for success. The framework facilitates predictions concerning how the stakes of successful competition may be consciously changed to a firm's advantage through skillful use of cooperative strategies.

Joint ventures (and other forms of cooperation) are an important change in the way that firms do business. They require a different approach to management by virtue of their complexity. If managed skillfully, joint ventures offer sponsoring firms a wider range of strategic flexibility than they could hope to develop by going it alone.

Acknowledgments

F unding for travel, telephone interviews, research assistants, and typing was made possible by grants from the Strategy Research Center and the Committee on Faculty Research, Columbia Business School. Thanks to Dean John C. Burton for this generous assistance. I am especially grateful to the corporations that support the Strategy Research Center; their funding greatly facilitates our scholarly investigations of strategic management issues.

Enthusiastic research assistants at Columbia Business School collected photocopies and background materials for each industry examined in this book. My assistants include Holly Wallace, M.B.A. 1983 (of Teleport Communications), Elizabeth J. Gordon, M.B.A. 1983 (of Norton Company), John Richardson Thomas, M.B.A. 1983 (of Topaz, Inc.), Mary Ellen Waller, M.B.A. 1982, and Stanley Seth, M.B.A. 1983. Special thanks are due to Harold Hamman Martin, J.D., M.B.A. 1982 (of Shearman & Sterling) for legal research assistance and to Carlos Garcia, M.B.A. 1984 (of Pfizer, Inc.) for computer programming and other valuable assistance.

Nida T. Backaitis and John G. Michel, doctoral candidates at Columbia University, deserve extraordinary recognition as research assistants, for they carried the burden of exhausting hours of photocopying, assembling industry briefing papers, and providing helpful summaries of these materials to supplement my field interviews. John and Nida are also much appreciated for their labors as my teaching assistants, for they ensured that I was well prepared to teach my M.B.A.-level business policy classes, as well as my M.B.A.-level and doctoral-level seminars on competitive strategy.

Many colleagues helped me by providing materials, suggestions, and comments on the manuscript at various stages of its development. At the risk of slighting helpful questions and other academic assistance received, I thank in particular William H. Newman, Samuel Bronfman Professor of Democratic Business Enterprise and Chairman of the Strategy Research Center (Emeritus), for his valuable ideas on how to improve every chapter and his encouraging comments all through this research program, and Donald C.

Hambrick. I thank my colleagues at Columbia, Robert Drazin, James W. Fredrickson, Leonard Sayles, Michael Tushman, E. Kirby Warren, Samuel Bronfman Professor of Democratic Business Enterprise, and Bob Yavitz, Paul Garrett Professor of Public Policy and Business Responsibility, for their comments on my manuscript. I thank Richard E. Caves and Michael E. Porter of Harvard University, Sanford Berg of the University of Florida, Jerome Duncan of the University of Manitoba, Barry Haimes (Kidder, Peabody), Richard Rumelt, William Ouchi, Mitchell P. Koza and Srinivasan "Cheenu" Balakrishnan of the University of California at Los Angeles, Henry Mintzberg of McGill University, Robert Dickie, Ted Murray, Farshad Rafii, Liam Fahey, Ken Hatten, and Anil Gupta of Boston University, John R. Schermerhorn, Jr., of Southern Illinois University, Cynthia Spanhel of the University of Texas, Ram Charan, and Milton Handler of Kaye Scholer, Fierman, Hays & Handler for their contributions of materials and suggestions.

Dr. Mary Anne Devanna, the administrator of the Strategy Research Center's funds, and Gayle Lane managed the financial details of this study. Maxine Braiterman, Maureen Gelber, and Lisa Lowell typed endless versions of this (and the earlier) manuscript under great time pressures while maintaining their sense of humor. Lydia Fatjo-Santiago remained composed and efficient as she managed the spider's web of telephone messages we created. Carol Landes and Linda Brodzinski in the Office of Support Services provided extra helpers—additional typing, transcribing, and telephone assistance for which I am grateful. Most notably, I am grateful for the help of Joy Glazener, the superstar who typed original manuscripts, transcribed tapes, input industry studies into my personal computer, coordinated the mailings, synchronized the photocopying with my eleventh-hour demands, immersed herself in the word processing challenge and performed other herculean tasks to ensure the manuscripts's timely completion. With this book, Joy learned yet another word processing system with the same grace and willingness to be helpful that has contributed to the timely completion of my other books.

This study could not have been completed without the assistance and information provided by many executives (who must remain anonymous). They completed my questionnaires, answered my telephone questions, unearthed archival data, commented on several versions of background papers, chapter drafts and other materials, and granted me their precious time for personal interviews and for other tasks associated with the Delphi study. Their feedback has been extremely useful in clarifying points about the use of joint-venture strategies. I commend their enthusiasm in responding to each iteration and their willingness to help academic researchers study complex and sensitive topics in strategic management. I especially thank Renata Karlin (*Business Week* Executive Programs), Harry Ashbridge (Control Data), Howard Harris (Montedison) and James Fiedler (MCA-DiscoVision Associates) for sharing their joint ventures' experiences at the 1985 *Business Week* Conference on Corporate Survival Strategies.

Don Hambrick was extraordinarily helpful in reading chapter drafts and giving me timely and constructive criticism. I especially thank him for suggesting the diagram for figure 3–5. I commend his willingness to help junior researchers, for Don's example sets the tone for colleagial behavior that makes the Columbia Business School a leading forum for research in management.

Again I acknowledge the enormous intellectual debt owed to William H. Newman, a paragon and pioneer in the field of strategic management. As Director and Chairman of the Strategy Research Center, he funded my research. As a colleague, Bill always found time to give me great ideas and thoughtful, detailed comments on chapter drafts (even under impossible timetables). Chapters 3, 4, and 5 have improved markedly through exposure to Bill's ideas. I especially thank him for suggesting many of the figures in these chapters. Bill's unabashed enthusiasm for this research effort and for the idea of doing research is inspiring to young faculty. His candor in giving feedback concerning findings and their presentation greatly accelerated the progress of my work. Bill's zeal in finding a clear way to explain a complex model has been both encouraging and awe-inspiring.

The Columbia Business School and its Management of Organizations faculty are uniquely positioned to support empirical research in Strategic Management. I have benefited greatly from exposure to its culture. Flaws in this manuscript are mine alone; excellence is due to the splendid colleagues, the generous support, and the many other virtues of Columbia University.

1
Domestic Joint Ventures

A s business risks and competition become more volatile, firms are embracing cooperative ventures with increasing frequency. This pattern is not surprising. Joint ventures have long been used by entrepreneurial firms to expand into new businesses and to tap new markets, particularly in industrializing nations. What is surprising, however, is a pattern that indicates that cooperative ventures are now being used voluntarily as a strategy option within mature economies such as that of the United States. Joint ventures have become a way to diversify, enter new markets, introduce new products, acquire process (or product) technologies, expand (or shrink) productive capacity, and integrate vertically, among other activities, all within a firm's home market.

This new use of joint ventures is a change in corporate practice that has not been chronicled adequately, resulting in a shortfall in the strategic management literature that reflects a serious weakness in what managers know about cooperative strategies. Investigations into the efficacy of joint ventures (and other forms of cooperative strategy) are especially timely now that some governments have taken a friendlier attitude toward the use of cooperative ventures.[1] Moreover, cooperative strategies can change industry structures in a manner that could lead to significant changes in competitive behavior. Their widespread use could exacerbate competition or stabilize profit levels, depending on how domestic joint ventures are lawfully used.

This chapter sketches how the use of joint ventures (and other cooperative strategies outlined in the appendix) has changed over time and why this strategy is now of increasing interest in a firm's home market. Chapter 1 also presents an overview of the theory presented in chapters 3, 4, and 5 that was tested using industry examples.[2]

Joint Ventures in Mature Economies

Analyses of joint ventures often have considered cooperative strategies from the perspective of firms that were expanding their domains overseas.[3] U.S.

firms entering overseas markets frequently had to take local firms as partners. Asymmetries in such partners' resources, technologies, managerial systems, and experience translated into asymmetrical managerial control over the ventures in these cases, although proceeds were split among partners in proportion to equity shares or other agreed-upon bases. Decision making was not truly shared in their joint ventures; one partner frequently took a passive role. (In earlier studies, passive partners often were considered the *best* joint-venture partners; they caused fewer hassles.[4])

However, when cooperative ventures are entered into voluntarily and are meant to be *more* than merely risk-sharing or financing arrangements, strategists must leave behind the old view of them as inadequate. A different set of issues becomes germane when shared decision making and ownership is considered as a strategic option. Past studies, for example, have devoted little attention to the use of ventures as a competitive weapon in mature economies. They overlooked the use of joint ventures as a new approach to global competition, technology transfer, or other strategic challenges. There has been no discussion of whether the presence of different competitive circumstances or environmental conditions make the use of joint ventures more (or less) appropriate as a strategy option. Little thought has been given to the question of how domestic firms in mature economies might best respond to the plethora of new alliances they may face as competitors if the use of joint ventures becomes widespread. The issue of joint-venture viability has received scant attention.[5]

These questions are of interest because analyses of different competitive practices (like those of Japanese firms, for example) have revealed differing attitudes toward interfirm cooperation than those traditionally harbored by western competitors. There is curiosity regarding whether such cooperative strategies are in any way superior to how firms usually approach competitive strategy formulation and many managers are wrestling with the evaluation of the pros and cons of joint ventures in their home markets. The news media make the recent burst of joint-venture announcements within the United States look like a stampede. Consequently, novice firms are plunging into cooperative strategies without looking at the pitfalls these strategies may entail. These problems arise because few firms based in countries with mature economies used domestic joint ventures prior to the 1980s. Firms forging first-time alliances in such economies are often unaware of the strategic issues surrounding cooperative ventures.

Joint Venture Defined

Joint ventures are separate entities with two or more active firms as partners. The examples used to illustrate the joint-venture strategy framework of chapters 3, 4, and 5 are those of firms cooperating in ventures to serve the U.S.

marketplace, regardless of partners' national origins. Several cooperative arrangements other than joint ventures are discussed in the appendix, but the primary focus of this book is on those ventures that create a distinct entity with its own assets and management team.

Operating Joint Ventures. This book concentrates on *operating joint ventures*—partnerships in which two or more firms create a separate entity to carry out a productive economic activity and take an *active* role in its strategic decision making, if not also in its operating decisions. Not included are passive financial investments made by parties not involved in the new entity's strategic business decisions. Thus, most real estate partnerships are excluded. Limited partnerships undertaken to drill for oil or make movies are also excluded.

Like the joint ventures U.S. firms undertake overseas, access to distribution networks is of most importance among the resources actively involved owners contribute to their ventures. (If neither partner controls such access, the likelihood of success for the joint venture will be reduced, as is explained in chapters 3, 4, and 5.) Access to local markets is a necessary ingredient for success and historically has been the primary motivation of U.S. joint ventures overseas.

Suggestions concerning joint venture success could also be applied to cross-manufacturing arrangements (for example, the 1976 agreement among McDonnell-Douglas, Boeing, Dassault-Brequêt Aerospace, Mitsubishi, Kawasaki, and Fuji to make jets) and cross-distribution arrangements (for example, between Hoffman-LaRoche and Glaxo to sell the latter's antiulcer drug Zantac in the United States) as well as research and development arrangements (such as the Microelectronics and Computer Technology Corp., or HP Genenchem, which is owned by Hewlett-Packard and Genentech). These guidelines apply to any venture where each partner makes a substantial managerial as well as equity contribution in the form of physical assets, capital technology, marketing experience, and personnel.

Spider's Web Joint Ventures. *Spider's web ventures* link many firms to one pivotal partner. Depending on the needs of each partner and the sensitivity of information and resources to be exchanged, a firm could forge a variety of patterns for cooperation to keep competitors at bay while strengthening its own position. In this manner, a smaller firm might establish ventures with several different large firms to form a counterbalancing pattern of agreements. Thus, managers can hedge their bets concerning which firms will eventually attain dominance in a particular industry. The spider's web of ventures is the opposite of a strategy whereby a firm picks the future industry champion early and bets all resources on it to get an "exclusive" joint-venture relationship. Powerful firms can form spider's webs of ventures with themselves at the hub of the web, holding their partners to exclusive partnerships with them alone. Chapters 3, 4, and 5 suggest when firms that could enforce monogamous relationships should let their partners practice polygamy instead.

An Emphasis on the Venture. The joint-venture framework of this book emphasizes the viability of the venture, the entity created by partners for a specific activity. This topic needs investigation because insufficient thought was given to making the venture capable of standing on its own in many U.S. ventures that failed (or never came to fruition). The nature of owners' relationships with their venture is important to joint-venture success, but, as chapter 3 explains, owners must sometimes make certain adjustments to their own strategies in order to make their cooperative venture into a viable competitor in its respective marketplace. I argue that the dynamics of partnership relationships, which sometimes dominate joint-venture negotiations, should be subordinated to issues of competitive strategy. Preconceived notions about the competition must be reworked to recognize the interdependencies that may exist (and may be exploited) among the owners of joint ventures (and between owners and their venture) when managers face competitors with several strong backers.

Other Forms of Cooperative Strategy

In addition to joint ventures, cooperative strategies could encompass several arrangements that range from just short of acquisitions (when one firm absorbs most of the stock of another) to informal agreements to work together where firms pool their resources and knowledge. As table A–1 indicates, cooperative strategy alternatives can differ in their proportions of shared ownership equity and control over joint activities.

Some firms attain their objectives through *wholly owned* business units that have been obtained (or developed) through mergers, acquisitions, or successful programs for internal venture development. These arrangements give firms *full equity ownership* of assets and skills, as well as full responsibility for the risks they face when diversifying.

At the other extreme in table A-1 are nonequity arrangements such as cooperative agreements, R&D partnerships, cross-licensing (or cross-distribution agreements), and other joint activities. These arrangements do not create a separate entity, and they involve no shared equity ownership. Consequently, they provide the least control over the assets and skills firms may seek. Between these extremes are minority investments and operating joint ventures, options that give firms partial equity control of the resources needed to diversify. Shared equity arrangements may provide for contractual controls over operations as well, but only joint ventures will create new entities with the potential to exploit shared ownership and shared managerial controls.

The benefits and costs of joint-venture strategies are contrasted with non-equity ventures in the appendix.

Joint Venture as a Key Strategic Decision

The decision to enter into a joint venture (or another form of cooperative strategy) is a key competitive strategy decision, but, despite its importance, has not been well understood. Managers need guidelines to cope with joint ventures if they expect to use this strategy effectively. They need a calculus to help them make the cost–benefit tradeoffs with which they are confronted when evaluating joint-venture proposals. Managers must understand the forces that increase the value of a joint venture (or accelerate its dissolution) so they can manage these forces to their best advantage. They must also realize how their parochial concerns may prevent joint ventures from being viable. These, and other issues concerning joint-venture strategies, are explored in this book.

A New Look at Joint Ventures

To set the stage for the framework presented in chapters 3, 4, and 5, a historical view of domestic joint ventures is contrasted with how firms now use joint ventures and other cooperative strategies in mature economies such as that of the United States. Briefly, firms use ventures differently than they have in the past because they have found that joint ventures offer better ways to cope with the competitive challenges of rapid technological change and increased interdependencies in some industries than venturing alone does.

A Brief History

In the past, joint ventures were defined in law as partnerships. (Many early studies of joint ventures did not distinguish between active and passive partners; few were interested specifically in how joint ventures were managed.) Some early ventures were firms whose stocks were owned by at least two other firms and that engaged in a business different from that of their owners (even if the difference was merely geographical). Sometimes joint venture were incorporated and issued their own securities.

Joint ventures originated as commercial or maritime enterprises used for trading purposes. They were one of the oldest ways of transacting business and originally were used as a commercial device by the merchants of ancient Egypt, Babylonia, Phoenicia, and Syria to conduct sizable commercial and trading operations, often overseas. Subsequently, joint ventures were used by the merchants of Great Britain in the fifteenth and sixteenth centuries, and companies of leisure class adventurers were organized through such ventures to carry on trade and to exploit the resources of various corners of the globe such as the Americas and India.[6]

Use of cooperative ventures in the United States dates back at least to 1880 when railroads used them for large-scale projects. Mining partnerships may be even older. Early in the twentieth century, joint ventures were formed to pool risks in shipping, gold exploration, and other undertakings. One of the largest projects ever to be conducted as a joint venture involved the apportionment and development of crude oil reserves in the Middle East by four U.S. oil companies in ARAMCO.[7] During the 1950s, joint ventures became more popular as vehicles for U.S. business enterprise, and by 1959 at least 345 domestic joint ventures were operated by the 1,000 largest U.S. corportions.[8] These early joint ventures were often vertical arrangements undertaken by two or more competitors to share the outputs of a supplying facility. Firms shared their supplier's capacity because the minimum efficient scale of an upstream plant often was so large that no firm could utilize its full output alone. Moreover, there were substantial scale *diseconomies* in running these plants below their engineered capacities.

Joint ventures have become a way of life for some U.S. industries such as offshore oil exploration or the manufacture of jet engines. Joint ventures of all types bound in the entertainment industry: co-production in motion pictures and television, joint production of phonograph records, joint holdings of theaters, jointly owned videotape programming producers and/or programming distribution firms, videodisc hardware and software manufacturers, and so on. When the Federal Trade Commission (FTC) examined U.S. joint ventures during the 1960s, it found that 66 percent of them were in the manufacturing sectors, with 72 percent of that subset in four industry groups: paper products (SIC 26); chemicals (SIC 28); stone, clay, and glass (SIC 32); and primary metals (SIC 33). Over half of the FTC's list was comprised of chemical ventures, and 90 percent of them were engaged primarily in the production of fibers, plastics, and rubbers (SIC 282), basic chemicals (SIC 281), or drugs and medicines (SIC 283).[9] During the years 1960 to 1968, the FTC reported that at least 1,131 U.S. firms were involved in the formation of over 520 domestic joint ventures, and that these were primarily in the manufacturing sector. By the mid-1980s, many U.S. joint ventures were in service industries such as financial services and entertainment programming, among others.

The experiences of U.S. firms in forming and managing domestic cooperative strategies are few when compared with those of firms based in the European Economic Community (EEC). (It is difficult to compare the venturing experiences of U.S. firms with those of European firms because records of the exact number of domestic EEC joint ventures are not highly reliable; one effort to register such arrangements flooded regulators' offices with between 60,000 and 120,000 notifications of joint-venture activity.)[10] U.S. firms are just now beginning to consider the evidence concerning the attractiveness of joint-venture strategies.

An Explosion in Joint Venture Activity

Since 1978 the use of joint ventures within mature economies has blossomed due to the many technological and economic changes that precipitated deregulation, globalization, and increasing emphasis on the need for product innovation. In 1983 alone the number of cooperative strategies announced in some industries, such as communications systems and services, exceeded the sum of all previously announced U.S. ventures in that sector, as table 1–1 illustrates. By the mid-1980s domestic joint ventures had become an important means of supplementing strengths and covering weaknesses of firms in mature economies. The willingness of managers to contemplate cooperative strategies where previously they did not do so represented a watershed in their way of thinking about competitive strategy. It also raised a warning flag for firms whose managers had not yet considered the implications of this strategy option. (The other new trend in domestic joint-venture practice during this era was the unwillingness of U.S. owners to take passive roles in governing their ventures.)

More joint ventures and other forms of cooperative strategy undoubtedly will be launched in the United States in the wake of increasingly rapid rates of technological change, deregulation, and globalization. As boundaries blur between industries—especially where the enhanced capabilities of information processing and data transmission technologies link together formerly disparate products and competitors—managers need to understand how changes like these will affect their need for joint ventures.[11]

Given that interfirm cooperation has suddenly become prevalent in certain competitive environments, it would seem that managers need a way to consider what effect this structural change will have on their industries, on their firms, and on the new ways in which their firms must compete. For example, it is doubtful that military aircraft will be made or sold in the future without the assistance of partners. Cooperation is becoming mandatory in the automotive industry. Risky ventures, like satellite comunications, coal gasification, or other undertakings involving costly and untried technologies such as genetic engineering, are the inevitable forums where many types of joint ventures will occur.[12] In light of this, managers need a new way of thinking about cooperative ventures as a strategy option. As economic growth slows, markets shrink or become crowded, and technological change accelerates to speeds at which individual firms cannot recover their initial investments alone, a new language of cooperation (not warfare) is mandatory. Otherwise, firms may encounter difficulties in delivering adequate value to their

Table 1–1
Announced Joint Ventures per Year

Industry	Pre-1969	1970	1971	1972	1973	1974	1975	1976
Coal extraction	—	—	1	1	—	3	1	7
Oil extraction	2	1	—	2	2	4	2	5
Alternative energy (includes synthetic fuels)	2	1	—	1	—	4	2	4
Other mining activities	2	—	2	1	1	—	—	6
Food processing	1	1	1	1	—	1	2	2
Pulp and paper	—	—	—	—	1	1	1	1
Printing, publishing	—	—	—	1	—	—	1	1
Chemicals	1	2	1	1	1	3	3	10
Pharmaceuticals and cosmetics	1	1	—	—	—	—	1	1
Medical products	1	—	—	1	1	—	1	1
Metals processing	1	1	—	1	—	2	—	2
Steel	—	—	—	—	—	1	2	1
Metals fabrication	2	—	—	—	—	—	—	2
Light machinery	—	—	—	—	—	—	—	—
Heavy machinery	—	—	1	1	—	—	—	5
Engines	1	—	—	—	—	2	—	—
Automotive	—	—	1	—	—	—	—	1
Aerospace	—	—	—	1	—	—	1	—
Electronic components	1	—	—	2	—	—	—	1
Electronic equipment	—	1	—	—	1	—	—	3
Precision controls	—	—	—	—	—	—	—	—
Robotics	—	—	—	—	—	—	—	—
Software	—	1	—	1	—	1	—	1
Computers and peripherals	—	—	—	—	—	—	1	1
Electronic consumer products	—	—	—	—	—	—	—	—
Videotape and videodisc	—	—	—	—	—	—	—	—
Photocopy and office equipment	—	1	—	—	—	—	1	1
Electrical equipment	—	—	1	—	—	—	—	1
Communications equipment	—	—	1	—	2	1	1	2
Motion pictures	—	—	—	2	—	—	—	—
Programming, cable communications	1	1	2	1	—	—	—	2
Cable communications services	—	—	—	2	—	—	—	—
Communications systems and services	—	—	—	—	—	—	—	—
Financial services	—	1	2	—	4	9	2	4
Advertising services	—	—	—	—	—	—	—	—
Pipelines	2	—	—	—	—	—	2	—
Database services	—	—	—	—	—	—	—	—
Leasing services	—	—	—	—	—	—	—	—
Wholesaling, retailing, distribution	—	—	—	—	—	—	—	—
Other services	—	—	—	—	—	—	—	—
Totals	18	14	13	20	13	31	23	65

1977	1978	1979	1980	1981	1982	1983	1984	Totals
2	1	1	3	3	na	na	na	23
3	4	1	3	1	na	na	na	30
3	3	—	5	5	na	na	na	30
4	1	—	1	1	1	—	—	20
1	—	1	3	na	na	na	na	14
4	2	—	3	na	na	na	na	13
—	2	—	3	1	na	na	na	9
5	7	4	6	3	4	27	1	79
3	1	1	—	8	1	3	5	26
1	3	1	1	3	—	4	5	23
2	1	2	1	—	1	1	—	15
—	1	1	—	—	1	1	7	15
2	3	3	2	1	—	4	—	19
—	—	—	2	—	—	7	—	9
4	2	2	1	2	—	7	—	25
1	—	1	2	1	—	4	7	19
1	1	2	2	2	—	6	1	17
1	—	1	1	—	1	6	—	12
1	—	1	—		2	5	9	22
—	2	1	1	—	—	2	na	11
—	1	3	—	1	1	1	1	8
—	—	—	—	2	2	2	4	10
2	1	—	3	5	—	8	4	27
—	2	2	2	—	—	3	8	19
—	—	—	—	—	—	4	—	4
—	—	1	4	1	5	—	1	12
—	1	2	—	2	—	2	1	11
1	3	1	1	1	1	1	—	11
2	—	1	2	—	3	20	17	52
—	1	—	2	—	1	4	—	10
1	1	—	—	3	7	10	3	32
1	1	1	6	4	9	7	3	34
—	—	—	—	1	10	53	3	67
3	7	1	2	2	2	36	18	93
—	—	—	—	—	1	4	na	5
1	2	—	—	—	1	na	na	8
—	—	—	—	—	—	10	1	11
—	1	—	—	1	—	2	na	4
—	—	—	1	—	—	10	na	11
1	3	1	—	—	—	15	na	20
50	58	36	63	54	54	269	99	880

customers, replenishing their base of skills, and safeguarding their abilities to increase long-term shareholder value.

A Paradox

This book is the result of the observation of a paradox. Joint ventures (and other forms of economic cooperation) are being formed in settings where firms choose to cooperate *without* duress from sovereign governments. Where regulations prevented joint activities, some managers lobbied for relaxation of these constraints so that they might form joint ventures. However, despite their apparent eagerness for the freedom to cooperate, many managers seem to pursue a knee-jerk approach to such strategies; they jump in without thinking through their motivations for cooperation or how the venture will fit with the ongoing activities of the firm or into its scheme for strategy implementation. Integration has rarely occurred (or has occurred badly). An adversarial attitude among owners (as well as between owners and their ventures) has replaced some of the zeal of true entrepreneurial efforts to cooperate. These tensions show little sign of abating because U.S. managers are not inclined to accept a *passive* role in siring and rearing cooperative ventures when they operate within the United States. Managers must find a way to sort through the tensions of shared decision making if this strategy option is to succeed.

A Global Challenge

For some applications, cooperative ventures must have more of the feverish intensity of underdogs trying to break into closed (but attractive) markets and less of the opportunistic coupling (and uncoupling) behavior that has characterized recent joint-venture arrangements. Deregulation, the electronics and communications revolution, and blurring national industry boundaries make all firms vulnerable to the threats posed by cooperative strategies. As they evaluate whether (and how) their firms should cooperate in forming joint ventures in such settings, managers must make a variety of tradeoffs among gaining new skills, entering new industries, helping their nations' domestic economies (by creating or saving jobs), creating new competitors, or risking the atrophy of in-house capabilities by relying on partners and ventures to perform some tasks. Since joint-venture partners could include domestic competitors, local firms who are new to the venture's industry or foreign firms (who may already be competitors in the venture's industry), the tradeoffs involved in choosing joint-venture partners should be evaluated in the context of global competition as well as in simple competitive terms.

As the national champions in the maturing markets of Japan, the EEC, and the United States seek new markets to conquer, the challenge of learning to use domestic joint ventures effectively becomes even more acute—for these competitors see the greatest payoffs in invading each other's markets. One of the most important new uses firms can make of cooperative ventures is in forging global strategies within mature economies. (*Global strategies* are those that recognize that competition can no longer be confined to a single nation's boundaries.)[13] Integrating the wholly owned, partially owned, and cooperatively coordinated business units of a firm within a global system poses a major strategic and managerial challenge for the future.

In the past, most cooperative ventures involving U.S. firms were regarded as a means to enter *foreign* markets; they were not considered a part of the network of business units that firms used to cope with worldwide competition, and they were especially not used in domestic markets. Managers now must consider this additional use for joint ventures. *This is a novel way for U.S. firms to think about their use of cooperative strategies.* Although firms will often think of production scale economies, technological innovation, and new sourcing arrangements as a means of meeting their oncoming challenges, fewer managers may recognize the potential advantages of joint ventures. This myopia may be due in part to the way such ventures have been used historically by U.S. firms. It may also be due in part to a recognition of the many difficulties inherent in coordinating the activities of cooperative ventures with those of its owners if the venture is to stand alone as a viable economic entity.

Questions Regarding Joint-Venture Strategies

If managers are to use joint ventures effectively, they need a way to assess the best partners for their firms, and they need guidelines on how to manage relationships with their venture. Cooperative relationships will be most effective if managers can spark (and sustain) some chemistry between partners to the venture. Because making ventures work is largely a matter of managing the chemistry among partners, their venture, and the industry in which it will compete, managers must discover how they can best enhance the benefits of these relationships within their joint ventures. Because cooperative ventures tend to last no longer (often less) than they must in order to obtain their owners' strategic purposes, managers need a way of telling in advance if joint-venture chemistries between their firm and a potential partner are likely to succeed or if the chemistry is not well matched.

Strategic Symmetry—Resource Asymmetries

Symmetry occurs when partners possess complementary strategic missions, resource capabilities, managerial capabilities, and other attributes that have a strategic fit such that the relative bargaining power of the partners is evenly matched. Symmetry of need to be engaged in ventures is a stabilizing force, for example, as is agreement among partners in their vision for the joint venture.

Assymmetry develops when attributes are not complementary or bargaining power is unevenly matched. Asymmetries in the speed with which partners want to exploit an opportunity, the direction in which they want to move, or in other strategic matters are especially *destabilizing* to joint ventures. If managers are to use cooperative strategies effectively, all parties—managers within the partners' firms and managers within the venture—must understand how asymmetries in skills, resources, and objectives will affect the joint venture's ability to thrive or languish. Moreover, managers must develop ways to nurture good relationships among owners and between owners and their ventures to reduce the effects of tensions from asymmetries created by exogenous forces such as those covered in chapter 3.

Reasonable Expectations

Experience in using domestic joint ventures in the United States has been limited, therefore, it is not yet clear which objectives managers can reasonably expect to achieve through cooperative strategies. But it has been estimated that over half of the cooperative ventures forged since 1975 were ill-conceived at birth because the objectives of the joint venture were unclear, because owners' capabilities were poorly matched, or because owners aspired to achieve more than was possible in the industries in which their joint venture competed. Managers recognize that their ventures must compete in hostile industries in the 1980s, but they need to understand why some industry conditions will make the use of joint ventures more risky than others. They need to understand why joint ventures can achieve better performance in some environments than in others. Managers must also be able to recognize whether their particular joint venture was well conceived and whether its implementation is well timed. Does their firm gain a first-mover advantage by venturing now? Is it necessary to venture early to overcome the advantages of those stronger rivals that often enter late?

Timing

Timing is an important part of effective joint-strategy formulation in situations where environments change rapidly, because firms that move first often can gain access to better partners, which in turn can give them a competitive advantage that late entrants could not capture as easily. Moreover, managers need to understand how the evolution of an industry's structural conditions (and competitive conduct) can make ventures seem more (or less) attractive, as in the example of petrochemical joint ventures, which were previously vertically related to their owners, as contrasted with the horizontally related petrochemical joint ventures of the 1980s that rationalize productive capacity. Managers must be able to recognize the penalties for entering cooperative ventures in home markets too late (as in the example of the automobile industry, where the best partners may already have been taken) as well as the penalties for holding on to a particular form of venture too long (as in the example of Skagg-Albertson's combination of food and drug stores). Managers must consider *whether* moving early through joint ventures will offer their firms opportunities to create synergies. Managers must consider whether early joint ventures help would-be competitors *too much* by performing missionary tasks to create demand, just as they would contemplate the timing of any other type of early entry and/or diversification investment. Finally, managers must consider *when* they could best leverage the relationship between joint venture and owner to strengthen their firm's competitive advantage.

In summary, managers need to understand how joint ventures can help them supplement internal resources and capabilities to build strengths and bargaining power by responding faster to competitive challenges. They need to realize whether cooperative ventures can create synergies—through vertical relationships or by sharing resources—and what limitations will be placed on the synergies they desire by the venture's needs for operating autonomy. If joint ventures and other cooperative strategies are helpful in solving technological problems and increasing value-added margins, managers need to realize how they can best enhance these sources of competitive advantage. Managers must understand how to use constructively the inevitable technological bleedthrough that occurs among joint-venture partners to their respective best advantage, as well as how to overcome the "not-invented-here" jealousies of personnel within wholly owned business units when transferring technology between owner and venture. Finally, managers must be able to assess which firms are the right partners in each of the diverse competitive environments they face, and they must learn to manage their relationships with these partners as carefully as they would manage other treasured corporate resources.

Managers need a framework to use in assessing whether their joint venture is realizing the best potential of this strategy option or whether something is awry. The effective use of joint-venture strategies requires managers to consider many questions about cooperative strategies that have been unanswered until now. Several forces (that previous empirical studies have never addressed) contribute to the differences between well-formulated ventures and those that fail. Chapters 3, 4, and 5 detail those forces in a framework that has been tested using industry studies.

Overview

Joint ventures will be increasingly important in the development of new industries, the revitalization of mature industries, the rationalization of a firm's portfolio, and the enhancement of a firm's competitive advantages. Given the accelerating pace of industry evolution and the increasing interdependencies among players within previously independent industries, managers must evaluate *all* of their strategy options carefully, including cooperative strategies.

Given the importance of joint-venture strategies and the many unanswered questions remaining, there is a need for a rigorous inquiry that distinguishes among environments where ventures might be undertaken with varying expectations for success. It is important to recognize that firms have varying strategic objectives, strengths, and other important differences that will temper their choices of which industries to enter, which joint-venture partners to choose, how to manage their ventures, and other decisions concerning cooperative strategies. It is also important to recognize the nature of those differences that push partners apart and divide their venture's loyalties among owners at times when all actors should be working together for mutual gain. Finally, it is important to distill the experiences of managing joint ventures into patterns that suggest which cooperative arrangements are most likely to prosper and to relate these patterns to a framework for creating and managing ventures successfully.

This book offers such patterns and frameworks. Chapter 2 reviews the benefits managers seek in forming cooperative strategies. Chapters 3, 4, and 5 (representing the relationships among owners, between owners and venture, and between the venture and its environment, respectively) develop a theory of joint-venture formulation, operation, and termination. These chapters construct a framework of the dynamics of partners' motives, strengths, and behaviors in working with each other (and with their ventures) as these must be tempered by the particular success requirements of the venture's competitive environment.

Three levels of analysis are presented: the linkages of owners to their joint venture, the linkages of owners to each other, and the special attributes endowed on the joint-venture entity in its own right to make it an effective industry competitor. This analytical approach is appropriate because it incorporates the capabilities that each owner brings to competition in a potentially alien industry as well as the synergies that may be created by joining with partners in a joint venture.

Chapter 6 summarizes findings concerning owner-venture relationships, and chapter 7 focuses on the use of joint ventures as technological change agents. Chapter 8 is devoted to guidelines for creating and managing joint-venture relationships.

This inquiry concerning the effective use of domestic joint ventures coincides with a decrease in the expected life of technological innovations and an increased blurring of industry boundaries. The insights it offers should be of interest to managers who contemplate joint ventures as well as those who face jointly owned competitors.

2
Motives for Joint-Venture Formation and Termination

M uch has been written about the use of joint ventures (and other cooperative strategies) as risk-sharing arrangements, but it has been largely descriptive, not analytical. It has not addressed questions concerning *what makes for an effective domestic joint-venture strategy,* such as why managers should consider using them, what advantages can be captured through cooperation, and why domestic ventures have been avoided until recently in many U.S. industries. Much has been written about why such ventures seem unattractive (even when legal barriers do not prohibit their use), but little has been written about *how these drawbacks might be overcome* while still maximizing the benefits of cooperative ventures.

To understand why domestic joint ventures have not worked well in the past, we must review what managers hoped to attain by their use. This chapter will consolidate and summarize joint-venture concepts used in earlier studies. It takes the form of a literature review. Some of the uses researchers found for joint ventures are summarized in table 2–1. New uses for cooperative ventures are also suggested in the table, and these competitive and strategic uses anticipate the material contained in chapters 3, 4, and 5 that deals with vital aspects of joint ventures that have yet received scant attention. These issues provide the basis for the analytical model that is developed in the next three chapters. Thus, chapter 2 anticipates questions (covered in chapter 3) concerning how firms should combine their strengths with the reciprocal strengths of the partners. It anticipates questions (covered in chapter 4) concerning how firms should maximize the potential for synergistic benefits of their relationships between their ventures and their wholly owned business units. Finally, table 2–1 anticipates questions (covered in chapter 5) concerning how the *venture*—as the embodiment of its owners' joint-venture strategy—should be used to compete within diverse industry environments.

As table 2–1 indicates, there are many situations where joint ventures could be useful, and these have been grouped into *internal benefits* (such as risk-sharing, no markets, scale economies, better information and practices, and reduction of turnover), *competitive benefits* (such as influence over in-

Table 2–1
Motivations for Joint-Venture Formation

A. Internal uses
   1. Cost and risk sharing (uncertainty reduction)
   2. Obtain resources where there is no market
   3. Obtain financing to supplement firm's debt capacity
   4. Share outputs of large minimum efficient scale plants
      a. Avoid wasteful duplication of facilities
      b. Utilize by-products, processes
      c. Shared brands, distribution channels, wide product lines, and so forth
   5. Intelligence: obtain window on new technologies and customers
      a. Superior information exchange
      b. Technological personnel interactions
   6. Innovative managerial practices
      a. Superior management systems
      b. Improved communications among SBUs
   7. Retain entrepreneurial employees

B. Competitive uses (strengthen current strategic positions)
   1. Influence industry structure's evolution
      a. Pioneer development of new industries
      b. Reduce competitive volatility
      c. Rationalize mature industries
   2. Preempt competitors ("first-mover" advantages)
      a. Gain rapid access to better customers
      b. Capacity expansion or vertical integration
      c. Acquisition of advantageous terms, resources
      d. Coalition with best partners
   3. Defensive response to blurring industry boundaries and globalization
      a. Ease political tensions (overcome trade barriers)
      b. Gain access to global networks
   4. Creation of more effective competitors
      a. Hybrids possessing owners' strengths
      b. Fewer, more efficient firms
      c. Buffer dissimilar partners

C. Strategic uses (augment strategic position)
   1. Creation and exploitation of synergies
   2. Technology (or other skills) transfer
   3. Diversification
      a. Toehold entry into new markets, products, or skills
      b. Rationalization (or divestiture) of investment
      c. Leverage-related owners' skills for new uses

dustry evolution, timing advantages, and globalization, plus the opportunity to create more effective strategic postures), and *strategic benefits* (such as synergies, technology, or other skills transfer and diversification).

Evidence concerning the costs and benefits of cooperative ventures comes primarily from a literature that has described international experiences. Many of the same problems (and successes) will be encountered when joint ventures are used in *home* markets if the domestic economies are mature.

Except for industries such as oil exploration (where U.S. firms by necessity established ways of pooling interests, operating authority, and profits long ago), Asian and European firms have accumulated more experience in successfully using joint ventures than U.S. firms have.[1] The late 1980s will continue to be an era of rapid technological innovation and challenges from imports and deregulation, therefore, firms must increase their understanding of *why* joint ventures are desirable and *how* to use cooperative ventures effectively, and they must do so quickly.

Uses of Joint Ventures

Studies and observation of current management practices have suggested many uses for joint ventures, but they also have suggested ambivalence concerning the use of this capital- and risk-sharing strategy. If managers can overcome inhibitions regarding joint ventures and develop systems to use them effectively, their firms can build strengths and gain knowledge by cooperating. They can even preempt competitors from forcing the marketplace to change disadvantageously, as in the example of the U.S. automobile industry.

Internal Uses

As table 2–1 suggests, cooperative ventures should not be seen as a way to hide weaknesses. Rather, if used prudently, such ventures can *create internal strengths*. Joint ventures can be resource-aggregating and resource-sharing mechanisms, allowing firms to concentrate resources in those areas where they possess the greatest respective strengths. Companies have cooperated in building airline engines because they wanted a piece of the pie but did not care to risk financial indigestion by investing alone. Some projects, such as the Great Plains coal-gasification venture, would never have been undertaken without this means of spreading risks and costs. Joint ventures are particularly appropriate when projects involve great uncertainties, costly technological innovations, or high information costs as in the synthetic fuel industries. Through joint ventures, small firms gain access to larger quantities of capital than would otherwise be available through the ordinary licensing of their technology, as is the case with medical products or other products with very long payback periods.

Technology, distribution networks, and other assets that provide internal strengths *are not always for sale*. As the resource dependency literature has noted, firms sometimes form joint ventures when they cannot afford to acquire the resources and competence they need.[2] Frequently, the knowledge and assets that firms seek *cannot be purchased,* or firms *cannot penetrate markets easily.* In those situations, joint ventures can be a means of coping with uncertainties and building strengths. They can provide firms with resources for which there are no equally efficient substitutes.

Joint ventures can be a means of using a new manufacturing process, a by-product, or a new capability.[3] Co-production, common procurement, and other joint activities are becoming the means to attain increased efficiency, productivity, scale economies, and other benefits commonly attributed to interfirm cooperation, such as are exemplified by joint ventures in the petrochemical industry. Access to improved brands or distribution networks can increase sales force productivity, as in the example of ethical pharmaceuticals, and access to an economical source of low-cost, better-quality raw materials as in coal mining joint ventures can provide both partners with better profit margins.[4]

As table 2–1 suggests, cooperative ventures can build internal strengths by offering firms a window on promising technologies such as robotics, genetic engineering, and solar energy. In addition to providing access to modern technological information, joint ventures can offer opportunities for engineering units to exchange technical staff, saving firms costly and unnecessary duplicate R&D efforts. In summary, joint ventures can offer partners many technological, financial, marketing, and managerial strengths, if managed effectively. The trick is to realize those benefits.

If managers are open to change, joint activities can be a way of building strengths through innovation in their managerial practices and methods of diffusing technology. Managerial practices can be modernized through contact with innovative information systems and administrative techniques used by other firms, as with cooperative ventures that bring together international partners. Firms can become more flexible strategically, since joint ventures facilitate better information exchange and enhance communications, if they are managed effectively.

Finally, table 2–1 (and earlier studies) suggest that joint ventures build internal strengths by reducing personnel turnover, conserving a firm's most valuable resources—entrepreneurial talent. Joint ventures offer an excellent method for retaining managers who lack the capital backing required to launch their own business ideas. Owners can also advise their ventures' management teams, providing more than just cash.

Competitive Uses

Beyond the benefits noted by past studies, it should be clear that joint ventures have the potential to become an effective competitive weapon. Joint ventures can be used in pioneering new industries like videotex services, because they minimize the capital investments that firms must commit to embryonic and potentially volatile settings. Table 2–1, which suggests some of these competitive uses of cooperative ventures, indicates that a prospective strategic posture requires firms to *seize initiatives* and to *force their industries' structures to evolve* in a favorable manner.[5] Thus, managers should draw on the cooperative strategy experiences of firms in mature industries and apply their knowledge of joint ventures to emerging industries to accelerate the *pace* of infrastructure development and control the *direction* of structural evolution, as petrochemical firms have done in genetic-engineering ventures.

Table 2–1 suggests that cooperative ventures can *create competitive strengths* such as vertical linkages or consolidate firms' existing market positions. Joint ventures can tame potentially tough customers (such as the defense department when purchasing armaments) or gain technological assistance through access to innovations pioneered in other industries (such as applying the knowledge of customer needs in office equipment to the development of vertical software for such customers). Erratic competitors who threaten industry stability can be mollified by drawing them into cooperative arrangements that focus their efforts on longer-term objectives rather than the short-term gains obtained from price-cutting.

Table 2–1 also indicates that joint ventures can *rationalize mature industries*, like metals processing, automobiles, and steel. They can combine foundering partners in mature industries (to consolidate the industry's structure and permit competitors to survive in a new form) and eliminate excess capacity (which could exacerbate industry volatility, as in the example of terephthalates production) through such coalitions.[6]

Joint ventures can be a means of preempting suppliers or customers from integrating in a manner unfavorable to the firm, as in the example of software programmers joining forces with hardware firms to offer database services, and table 2–1 argues that ventures can blunt the abilities of ongoing firms to retaliate by binding potential enemies to the firm as allies. Thus firms can gain new competitive capabilities (or enter new markets) faster, gain market power, or stake out leadership positions in emerging industries such as robotics, data communications services, and retail through joint ventures.[7] Entry through joint ventures may occur more rapidly than individual entry (since less capital is required to enter), as in the examples of cable television programming, videotex services and fiber-optic communications systems. Properly structured cooperative ventures can allow firms to move faster toward innovations and to improve their competitive positions in global arenas. (Note that *timing* is an important part of using joint ventures as a competitive strategy; pioneering firms can gain access to the *best* partners, thereby gaining a competitive advantage that subsequent entrants cannot replicate by forming joint ventures later.) As chapter 5 notes, partners risk creating new competitors if they do not structure their joint ventures advantageously. But if cooperative ventures are destined to become an inevitable structural feature within their industries, then firms must *quickly* seek out the best partners available to preempt their competitors from linking up with these firms instead. Joint ventures may also offer salvation for older global industries where the joint activities of steel and automotive firms, for example, seem to point to a new trend—the exploitation of joint economies in order to ward off other competitors that are making inroads into key markets.[8]

The competitive benefits shown in table 2–1 that are enjoyed by firms that enter cooperative ventures will differ by their positions. Newcomers seeking to enter a new geographic market may see joint ventures as insurance against domestic trade barriers. For them, moving some operations to the target market may be a means of easing political tensions by overcoming trade barriers. Sometimes firms with technological complementarity may cooperate out of necessity to gain a local identity. For firms already engaged in the business that the proposed joint venture will encompass, the critical competitive question is often *whether* established players should trade access to their sales networks for the capabilities outsiders can offer.

Table 2–1 notes that joint ventures can defend current strategic positions against forces that are too strong for one firm to withstand. Through the combined internal resources of diverse firms, cooperative ventures can create more effective competitors.[9] They can provide a buffer to marry dissimilar cultures, providing larger firms access to innovations made by the types of researchers who prefer to reside in smaller organizations (like the genetic-engineering firms, for example), because they want no part of the culture of larger firms and the "professional management" practices that characterize them. In brief, the unexplored structural and competitive potential of joint-venture strategies could be immense if managed skillfully.

Strategic Uses

Table 2–1 suggests that joint ventures can be strategic weapons as well. They can be a way to implement *changes* in a firm's strategic positions. They can increase (or decrease) a firm's domain, stabilize a firm's existing domain, or help a firm achieve diverse strategy objectives.[10] The strategic objectives that can be attained by using cooperative strategies are numerous, provided they are managed effectively.

Table 2–1 notes that if relationships are managed correctly, joint ventures may create synergies with owners' activities. Cooperative strategies offer a means of leveraging synergies between the skills and resources of owners and venture as well as between owners. As an intermediate alternative between acquisition (or internal development) and dependence on outsiders, joint ventures represent a special, highly flexible means of enhancing innovation or achieving other strategic objectives that managers should not overlook.

As product lives become increasingly short and the rate of technological innovation accelerates, table 2–1 suggests that cooperative ventures could become increasingly important as a means of attaining "toehold" entries into new businesses that may be of long-term strategic importance to venture owners, such as cable communications for newspaper publishers or cable television services for motion picture distributors. They can allow firms to diversify into attractive but unfamiliar business areas. Joint ventures can help firms diversify from unfavorable businesses into more promising ones.

Table 2–1 also points out that ventures may be a means of entering (or divesting) businesses or of expanding internationally. In addition to providing a less risky means of entering new markets, ventures can provide a nondisruptive means of divesting substantial businesses that no longer fit corporate objectives.

In summary, as table 2–1 has noted, many *internal, competitive,* and *strategic* benefits can be gained through joint ventures if firms take partners in cooperative strategies. The strategic benefits of diversification and synergies with sister business units need further discussion, for these benefits attributed to joint ventures are particularly difficult to realize, even if careful thought has been given to them.

Diversification Uses

When a venture is used as a means of diversifying from or enlarging the scope of a firm's ongoing activities, the way in which the venture is related to its owners determines its *pattern of diversification*. If the joint venture is *horizontally* related to its owners, it performs the same product, market, or technology tasks that its owners perform, albeit in a different geographic arena. *Vertical* ventures are entities whose activities and outputs supply to or distribute for their owners. *Diversifying* ventures, on the other hand, are entities that do not duplicate the activities of the venture owners nor can the venture owners consume or distribute the products or services of the venture; there are no natural horizontal or vertical linkages to diversifying ventures.

Since there will be at least two owners, two or more types of relationships can exist between a joint venture and its owners. If owners are not competitors, then different patterns of diversification will relate each owner to the joint venture.

Horizontal Cooperation. A firm may form a venture that creates a horizontally related competitor to expand its market scope, expand or flesh out its product lines, or rationalize excess capacity. Innovation may be a firm's primary motive to cooperate. (When horizontally related partners join forces to create a supplier or distribution channel, it is classified as *vertical cooperation* in this book because the *venture* is vertically related to its owners.)

The issues associated with horizontal cooperation are those of creating new competition (a horizontally related venture) versus deterring potential entrants. These are tradeoffs that U.S. firms have faced several times in the past.[11] In the 1980s the major difference is that potential partners are often foreign horizontal competitors, who possess absolute cost advantages over ongoing domestic firms. These intruders need not create a joint venture to enter the domestic firm's markets successfully, as chapter 3 explains, but they may prefer a cooperative venture to ease their way in. The issue for domestic firms, then, is whether the cooperative advances of such potential entrants should be welcomed or rebuffed.

Vertical Cooperation. Vertical ventures (those ventures that are at a different stage of the transformation chain than where their owners are) often are formed to decrease dependency on outsiders and circumvent market imperfections. They can also be used to develop young industries.[12] Sometimes competitors join forces to build supplying plants that are larger than either firm could use alone to exploit scale economies, as in the example of steel firms sharing iron ore mines, or partners may pioneer new distribution channels together. If effective product differentiation could give their firms sustainable advantages (and if economies necessitate sharing a facility), managers will forge vertical ventures. Most likely, partners will do so because quality control depends on good relationships between production stages. Thus, suppliers (or buyers) may form a cooperative venture to improve raw material or component quality, to design new products, or to shore up domestic firms' positions against imports.

Earlier studies, which regarded joint ventures primarily as a means of entering industrializing countries (where infrastructures often did not exist previously), found many vertical ventures. Vertical integration often is necessary early in the development of an economy to build roads, electrical systems, potable water access, and other necessary infrastructures. Vertical integration is also necessary in embryonic industries if an appropriate infrastructure does not yet exist. Vertical joint ventures are most prevalent in new industries such as synthetic fuels, genetic engineering, or other products that satisfy new customer demands or provide technologies to accomplish unheard-of tasks as well as in young economies of newly industrialized countries.

Diversification and Cooperation Strategies. Diversifying ventures (involving owners who are neither horizontally nor vertically related to their venture's activities) are used to gain access to knowledge, technology, or other resources that firms seek, as well as to enter new and unfamiliar businesses where entry barriers are so high that firms could not enter alone. *Related* diversification ventures exploit some core skill or expertise of their owners—whether it is marketing, R&D, and production or managerial skills. (*Unrelated* diversifications do not.)

As with the horizontal and vertical diversifications discussed above, the true strategic benefits of cooperative ventures cannot be assessed until all sides of the triangle of relationships can be assessed. In brief, the strategic benefits anticipated from diversification (and associated synergies) depend on the dynamics of relationships between owners and their venture, between owners as partners, and between the venture and its competitive environment. Managers embrace ventures where they anticipate that synergies with their firms' wholly owned business units can be exploited or where they can attain scale or integration economies. However (as chapters 4 and 5 will explain), synergies and economies cannot be realized unless the appropriate managerial systems are in place and unless partners allow their venture sufficient autonomy to cope with competition effectively.

Drawbacks of Joint Ventures

Despite their many potential uses and benefits, ventures frequently go awry and create problems. There are dangers in using ventures, including antitrust problems, sovereignty conflicts, loss of autonomy and control, and loss of competitive advantage through strategic inflexibility. Some of these drawbacks are due to the relative inexperience of firms in using joint ventures. Others are due, in part, to governmental ignorance concerning this strategy option as well as to unrealistic trade policies. Finally, problems are created by owners' *inabilities to manage* ventures effectively, and these are the primary concern of this book.

Antitrust Problems

Because legislators cannot foresee all technological changes that may occur when they draft a law, a goverment's policies regarding economic regulation must be dynamic. Some industrialized nations, for example, the United States, in the past have enforced strict antitrust laws that prohibited cooperative strategies when they appeared to function as monopolies or if they behaved collusively.[13] But late in 1984, U.S. antitrust officials indicated that joint ventures might be tolerated (even among competitors in highly concentrated markets) if *efficiency gains* offset the harm to competition that such arrangements had previously been assumed to create.[14]

Note that until 1984, U.S. antitrust authorities preferred to treat many forms of cooperative strategy as though the partners had merged. (Judicial opinions suggested that *all* forms of cooperation were suspect and that strategists should prepare for antitrust challenges whenever planning corporate alliances within the United States.) When firms plan joint ventures within such legal environments, it is particularly important to show a procompetitive design and an antitrust-sensitive explanation of the (1) need for the joint venture, with convincing portrayals of the inability of *either* partner to go it alone; the (2) expected gains in efficiency from cooperation; the (3) stream of new products (or technologies) that the alliance could create; and (4) what role the joint venture would play in promoting the growth and international competitiveness of the national economy. Because cooperative strategies raise questions of market division and limited freedoms to compete vigorously,[15] aspiring partners must write their joint-venture agreements carefully, with thoughtful provision for the resolution of disputes and modifications to suit local antitrust agencies. Neglect of this aspect of joint-venture planning could result in costly litigation with public agencies (or private parties), wasteful exposure of company resources on litigation, exposure of the firm's innermost business secrets, and potential loss of competitive momentum.[16]

Sovereignty Conflicts

Traditionally joint ventures were used as a means of expanding internationally when firms were unwilling to license their competitive advantages to companies in the country to which they wanted to expand but local laws prohibited majority ownership by foreign firms.[17]

Often the objectives of host nations were different from those of the joint-venture partners, and this conflict was likely to persist even in mature industrialized economies, especially when the local partner was a state-owned enterprise. For example, domestic partners would want to import highly advanced technologies and leading global brand names into their home markets as a sort of instant remedy that would give them overwhelming advantages over local competitors, but host governments would want those technologies that created jobs for the greatest number of workers. Alternatively, foreign partners may have formed joint ventures with local firms to use technologies that exploited the advantages of lower wages. However, host governments may want the most modern technologies for reasons of national pride, rather than those technologies that would make the most economic sense from the partners' viewpoints. Thus, a state-versus-firm conflict results from different perspectives concerning the timing of exploiting innovations or transferring technology between owner and venture.[18] (The same kind of conflict may occur between firms even when the partner is not a government entity.)

These types of conflicts between partners may result in problems in day-to-day operations or in capital recovery if the foreign partner is unwilling to accommodate the local government's (or local partner's) economic development plans.[19] In brief, decisions whether to license technology (or brand names) or to take local partners in cooperative ventures cannot be analyzed using traditional schemes of technology transfer if host governments exert substantial bargaining power, especially if the local partners are nationalized firms.[20] If local partners exert such bargaining power, they can disrupt the schedule by which their global partners had intended to share the very knowledge that gave them competitive advantages overseas.[21]

The problems that U.S. firms have encountered in managing their international ventures suggest the types of difficulties that could arise domestically as well. In particular, joint ventures with global partners may be tolerated by the host government only as long as the global firm is required to have local partners by law *or by inexperience.*

Loss of Autonomy and Control

In addition to local regulation problems, many conflicts within ventures arise from the simple fact that *there is more than one owner.* Each owner wants to coordinate the venture's activities with its own, and owners often have not created adequate mechanisms to resolve day-to-day deadlocks in decision making. Poorly structured ventures encourage political behavior problems, especially where owners find they differ in their *long-term* objectives, time horizons, operating styles, and expectations for the venture (especially how to realize potential synergies with the joint venture), as in the example of research-oriented firms teamed with marketing-oriented firms. Owners' fears that they will lose competitive advantage prevent such ventures from being effective, and owners' fears often exacerbate the difficulties of coordinating the venture's daily operations, especially in industries where technologies change rapidly.

The costs of cooperating in a joint venture can be sizable, requiring a multitude of resources to be committed, including time, money, materials, personnel, and communications. There can be drawbacks to joint ventures from opportunities forgone, and partners will often be concerned over their *perceived* loss of control over invested capital, technical resources, proprietary information, and other advantages that might be disseminated to third parties. Commitments to one set of partners may reduce a firm's future opportunities to forge alliances with other partners.[22] Fears concerning a firm's loss of strategic flexibility can weigh most heavily of all; thus some firms refuse even to discuss the use of joint activities as a means to supplement their ongoing strategies. Their managers prefer to let their firms fall behind rather than risk the loss of autonomy in decision making and control over cooperative arrangements.

Strategic Inflexibility and Loss of Competitive Advantages

Many internal benefits can be enjoyed if joint ventures are used effectively, but since managers seek diverse strategy objectives when forging ventures, there will be limits to what their firms should expect to achieve through them.

Past studies suggest that in their eagerness for gain, managers often have invested too little of the appropriate time or resources in formulating and monitoring cooperative ventures. Most frequently, owners expected synergies between their firm and their venture to accrue without explicitly managing for these synergies. Owners that served on their ventures' governing boards devoted too little attention to the strategic direction of the joint venture, perhaps because the wrong managers were involved. Some owners maintained too much control over the venture's investment decisions, business expansions, or other important decisions, perhaps because they were uncertain what the venture should achieve and were reluctant to trust the venture's managers to make these decisions correctly. Participation in joint ventures could have adverse effects on the corporate prestige, identity, or strategic positions of owners, because the venture's activities may sap the motivation and innovative fervor of their personnel in ongoing business units, especially if the management systems that integrate owner and venture do not arbitrate between their needs adequately. Giving half-hearted attentions to cooperative ventures is as bad as giving too much attention and often creates handicaps for owners and their ventures.

If the reasons for forming cooperative strategies are poorly conceived, if partners are not selected carefully, if firms have overestimated their partners' strengths, or if the agreements and systems used to control the venture are inadequate, such that each owner believes the others are shortchanging it, firms may often be worse off than they were before entering joint ventures. Some firms found that when resources and capabilities were commingled, the weaker partner often benefited the most. If joint ventures were horizontal, strong firms found that they had more to lose than to gain by cooperating, especially if the knowledge comprising their technological core was highly appropriable. If linkages were forged with specific suppliers or distribution channels, firms often increased (rather than decreased) their exposure to shortfalls and bottlenecks because doing so meant alienating vertically related outsiders that might have served as safety nets when shortages (or surpluses) occurred.

Some ventures want to move faster or further afield than their owners had intended. Sometimes ventures want to enter markets where owners had not anticipated they would be competitors. Worst of all, poorly structured joint-venture agreements can spread the firm's expertise to third parties that are not members of the joint venture. This inadvertently occurs where cooperative ventures are structured loosely in terms of policies for personnel rotation and other ways of repatriating knowledge.[23] (Grappling with these strategic issues is crucial for joint-venture success; they are covered in chapters 4 and 5).

Previous studies have noted that having partners means the decision-making process will be more cumbersome.[24] Revisions to production plans are difficult, and plant closings become a frequent source of conflict in many cooperative ventures, especially in unionized industries. Historically, the difficulties owners encountered concerning controversies with their partners· about new product designs, production scheduling (and locations), and vertical integration arrangements explain, in part, why many firms that entered ventures overseas have disposed of their partners as soon as was feasible, rather than perpetuate an ill-fitting alliance.[25] Joint ventures even have been considered impediments to the flexibility of a firm's global strategies because effective competition requires manipulation of *all* parts of a firm's global networks—yet consider the examples of the petrochemical, oil, or other global industries where transshipments must be frictionless in order to be effective. Why have joint ventures played an important role in these industries for so long? What accounts for these differences in industry experiences? Has one partner been passive, or have these successful firms found a way to coordinate their ventures to attain the best advantages of cooperation?

A Timely Managerial Challenge

Merely knowing the potential uses and drawbacks of joint ventures is not adequate for managers who will forge cooperative strategies. Literature searches describing the costs and benefits of ventures are fine, but they do little more than point out to managers the challenges that must be overcome when using joint ventures. Descriptions do not go far enough in addressing how to manage the tensions of joint-venture relationships. *The missing link in understanding joint-venture strategies is an analysis of the dynamic interactions of the three key actors.*

Joint ventures have become so prevalent in the United States that all managers need to consider what effect this structural change will have on the way their firms compete. Joint ventures are an important structural trait of emerging industries such as alternative energy, communications services, and biotechnology. As such, they represent a key strategy decision that has the potential to force a firm's industry to evolve in an unfavorable way if managers are not alert. Joint ventures bring the viewpoints of new players (partners) into the competitive arena, and they result in a stronger, hybrid champion if managers can channel the interactions between owner and venture, and between owners, into an effort to make the venture a formidable player within its industry. However, unless managers understand these dynamics, they cannot formulate effective joint-venture strategies.

Past studies indicate that managers often have disparaged joint ventures, believing them to be too complex, too ambiguous, or too inflexible to be useful.[26] But as the challenges of competition increase, as projects grow larger and more risky, and as technologies become too expensive to afford alone, managers must learn how to use cooperative strategies, even in their home markets.[27] Despite the reluctance of many firms to participate in them and their relatively high mortality rates, joint ventures are becoming common entry strategies, even in industries that have become global. Yet their shared ownership suggests that strategic tradeoffs must be made when joint ventures are employed. Compromises will be necessary. The next three chapters describe these compromises.

3
Interactions among Joint-Venture Owners

G iven shorter product lives, maturing domestic economies, the explosive effect of technological improvements on communications, computers, biotechnology, and other arenas where industry boundaries were formerly distinct and given that many industries have become global in their scope of competition, how do managers analyze the use of joint ventures in mature economies? From a sponsoring firm's perspective, when do cooperative ventures make sense? Which firms are most appropriate as partners? What should they offer the venture? How should each partner's contribution to the joint venture be valued? When are there timing advantages in forging cooperative ventures early, and how will changes in relationships between partners affect the joint venture's fate?

These and other questions concerning cooperative strategies are addressed in the joint-venture framework presented below. The framework covers the dynamics of relationships between (1) owners as partners, (2) between owners and their ventures, and (3) between the venture and its competitive environment as these concerns affect the viability of joint-venture strategies for its owners. Because the joint-venture framework is complex, portions of it are developed in three separate chapters that correspond to its three perspectives. As the heavy arrows in figure 3–1 indicate, after the framework has been presented, chapter 3 will elaborate on the first of these relationships—that of partners coming together in an agreement to form a joint venture (or other form of cooperative strategy). Chapter 4 addresses owner–venture relationships and chapter 5 presents a framework that relates the venture to its competitive environment. First, an integrated overview of the framework is presented below.

Overview of the Joint-Venture Framework

Most joint ventures formed today are complex and the cost-benefit analysis done to decide whether or not to form joint ventures is also complex. Man-

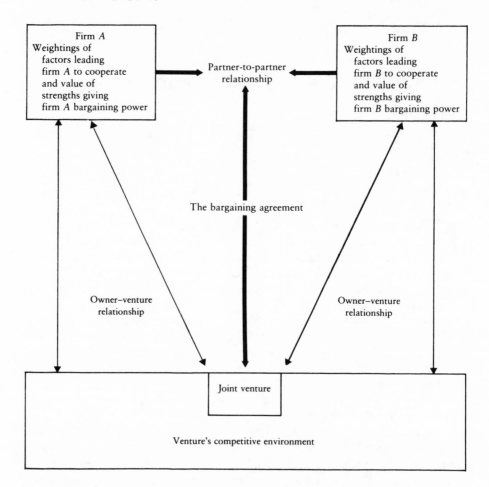

Figure 3–1. Owner-to-Owner Relationships Creating a Joint Venture

agers expect to reap attractive benefits by cooperating, but at the same time they hesitate when evaluating cooperative ventures because their firms may have to make significant sacrifices. Faced with the disadvantages that can be associated with shared ownership, many managers prefer *nonequity* ventures. Nonetheless, assuming that some form of cooperaion will be necessary in order for firms to achieve their strategic objectives, it would be helpful for managers to have a framework that suggests which forces influence the viability and durability of joint ventures or other forms of cooperative strategy. It would be helpful also to understand how managers might design and run cooperative ventures to be most effective in light of these forces.

An analytical framework that identifies the primary factors to consider in forming joint ventures and structures a set of relationships between these factors is presented here. The framework is dynamic, and discussion of it from the partner's perspective will progress from a single-firm analysis of the pros and cons of entering into a joint venture, through the meshing of two (or more) firms' bargaining positions to form a joint venture, to the interrelationships of owners with their newly created ventures, and, finally, to the forces that are likely to precipitate a revision of their design for cooperation.

The joint-venture framework begins by considering *whether* a particular set of partners is likely to cooperate. *How* the venture will be structured and integrated with the ongoing activities of its owners is considered in chapter 4. The framework assumes that all ventures require access to certain inputs and healthy markets for their outputs in order to be viable.

The resources and attributes that partners will share with their venture affect both their *willingness* to form a joint venture and each partner's *relative bargaining power* therein. Whether the bargain that partners strike in cooperating will take the form of a joint venture (or other form of cooperative arrangement) depends on the bilateral bargaining power among partners and on other forces discussed below. This initial *balance of power* will evolve over time due to the effects of many internal and external change forces. Although joint ownership can endure in some ventures for decades, partners will often resolve the tensions of shared decision making by dissolving their joint-venture partnerships earlier rather than later. Thus, many cooperative strategies are, at best, transitory organizational arrangements. If managers can accept the premise that the transitional period when a joint venture is necessary may last only a few years—or months—they can look in an informed manner at this organizational arrangement and regard it as being one of several means to their ends.

Figure 3–1 suggests that the joint-venture relationship is a strategic triangle (or quadrangle). The motivations and fears of potential partners as well as their strengths and shortfalls must be considered when evaluating them. The following is an overview of the full joint-venture strategy model.

Single-Firm Considerations

Fundamental to any analysis of a joint venture that might be formed is an assessment of the willingness of firms to embrace the "shared-ownership" strategy option.[1] Why would managers consider an inevitably complicated arrangement like a joint venture when performing the contemplated activities themselves would be a much simpler administrative task? The answer to this question is found in some combination of faster and/or less costly access to desired markets or resources. As figure 3–2 suggests, the willingness of firms to cooperate is influenced by the sacrifices involved, available inputs required, urgency and the like.

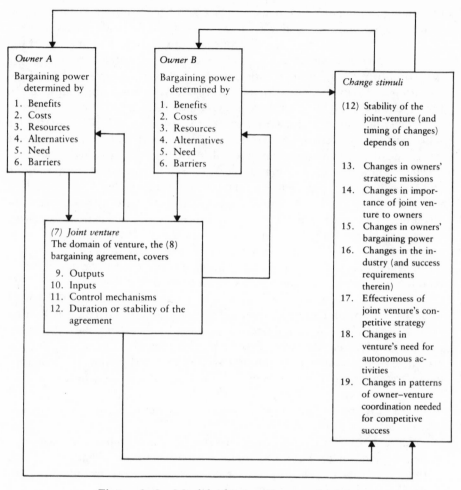

Figure 3–2. Model of Joint-Venture Activity

Briefly, in figure 3–2 firm *A* seeks certain (1) benefits from affiliating with firm *B*. These benefits are its reasons to cooperate with any partner. Firm *A* also faces (2) costs in using joint ventures that may be too significant for it to accept. If firm *A*'s costs exceed expected benefits, negotiations to form agreements with firm *B* become fruitless or will take forms other than a joint venture. But if firm *A* sees benefits to joint ventures such as synergies, scale economies, or other benefits sketched in chapter 2 that exceed its costs, a bargain may be struck. Thus, the first premise of the joint-venture framework is that effective ventures will be formed *only* if each firm believes that there is greater advantage in cooperating than there will be costs. (Firm *B* also performs this analysis before it is ready to strike a bargain.)

Next comes an evaluation of the potential chemistry between two (or more) specific partners. What does each firm want and have to offer? The primary issues in assessing this chemistry are *fit* and *compatibility*. In an operating joint venture, neither partner is passive; each partner contributes and receives.

Each firm in figure 3–2 possesses resources and skills that could serve as potential inputs to a joint venture. The inputs a partner offers and the outputs it desires are highly individualistic and diverse in nature. Finding a partner who is an attractive fit is much more exacting than just describing the general willingness of a particular firm to cooperate.[2]

When the chemistry of matching firm *A* with firm *B* is assessed, issues of *relative bargaining power* arise. The greater a particular firm's (3) resources and (4) alternatives for attaining its objectives, the greater its potential bargaining power. But the greater its (5) need to cooperate with a particular partner, the less its relative bargaining power will be in negotiating the joint-venture agreement. Some firms are skittish as partners. The greater the magnitude of opportunity costs or other disadvantages such firms perceive in cooperating, the higher will be their (6) barriers to cooperation. (It will be necessary to overcome these barriers if a joint venture is to be formed initially. After the agreement is consummated, another set of barriers will impede *re-negotiations* of the bargaining agreement, encumber partners' abilities to use their venture effectively, and limit the venture's ability to compete advantageously. Throughout their relationship as partners, firms must manage the impediments to strategic flexibility that prevent them from realizing this strategy option's full potential.)[3]

Bargaining Agreement Considerations

In figure 3–2, the *form* of the venture is the net result of the bilateral bargaining power of its owners. Effective cooperative efforts generate results that neither owner acting alone could achieve. However, there will be questions about how the venture's results (both good and bad) are divided among the owners. Questions concerning how much of what resources each owner contributes, and under what conditions, must be resolved as the agreement is forged. Bargaining power is a critical factor in finding answers, and it arises out of relative urgency, available resources, other commitments, possible alternatives, and similar strengths and weaknesses of each owner. Thus, the attractiveness of any potential partner is strongly conditioned by a projection of how much power it wields and how the power is likely to be used in managing the joint-venture relationship.[4]

The agreement to cooperate will be defined by the terms of a legal document, (8) a bargaining agreement that defines the venture's domain of activities, its (9) outputs, and possibly its customers, as well.

The bargaining agreement that partners forge sets forth the venture's objectives, scope, degrees of freedom, and constraints. It represents the compromise that has been hammered out by partners on the basis of their willingness to cooperate and their relative bargaining power. The agreement should represent the intentions of the venture's owners concerning its autonomy to take the actions necessary to compete effectively, as well as the owners' limitations on actions.[5] (Unfortunately, as chapter 8 explains, too often negotiations to forge such agreements tend to focus on financial arrangements, valuations of partners' contributions, and how to file for "divorce.")

The bargaining agreement should specify which (10) inputs are necessary for the joint venture to attain its objectives. These inputs may be provided by the venture's owners through a variety of vertical integration arrangements, or they may be obtained from outsiders. The venture cannot be viable, however, if its owners do not provide for an *economic* source of (or means of attaining) these inputs.

The (8) bargaining agreement also specifies the (11) control mechanisms that owners will use to ensure that the benefits they desire were indeed received. These control mechanisms provide for development of managerial resources, the method that will be used by the board of directors to control the partners' interests, the manner in which disputes will be resolved, and other operating details. Thus, the formal agreement provides ways of maintaining the (12) *stability* of the joint venture. (In fact, the stability of cooperation between partners will be established by their subsequent behavior patterns, not by what is written in their agreement. Nevertheless, partners should articulate the bargaining agreement's terms in order to think through how the venture can fit into their other activities.) The bargaining agreement provides owners with a guide—a touchstone—for assessing whether the venture has deviated from their purpose in an unacceptable way.

Control mechanisms are discussed at length in chapter 4, which treats the owner–venture side of the model. As chapter 4 explains, owners' trade-offs between coordination and autonomy affect which integrating mechanisms they will employ, whether the venture will be horizontally or vertically related to its owners, and whether owners will share any facilities with their ventures.

Change Stimuli

The joint-venture framework recognizes that changes will occur in every venture's design because managers rarely can anticipate exactly how their agreement to cooperate will evolve. Figure 3–2 notes that several factors could force changes in terms of the bargaining agreement before its original objectives are attained. The needs and strengths of each partner's major business activities are subject to continual change, and these changes often enhance or diminish that partner's interest in the joint venture's activities. The formal bargaining agreement is unlikely to capture all of the changes in how partners realize their respective desires for synergies with the venture. The covenants of the joint-venture agreement rarely recognize how the venture's needs for autonomy may change.

The venture faces dynamic competitive forces in its target market, and these changes affect the venture's ability to satisfy the desires of its owners. As a result of the many forces that affect the desires and abilities of the parties to the joint venture to attain the venture's purpose, the original terms of the bargaining agreement become less satisfactory for at least one party.

These dynamics will be destabilizing to joint-venture relationships because the tensions force owners' relationships to change vis-à-vis their venture. In figure 3–2, changes in the circumstances surrounding either partner, such as (13) changes in partners' strategic missions or in their (15) bargaining power with respect to each other, changes in owners' relationships with their venture, such as (14) changes in the joint venture's importance to owners' strategies), or changes surrounding the venture itself, could upset the balance and lead to renegotiation of the (8) bargaining agreement or even to an end to the (7) joint venture. The revision process is complicated because relative bargaining power has changed. The venture's (16) industry structure and success requirements may also have changed. The venture's strategy may no longer be (17) suitable for serving its customers, or the venture may be less effective in implementing its chosen strategy.

Performance may falter because success requirements change within the venture's industry, due to past competitive behaviors or other exogenous forces. The venture's abilities to command resources or satisfy its customers may deteriorate or improve, depending on its past performance and its ability to respond effectively to these changes. Changes in the competitive conditions sketched in chapter 5 will influence the (19) venture's need for close coordination with the owner that contributed needed resources and skills as well as its (18) need for autonomous activities.

The ultimate disposition of the venture will depend on (13) changes in owners' strategic missions, (14) changes in the strategic importance they attached to their venture, and (15) changes in their respective abilities to attain their objectives in other ways (a source of bargaining power). If partners can no longer cooperate by renegotiating on the points of their agreement, the venture may be spun off, or its configuration may be changed to another form. Although the discussion of change suggests that joint ventures are an unstable form of organization, the conclusion to shy away from them does not necessarily follow. Cooperation is useful as a strategy option if its purpose can be attained during the time when partners work together. As conditions change, firms reevaluate their internal analyses. Their conclusions precipitate negotiations among partners to change the bargaining agreement. Consequently, the ownership split, relationships with partners' business units, or other dimensions of the joint-venture agreement are readjusted to accommodate partners' evolving needs.

A Single Firm's Perspective: The Cost-Benefit Analysis Determining Its Willingness to Cooperate

From a particular firm's perspective, analysis of joint-venture strategies encompasses *whether* to cooperate, how to cooperate (what form of cooperation) and *for how long* to cooperate with a particular partner. Each firm makes a private cost-benefit analysis by weighting assessments of the (1) benefits the firm expects to receive by cooperating against the (2) costs it sees in cooperative ventures. Although some costs may be weighted heavily as disincentives when managers initially assess their positions on joint-venture formation, changes in the firm's competitive environment may later push them into a different, more tolerant position concerning cooperation. Joint ventures may look more attractive in light of the firm's (5) need to cooperate or the (4) alternatives to cooperation that are available. Firms may be more (or less) demanding because of the (3) resources they hold as bargaining chips in forming agreements to their liking.

If firms already possess the resources needed to compete effectively, they will not form joint ventures as readily as if they lacked such resources. Shared decision making often is so difficult to manage that firms would rather deal on a contractual basis in short-term relationships than try to cooperate. When firms conclude that they are willing to cooperate, they do so because the benefits they desire exceed the problems they anticipate and because they have no better options.

Willingness to Cooperate

Although there are exceptions, the most likely candidates for joint ventures are firms that *lack* the capabilities, strengths, or resources needed to exploit business opportunities alone. Firms will attempt to link up with the strongest partners they can win, but they may have to settle for those partners that their bargaining position qualifies them for.

Benefits and Needs. The opportunity to satisfy a variety of internal, competitive, or strategic needs motivates firms to consider some form of cooperative strategy. Firms that contemplate cooperative strategies want access to particular value resources—access to a specific distribution channel, use of a certain patent, access to employees with unique knowledge and capabilities, use of an efficient manufacturing plant, a brand name, a process—that they cannot develop themselves. Analysis of competitive conditions may suggest that such ventures be undertaken quickly to preempt competitors or simply to catch up. Cooperative strategy may be needed because suppliers or customers are integrating vertically to become competitors. Cooperation may be the best way to blunt the retaliation of competitors as firms expand their domains.[6] Binding potential rivals through cooperative ventures makes them allies.

The benefits that a particular firm envisions in cooperative strategies will be influenced by competitors' activities. The weightings that firms assign to the benefits of cooperation depend on whether they have promulgated their equipment standards successfully or not. If the competitor's product designs are becoming dominant, the only way to recapture a share of the market is to enter into a joint venture with partners who want to take on the industry leader. Together, such partners can realize the scale economies enjoyed by firms with larger market shares. The benefits of cooperative strategies are even greater if the dominant firm will not license its standards to competitors or to manufacturers of peripheral equipment until long after it has captured a commanding lead and established high switching cost barriers among its customers.

Timing is an important part of cooperative strategies in situations where environments change rapidly because firms that move first can gain access to *better partners,* set *technological standards,* and exploit *experience curve advantages.* The urgency with which partner firms forge joint ventures (or other forms of cooperative strategy) depends primarily on their assessment of competitive conditions in the markets where the venture will operate. Some firms must move earlier than others because they have less bargaining power than other firms. Fleeting advantages should be exploited quickly while they still create valuable bargaining positions in gaining access to innovations, cost reductions, and other desired improvements.

Barriers. Joint ventures will not be formed unless firms need to diversify, acquire new skills and resources, consolidate their positions, or attain other objectives that they cannot reach *alone.* Many firms reject cooperative strategies as a way to supplement flagging strategic postures because recognition of their weaknesses does not come easily to them.[7] Their unwillingness to see that the nature of competition is changing creates *barriers* to their effective use of joint ventures or other cooperative strategies.

The principal barriers to forming cooperative ventures are *strategic* in nature. Firms are unwilling to share information and access to resources in areas that are of strategic importance to them. Thus, the likelihood that a firm is willing to form a joint venture depends, in part, on the strategic importance that its managers attach to the proposed activity. Activities that are close to a firm's strategic core (xerography for Xerox, for example) are not likely candidates for joint-venture strategies. Externally imposed barriers to forming cooperative ventures include political restrictions on ownership, patent restrictions, competitor retaliation, or other conditions. These external barriers may be easier to overcome than a firm's own attitudinal barriers against cooperation.

Each firm has a calculus for assessing the attractiveness of opportunities that joint ventures can offer. Depending on the weights that managers attribute to the firm's need to cooperate and the benefits to be received by doing so, the firm's *initial bargaining position* is created.

Analysis of Strengths

If a firm hopes to attract a needed resource through cooperation, it must offer an offsetting inducement to its potential partner. The manager of any firm contemplating cooperative strategies must assess what that particular firm can "bring to the party." Each firm has strengths that must be evaluated in light of its relative attractiveness to other firms. Possessing relative strengths—resource abundance, opportunities to exploit synergies, strong market position or other successes that outsiders may covet—should give a firm a stronger bargaining position in joint-venture negotiations.

When managers entertain a proposal for their firm to form a joint venture, they have clearly in mind what it hopes to achieve by cooperating. They must be careful to guard, rather than squander, the competitive advantages that give the firm its relative strengths. Joint ventures are the obvious strategy choice for risky undertakings where required investments are large (as in oil exploration or turbines), and firms cannot afford to bear such risks and costs alone. They are a less obvious strategy choice when firms already possess the internal strengths needed to cope adequately with competition on their own.

There is value in having a strong firm as partner because its ongoing management system and organization culture enable it to solve problems more effectively. Such a firm's bargaining position in negotiating a joint venture should reflect these managerial advantages.

A strong firm will be courted by many potential partners who want to leverage the firm's strengths for their own benefit. If the courted firm were entertaining takeover bids, its asking price would be high. Accordingly, the value of its participation in a joint venture will be equally as high.

Resources. The balance of power favors the firm that controls the resource that is most desired at a particular time. Some managers use joint ventures preemptively to protect turf that is of strategic importance to their firms because they realize that their sources of competitive advantage are *not* enduring strengths. Such managers use their current control over crucial resources and their current access to technology and markets as bargaining chips to gain timing advantages through cooperation.

Although bargaining power may come from a firm's high-quality products, from scarce or proprietary technology, from access to markets, personnel, resources, or capabilities, or from commitment to the business activity in question,[8] the most important attribute to control in most joint ventures is market access. Management talent, experience, local contacts, and financial resources are important, *but secondary,* in determining the balance of power within ventures and how to value each firm's contributions. (This premise should not be surprising. Access to geographically remote markets has been the primary motive for many U.S. joint ventures in other countries in the past.)

Market access is the most attractive resource to control (or develop) because it provides a competitive advantage that is *more durable* than most technological resources, especially where product and process technology changes rapidly. (Technological prowess provides more enduring advantages where proprietary skills *can* be effectively protected, as in the ethical pharmaceuticals industry, just as marketing and product-differentiation skills provide more enduring competitive advantages where they can be protected, as in industries where products are *not* growing commoditylike and customers are *not* becoming increasingly discerning and powerful as buyers. These points are developed further in chapter 5.)

Firms whose products have recognizable brand names or who have reputations for quality products can protect this advantage. They can effectively expand their product lines (or market access) without creating new competitors because they can distribute the products of outsiders under their own brand names or parlay their quality image into access to new geographic regions or marketing channels. Firms possessing technological prowess, patents, and an image of success in research will have more chips for bargaining advantageously if their partner cannot adequately evaluate their contributions or emulate them.[9] Again, if a firm's strengths and resources provide transitory advantages, it should exploit these advantages *faster* by using licensing agreements, ventures, and other ways of leveraging them to build more enduring competitive advantages for the future.

Alternatives. The importance attached to forming a joint venture depends, in part, on the availability of other ways to obtain the desired resources or to employ underutilized existing resources. Alternatives reduce dependence on one course of action. Firms bargain from a base of strength if they have alternative ways to satisfy the needs that are motivating them to consider joint ventures. Stronger firms—those with superior resources—will be sought after as a joint-venture partner by more firms. Strong firms can exploit their dominant positions by forging "spider webs" of ventures, if they wish to do so. They may also be able to force weaker firms to deal with them on an *exclusive* basis, while they play the field by cooperating with many partners. (Chapter 5 addresses the question of how firms that possess great bargaining power should exert it.)

Firms do not need joint ventures if they can exert their influence and treat suppliers or distributors as if they were extensions of their corporate entities. If a firm can license technologies at reasonable royalties or obtain other needed resources, there is no need to form a cooperative venture. If other arrangements are available that give firms the internal benefits sketched in table 2–1, most managers will *not* make joint ventures their first choice of strategy. (When managers negotiate with outsiders to obtain needed skills and resources, joint ventures are selected as a *compromise*. Many managers prefer mergers and acquisitions to shared-equity arrangements.)

Managers resist the use of joint-venture strategies because they fear loss of control over strategic resources. If analysis suggests that some form of cooperative venture is needed, managers will usually evaluate their firm as being highly attractive because they overlook the second step in assessing its initial bargaining position: a potential strength becomes a relative strength only when it is compared with the attributes of a partner.

The Initial Bargaining Position

A manager establishes a threshold for cooperation based on internal assessments of the firm's need for cooperation, the amount of risk the firm can cope with alone and other factors of importance to the firm. The manager also assesses what benefits the firm wants from a joint venture, what resources and strengths the firm will contribute to receive those benefits, and what constraints on management's freedom to take appropriate actions will be tolerable. This threshold is the firm's initial bargaining position.

The *strategic importance* that partners assign to their cooperative strategies will suggest how the terms of ventures are negotiated. The key to maintaining strategic flexibility in using joint ventures effectively is a firm's bargaining power and attention must be devoted to sustaining this power. If a joint-venture proposal is close to a firm's strategic core, that firm will *not* want to cooperate. A firm's negotiating team may move from an initial position of noncooperation to one of accepting a joint venture if it becomes clear that the market access, technology, or resources, inputs or services it desires will not be available in any other way. But the firm's managers will bargain very cautiously when the venture's activities touch their strategic core.

Firms are often unwilling to accept minority positions in ventures that they value highly. Thus, their negotiating team will ask for 51 percent of the equity and to be the "operator"—the partner in charge of day-to-day operating decisions—in such ventures. They often move to a position of 50%–50% ownership and an operating committee. These concessions are part of the negotiations that move firms from their initial bargaining posture of noncooperation to a compromise with respect to a particular partner. It is a discovery process. Firm *A* may not know firm *B*'s positions on several dimensions that could define the joint venture's mission and/or may misinterpret what it does know. Similarly, firm *B* may have limited (or incorrect) information about firm *A*. Limited information (or misinformation) may be provided *intentionally* because managers do not reveal to their potential partners what their firms' true weightings matrix, which comprises the saddle points of cooperation in their bargaining position, looks like. In such situations, managers' *perceptions* about relative bargaining power become as important as the actual basis for such power. If a firm's managers want to cooperate and think their management teams can work together, they negotiate further.

Indifference (due to holding a business to be of low strategic importance) actually gives firms some bargaining power over partners that care deeply about the business activities under negotiation. Firms that do not hold a business unit to be as important (strategically) as its potential partners do might win other important bargaining concessions from eager partners who want to run the joint venture's operations. The indifferent partner could even be carried by its more eager counterpart.

Two-Firm Analysis: The Meeting of Minds

Partners should *complement* each other, as when technology-dominant firms seek market access or marketing-dominant firms seek technological skills, especially in industries where patent protection is strong or the knowledge that gives firms technological advantages is *not* highly appropriable. Bargaining power is based on the fit or interplay between the resources and needs of two specific firms. Bargaining power arises only when one firm wants something that another firm can dispense or withhold. Bargaining power is situation-specific because it arises in a one-to-one relationship in a particular setting. All cooperative strategies require firms to give up some control over strategic activities, especially where the risks and problems of acquiring resources (or of developing them in-house) leave few other feasible ways of doing a project. Each player possesses inherent strengths that give its negotiating team bargaining power in forming cooperative strategies. Firms' strategic missions will determine how their managers will use that bargaining power. Technology transfers, distribution agreements, and other details of owners' relationships with their joint venture will be determined by strategic motivations for the venture and will be subject to ratification by the owners.

Thus, firms signal their bargaining positions in negotiations and work out the details of their partnership in agreements that define relationships between firms as partners (as well as firms as owners) as explicitly as is necessary in order to make them comfortable with their affiliation. When partners negotiate a bargaining agreement, they provide for who will take the venture's outputs and in what volumes, who will provide raw material and supporting services to the venture and on what terms, and how partners will monitor and evaluate the venture's performance. Partners may also provide for the duration of the partnership agreement, or at least provide for "horizon" points (or milestones) for review of their relationship.

Finding a Basis for Agreement

Opposing tensions characterize a manager's decision to embrace a particular form of cooperative strategy. Negotiating teams from both firms approach the bargaining table, each seeking high equity ownership and managerial control in any alliance that might be formed. Negotiations frequently begin with each side trying to ascertain whether the other side can be acquired. When the managers discover this, round two (which encompasses negotiations that could lead to a cooperative venture) will commence. Factors previously important to one or the other of the negotiating parties but not of concern to both parties may drop out of the negotiations at this point and other factors of interest to both parties will become more significant.

Fears concerning loss of control will motivate a negotiating team to seek a greater proportion of ownership, especially if they believe the venture's activity to be of strategic importance to their firm. In such cases, joint ventures are more likely to be acceptable to them than arrangements that offer *less* control over operating decisions. Ironically, if a venture's activity is not of at least *medium strategic importance* to its owners, a joint venture may be formed, but the managers will not give it the attention it needs to thrive to its best abilities.

Subsequent Bargaining Positions

After the potential partners have assessed each others' valuations of the need to cooperate and the attractiveness of venturing together, some adjustments to their initial bargaining positions may be necessary to reach a final agreement. In reevaluating the attractiveness of cooperation, negotiating teams may mitigate their initial demands because (1) they cannot afford their potential partner's price; (2) they are unable to manage the joint venture as effectively as it has now become clear their partners could; or (3) for other reasons. A firm's demands will be mitigated by its relative bargaining weakness in the face of a partner that possesses the resources and strengths the

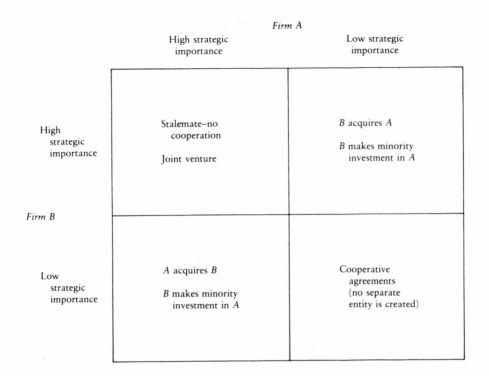

Figure 3–3. Strategic-Importance Relationship and Joint-Venture Formation (Assuming Firms Will Cooperate, Ceteris Paribus)

venture needs to succeed. In the interests of reaching an agreement, each partner may have to concede that its bargaining position is not as strong as it had asserted initially. Otherwise, an agreement may not occur.

Joint ventures are likely to be the equilibrium point that partners settle on as they negotiate, if their respective needs for cooperation are high. As figure 3–3 indicates, when both firms' bargaining postures have them valuing a business activity highly, they will reach a stalemate if they cannot reach a compromise. Joint ventures are frequently the compromise. If there is enough interest among partners once a compromise point is recognized, negotiations to flesh out the bargaining agreement will continue.

A firm's relative bargaining power in negotiating joint venture agreements translates into market power later on. If a firm has bargaining power, it is desirable as a partner—so desirable that other partners may permit it to act promiscuously and to form a spider's web of joint ventures. As figure 3–4 indicates, when the resources and strengths of potential partners are compared, the compromise may resemble that shown in figure 3–3; or one (or

Firm A

	High bargaining power	Low bargaining power
High bargaining[a] power	A and B can both form constellations of spider's web joint ventures or cooperative agreements at the hubs of their respective webs. One of these ventures will join A with B	B forms spider's web agreements with itself to the hub A cooperates exclusively with B
Low bargaining power	A can form spider's web agreements with itself at the hub A accepts B's minority investment B cooperates exclusively with A	Mergers and capacity-shrinking agreements

Firm B (label on left side)

[a]Where bargaining power is determined by market position, control of crucial resources, past performances, position in vertical chain of processing, and other attributes.

Figure 3–4. Bargaining-Power Relationships and Joint-Venture Formation Behavior (Assuming Firms Will Cooperate, Ceteris Paribus)

both) of the partners may engage in *several* cooperative agreements, ventures, minority investments and so forth. If two weak firms agree to cooperate, they would do best to merge and rationalize their production facilities, building one sleek but more efficient entity. In summary, the firm that possesses the greatest strengths when compared with its partner's needs can exploit positions of bargaining power by forming multiple agreements, even among competing partners.

When the effects of partners' needs to cooperate are combined with their respective bargaining power, normative propositions concerning their use of joint ventures can be advanced as in figures 3–3 and 3–4. Thus, partners form joint ventures when their need to share risks, costs, and strengths are greater than their concern about losing their basis for competitive advantage through cooperative strategy. (Where loss of competitive advantage is not an issue—perhaps because no firm possesses a clear advantage over another within a particular strategic group—firms are free to form as many ventures as they wish). The balance of power among partners will be apparent in the mechanisms used to control their interests in the joint venture, and in the vertical relationships they maintain with their venture. The balance of power among partners will be determined primarily by what each partner brings to the party, although some firms will be willing not to exert their bargaining power in order to take more home with them.

There is an *experience curve* associated with cooperative strategies; the more managers use joint ventures, the better they become at exploiting the benefits of shared ownership and shared risk. The most experienced firms make the best joint-venture partners. Indeed some managers are enthusiastic about the use of cooperative strategies to supplement their firms' capabilities because they have discovered how to use them effectively. When firms overcome organizational resistance to using joint ventures, and their managers have worked through agreements with a variety of dissimilar partners, they become *more adaptive* in their responses to competitive challenges of cooperation because joint ventures permit managers to be more creative in problem solving and are better supported by their owner's joint resources.

Successful joint ventures serve their purpose without disrupting their owners' strategic well-being. Until partners find that they have irreconcilable differences in their visions for the venture, cooperation can be a way to implement changes in their strategic postures or to defend their current postures against forces too strong for one firm to withstand.[10]

The equilibrium point in an agreement could change, of course, if one of the partners was willing to make a minority investment in the other or if partners agreed on an outright acquisition. (A different cooperative strategy could also result over time if partners' perceptions of the activity in question changed.) Assuming in figure 3–3, for example, that firm A operated in a geographic market where firm B valued a presence highly and that the business activity was of strategic importance to it, firm B would want to control firm A's activities through an equity investment, if possible. If the business activity were not of strategic importance to firm A initially, it might become important after firm B made a minority investment in firm A and exerted some influence over A's autonomy. As it questions firm A's decisions, firm B forces firm A to increase the attention it devotes to the activities where firm B has an interest. If firm A devotes more managerial attention to its relationship with firm B, that makes the activity more important for A and the equilibrium point of cooperation between firms A and B evolves to the joint-venture alternative shown in figure 3–3. (In effect, firm A spins off its geographic activities in the regions of interest to firm B to create a jointly-owned subsidiary with firm B.) If the activities of interest to firm B do not increase in strategic importance for firm A, the equilibrium point in their cooperation stays in the right-hand cell. Firm B will probably press firm A for the acquisition of the business units it desires until they can reach a mutually accept-able price. The point is that asymmetries in the importance partners assign to the activities where they cooperate are *destabilizing*. If a balance is not maintained, cooperation cannot endure.

Changes in the Venture and/or Its Owners

Joint ventures are inherently unstable. The forces that promote cooperation are often fickle; even the success of a joint venture may encourage one owner to undertake *by itself* (and sometimes in competition with) the activities pre-viously assigned to the venture. In figure 3–2, the stability of a joint venture—and timing of changes in its terms—depends on changes in owners' condi-tions: changes in (13) owners' strategic missions, changes in (14) the impor-tance of the joint venture to owners, and changes in (15) owners' bargaining power with respect to its partners. When the joint venture is formed, each owner receives benefits from it that aids their respective strategic missions. Environmental changes, competitive pressures, or other demands may force their missions to shift, making the venture's activities more, or perhaps less, important to their new strategic missions. As an owner's dependence on its venture's activities rises or declines, the balance of relative bargaining power between partners shifts, especially if the resources one partner contributes to the joint venture become more or less valuable than the resources contributed by other partners. The stability of the agreement that creates a joint venture also depends on the venture's success within its industry: for example, on changes in (16) the success requirements of the venture's industry, as will be evident by changes in competitors' strategic postures, and in (17) the effec-tiveness of the venture's competitive strategy in responding to industry suc-cess requirements. The venture's strategic posture, like that of its owners, must change as technologies change in its industry, as new competitors enter, as productive capacity increases, as government regulations change, and so on. As customers' needs change and the means of satisfying demand change, a venture cannot remain static. But as the venture strengthens its position in its industry, it almost inevitably creates strains with the missions, activities and relationships of its owners. A joint venture's stability also depends on changes in owner–venture relationships, such as (18) changes in the venture's needs for decision-making autonomy, and (19) changes in owners' needs for coordination with their venture (as well as changes in the venture's need for coordination with its owners and changes in other forces discussed in chap-ters 4 and 5.

In responding to the threats and opportunities of its industry, the venture inevitably needs more (or different) inputs than what its owners provide; the venture's outputs change to suit its evolving marketplace. Only by sheer luck will the actions that are optimal for the venture's competitive success fit neatly with the evolving needs and resources of its owners as they each adapt their activities to the changing needs of their respective marketplaces. The venture will likely be reconstituted or changed in response to these and other change stimuli if it is to be continued (see figure 3–5).

Successful joint ventures require the correct choice of partners and symmetrical partner outlooks; but because most partners have diverse strategic outlooks and their strategies evolve dissimilarly, the tensions that develop over time must be managed. It is unreasonable to expect that partners can preserve the relationships that existed when the joint venture was first created. Sometimes just a change in managers is sufficient to change how an owner values cooperative strategies. Joint venture may be terminated at that point, or they may be turned into new opportunities to cooperate. The key to successful use of the inevitable tensions created by change lies in remembering each partner's sources of bargaining power and each partner's original reasons for cooperating.

Joint ventures are a compromise. They are also an inherently fragile and transitory strategy because of the political difficulties inherent in sharing authority for the venture's operating decisions (described in chapter 4) and because of the venture's changing requirements for successful competition (described in chapter 5). Partners will leave joint ventures when they have no further need for them, especially when they have learned how to go it alone.

Because joint ventures are formed in dynamic environments, changes in circumstances surrounding either owner, changes in the relationship of owners to their ventures, or changes surrounding the venture itself could precipitate renegotiation of terms of the bargaining agreement or an end to the joint venture. As each owner's strategic mission, expectations, loyalties, and resource mixes change, the balance of power within the joint venture changes. When owners gain (or lose) the power needed to influence their joint venture's activities, it will be renegotiated or terminated. Joint ventures may be liquidated, spunoff, taken over by one partner, or sold to an outside firm. Alternatively, the venture may go on but managerial control will pass from one owner to another, or it may open up to include more partners. *These are healthy and inevitable changes.* Because joint ventures are inherently unstable organizational forms, they are ideal for implementing transitional strategies, such as fade-out divestitures, organizational restructurings, and so on.

Changes in Owners' Strategies and the Venture's Strategic Importance

The *stability* of joint ventures—that is, whether changes in terms of the bargaining agreement were necessary before owners' objectives were attained—depends on how long the cooperation embodied in the original agreement

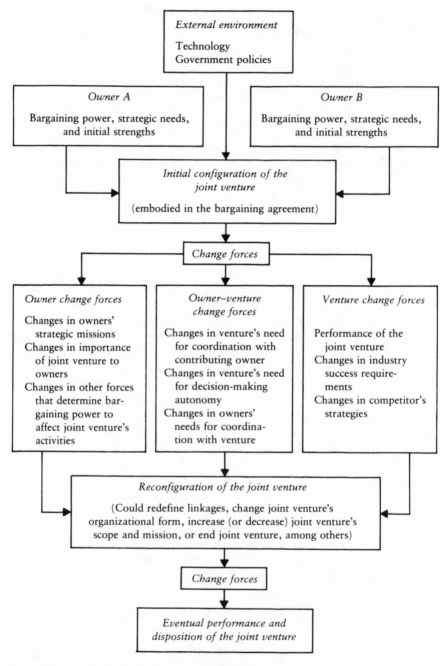

[a]I thank Donald C. Hambrick for suggesting this diagram.

Figure 3–5. A Dynamic Model of Joint-Venture Activity[a]

can be sustained. The stability of a joint-venture agreement will be affected by changes in owners' strategic missions, changes in the strategic importance owners attached to the venture, and changes in the alternatives owners may possess to attain the same benefits that the joint venture provided.

It is important to recognize when terms of a joint venture should be changed and when the affiliation should be terminated. Perhaps the venture no longer fits well with its owner's diversification plans, or perhaps partners can no longer agree on market allocations, the speed of product introductions, or other important points of cooperation. If firms diverge from their original vision for the joint venture or if their strategies evolve in a manner that lessens the venture's usefulness, it may be necessary to negotiate a "fade out" for one of the owners.

Chapter 1 notes that symmetry occurs when partners possess complementary strategic missions and visions for the role their joint venture plays with respect to their wholly owned business activities (for example, as a supplier, customer, or other affiliate). If the partners' strategic needs for each other are symmetrical, the relationship will be stable.

But as chapter 1 cautions, asymmetries in owners' visions for their joint venture are destabilizing to joint-venture relationships. The venture may be terminated because owners cannot agree on how much autonomy the venture should enjoy. The original agreement may be broken because the partners disagree on how the venture should relate to each owner's business units or how the venture's strategy should adapt to changes in its respective competitive environment. The opinions that each owner initially held on these and other points covered in the original joint-venture agreement tend to change as each owner's strategies change, or as other forces (sketched above) change.

Changes in Owners' Relative Bargaining Power

Joint ventures often have a built-in, self-destructing propensity because each owner is continually reassessing the tradeoffs of its investment. Joint ventures become casualties when one of the partners believes it has made a one-sided bargain that favors unreasonably the other partner.[11] When an owner becomes discontent with the original agreement, it often tries to enter the venture's markets through wholly owned subsidiaries so it can control these activities more tightly. Much depends on how each partner values the other partner's contributions and the operating policies that were originally negotiated.

Inequities may develop as ventures grow and require new infusions of capital; wealthier partners can better afford to increase ownership shares in the venture than can less prosperous partners. Wealthy owners will eventually gain dominance over the venture if parity cannot be maintained among partners. In oil exploration ventures, for example, when a joint venture seems unprofitable and one partner will no longer put up the cash needed to sustain operations, the other partner can increase its voice in operations and its ownership stake by contributing the full amount that would be needed to continue operation.[12] The latter firm may even acquire the joint venture outright if its partners are of unequal financial strength or if one partner becomes ill.

There could be valuation errors. Occasionally, both partners overestimate the value of distribution channels or other resources contributed to their joint venture and conclude that they could do as well without partners. However, joint ventures are more frequently terminated as the value of each partner's resources evolves asymmetrically. Their joint-venture agreement reflects the balance of power that formerly existed rather than the evolved balance of power, and partners are unwilling (or unable) to hammer out a new agreement that is mutually satisfactory.

Perceived parity in market power is important to joint-venture stabiity, but equivalent contributions of knowledge are often more important than many other types of asset contributions because innovation permits organizations to renew themselves. In order to maintain parity among partners, employees of the joint venture must learn to work together in creating knowledge, rather than to allow their ideas to be blocked by misplaced loyalty to the respective partners. As long as partners offer each other complementary strengths, which are amplified through their venture, each owner needs the joint venture. But a firm should be wary of developing strengths that duplicate those of its partner or venture, because jealousies could develop concerning the routing of business opportunities (to a partner or to the joint venture rather than to the firm). For this reason, joint ventures are more stable when market territories are delineated such that they do not let the venture compete against duplicate, wholly owned units of its owners. With at least three separate enterprises involved—two owners and their venture—there naturally will be some jockeying for priorities, protecting of turf, jealousies at the successes of the other parties, and so on. A push for parity by one enterprise will affect all other parties to the venture, perhaps with fatal results.

Changes in Owner–Venture Coordination and Relationships with Wholly Owned Business Units

Because joint ventures are often terminated after partners have gained knowledge of markets that they previously did not have, it is important for firms to find ways of cooperating without surrendering their competitive advantages to their venture or through it to their partners. If their basis for competitive advantage is easily appropriated, firms may *think* that they desire passive partners who will not intervene in the venture's operating decisions or share information with it. Such a position is unrealistic if owners are to realize the full potential of this strategy option. Active partners have two-way flows (between owner and venture) of (1) information and technological know-how; (2) products or services; (3) personnel; (4) marketing efforts; (5) training programs; and (6) other resources that provide for the enjoyment of synergies with their venture as well as financial assistance. Such synergies require both formal and informal coordination.

Because partners' relationships with their venture will determine whether they realize desired synergies and because owner–venture relationships exist at the sufferance of partners, it is important to understand that a means must be provided for sustaining good relationships between partners. Without this chemistry, owners will not realize the full benefits of joint ventures, and synergies will not accrue between owners and their ventures. If differences in strengths, performance, commitment, and other factors lead firms to create management systems (integrating mechanisms with their venture) that prevent their partners from enjoying desired synergies, their participation in the joint venture will not continue. The dilemma concerning owner–venture relationships is developed at greater length in chapter 4.

Changes in the Venture's Competitive Environment and Its Need for Autonomy

Industry differences will suggest how quickly ventures must evolve from loose cooperation to partnerships to stand-alone entities (if at all). As chapter 5 explains, volatile competitive conditions require shorter-lived and more informal liaisons. High demand uncertainty requires tentative affiliations, modest funding, and pilot plants or test situations. Because few industry structures are likely to remain unchanged in the future, few ongoing relationships between owner and venture (or between partners) are likely to match competitive realities for long. Change is inevitable, and resilient joint-venture agreements will recognize these dynamics.

Summary

Firms must anticipate not only how their own industry will evolve but also that of their venture if they hope to provide for all significant contingencies in how their relationships with partners might change in their joint-venture agreements. As chapter 8 notes, even partners that prefer to negotiate decisions as conflicts develop (rather than setting out divorce settlements in great detail in a prenuptial document) find it necessary to agree on the venture's purpose initially and to keep updating their expectations vis-à-vis the venture's performance and their relationships with their partners and their venture. Open discussions of these dynamics during the bargaining period often result in partners establishing ground rules for how the joint venture will operate, for example, with how much autonomy the venture may proceed as it matures or as strategic milestones are attained. Open discussion of these dynamics at the bargaining table during the courtship period often results in the creation of management systems that better anticipate the nature of changing relationships among parties and the tensions these changes could create.

4
Interactions between Owners and Venture

This chapter develops components of the bargaining agreement pertaining to each owner's relationship with the venture: the terms, resources shared, and management policies that create and define the venture. It assumes that owners have created a separate organizational entity, and it develops points concerning the horizontal and vertical relationships between owner and venture that could give rise to the creation of synergies. This analysis is appropriate for shared-ownership arrangements regardless of whether a separate entity is created or one partner takes a minority interest in the other. In either case, arrangements must be made to cover organization structure, management systems, and the ways of thinking about competitive strategy to reflect each partner's motives for cooperating.

Integration of owner and venture activities represents the second leg in the joint-venture strategy model, as the heavy arrows indicate in figure 4–1, and terms of these relationships are set forth in the bargaining agreement, which is often accompanied by a legal document that defines ownership terms, governance procedures, and divorce settlements. More important than these financial details, however, are the understandings developed between owners concerning (1) what relationships will be maintained between them and their venture; (2) what degree of autonomy the venture's managers will enjoy to modify those relationships; and (3) what levels of support the venture can rely on from its owners.

Chapter 3, which sketches each firm's privately weighted cost-benefit analysis, assumes that partners had specific benefits in mind when they agreed to cooperate in joint ventures. Many of these benefits are discussed in chapter 2 as being motivations for cooperative strategies. In order for owners to realize these benefits in their dealings with their venture, they must agree among themselves on the nature of horizontal or vertical relationships that each will enjoy with the venture, including their need for close coordination with the venture (for synergistic resource sharing), or for the venture to enjoy operating autonomy (for performance maximization). Partners must agree among themselves on which resources will be shared among owner and ven-

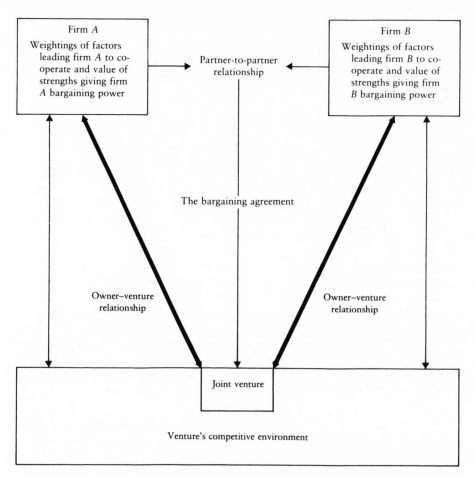

Figure 4–1. Owner–Venture Relationships in Managing a Joint Venture

ture (which resources will be duplicative of existing assets), how transactions will be channeled among owners' and venture's facilities when they run in parallel, and other issues determining how synergies and other benefits of joint ventures will be realized.

The Bargaining Agreement

The joint-venture framework assumes that the venture requires access to certain inputs and a healthy market for its outputs in order to be viable. Access to these inputs and distribution channels is provided for by terms of the bargaining agreement; many arrangements are possible. Owners may specify vertical as well as horizontal relationships, but a decision must be made concerning where the venture obtains inputs and sells its outputs or the joint venture will not be viable and cannot be expected to survive for long.

The Bargaining Agreement's Content

The resources and attributes that owners share with the joint venture determine its purpose and what types of synergies (if any) they expect to enjoy through its operations. These are the benefits that satisfy a firm's strategic needs that are discussed in chapter 3. These benefits are what motivated it to form the venture initially. As the content of the partnership's bargaining agreement evolves, these expected benefits are the touchstones against which owners will compare ongoing operations to ascertain whether the venture's operations continue to satisfy their objectives. Details of the joint-venture agreement are shown in figure 4–2, which recasts the dynamic joint-venture framework diagram. Each owner in figure 4–2 possesses resources and skills that could serve as potential inputs to the joint venture. Alternatively, the venture's managers may be given autonomy to go to outside markets to obtain needed inputs.

The bargaining agreement, which defines the venture's domain of activities, will specify its outputs (and it may specify the venture's customers, if one or more owners gives the venture a take-or-pay contract for the sale of some of its outputs). Operating relationships with owners are defined by provisions for *sharing facilities*.

The most commonplace sharing arrangement involves the use of an owner's sales force and marketing organization or the use of an owner's R&D facilities. These are the resources *least likely* to be duplicated in the joint venture because they constitute their respective owners' strategic cores. However, if firms do not share facilities with their venture, owners should agree on whether they themselves will be operating facilities that *duplicate* the venture's operations and whether their in-house organizations will have any *choice* in dealing with the venture for supplies, marketing services, or other products that the venture has been expressly created to provide.

Although this point is frequently spelled out in the bargaining agreement, it is helpful to articulate what *operating autonomy* the venture's managers may expect as their experience base increases. Similarly, it is helpful to articulate *how closely* the venture's activities will have to be coordinated with those of its owners to exploit any potential for synergies.

Finally, the bargaining agreement also specifies the control mechanisms that owners will use to ensure that the benefits they desire are indeed received. The control mechanisms provide for how owners will develop the venture's managerial resources, how the venture's board of directors will provide for

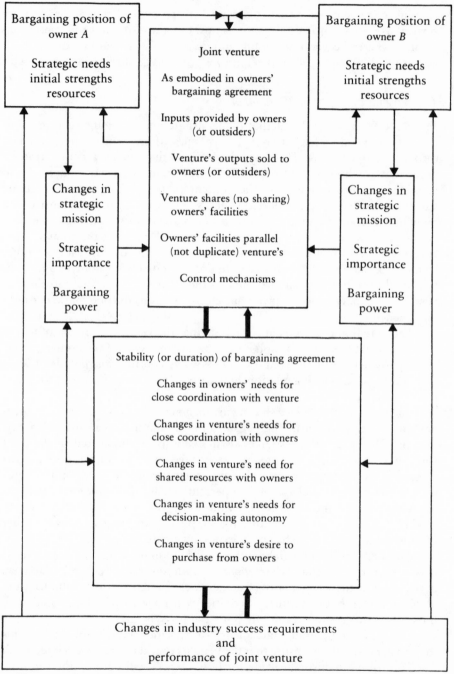

Figure 4–2. A Dynamic Model of Joint-Venture Activity (Venture's Perspective)

owners' interests, and how disputes between partners will be resolved. The formal document specifies divorce settlements when the venture ends, and it should also suggest ways of maintaining the joint venture's stability.[1]

In summary, the bargaining agreement document is frequently highly detailed in financial and legal matters. To ensure joint-venture success, more attention should be given to questions of owner–venture relationships and questions of operating autonomy. In particular, managers should devote some attention to questions of how the benefits that are expected of joint ventures will in fact be realized.

Provision of Inputs and Markets for Outputs

Chapter 3 notes that the most likely candidates for ventures are firms that lack the capabilities, strengths, or resources needed to exploit business opportunities alone. As table 4–1 indicates, the alliances they create will enable them to (1) share risks and costs with partners; (2) reach the external capital markets using the joint venture as an additional vehicle for raising funds; (3) gain scale economies and operating synergies from shared manufacturing facilities, technologies, and other physical assets; (4) build market share and fill out their product lines by sharing brand names, products, and support services; (5) gain scale economies and operating synergies by sharing distribution channels, sales forces, and marketing facilities; (6) exploit innovation synergies by sharing laboratories and scientific personnel; (7) share components, raw materials, or other supplies that require a plant of a minimum efficient scale far larger than a firm's internal component requirements; (8) exploit logistical synergies from shared service organizations, research activities, and other multiplant activities; (9) gain scale economies through pooled purchasing and provision of services, supplies, and other resources; and (10) enjoy other benefits and sources of synergy.

Vertical Relationships. Many other synergies and benefits of joint ventures are discussed in chapter 2. In table 4–1, these are depicted in a matrix of synergistic relationships that may be interpreted as inputs $(_j)$ and outputs $(_k)$ that could provide synergy $(_i)$ when taken from or provided to owner A (which gives and takes x_{ijk}), to owner B (which gives and takes y_{ijk}). The set of synergies was constrained to nine sources in table 4–1 for expositional purposes, and the inputs and outputs were each constrained to four per source of synergy—typically, personnel, technology, physical assets, and capital.

The x_{ijk}s, y_{ijk}s and z_{ijk}s that partners agree on will determine whether the venture is vertically or horizontally related to its owners. In figure 4–3, the vertical stages of processing are numbered consecutively to facilitate the discussion that follows. If in figure 4–3, for example, synergies accrue when owners A and B share the outputs from (6) their venture's plant and market

Table 4–1
Matrix of Synergies by Horizontal and Vertical Relationship of Owners to Joint Venture

Source of Synergy$_{(i)}$	Venture$_{(j)}$[a]	Venture$_{(k)}$	Owner A$_{(x)}$	Owner B$_{(y)}$	Open Market$_{(z)}$
1. Cost and risk sharing	. . . takes materials from	. . . sells outputs to	x_{111}	y_{111}	z_{111}
	. . . takes personnel from	. . . gives personnel to	x_{122}	y_{122}	z_{122}
	. . . takes technology from	. . . sells technology to	x_{133}	y_{133}	z_{133}
	. . . takes capital from	. . . gives capital to	x_{144}	y_{144}	z_{144}
2. External financial markets	. . . takes materials from	. . . sells outputs to	x_{211}	y_{211}	z_{211}
	. . . takes personnel from	. . . gives personnel to	x_{222}	y_{222}	z_{222}
	. . . takes technology from	. . . sells technology to	x_{233}	y_{233}	z_{233}
	. . . takes capital from	. . . gives capital to	x_{244}	y_{244}	z_{244}
3. Share plant, facilities	. . . takes materials from	. . . sells outputs to	x_{311}	y_{311}	z_{311}
	. . . takes personnel from	. . . gives personnel to	x_{322}	y_{322}	z_{322}
	. . . takes technology from	. . . sells technology to	x_{333}	y_{333}	z_{333}
	. . . takes capital from	. . . gives capital to	x_{344}	y_{344}	z_{344}
4. Share product lines	. . . takes materials from	. . . sells outputs to	x_{411}	y_{411}	z_{411}
	. . . takes personnel from	. . . gives personnel to	x_{422}	y_{422}	z_{422}
	. . . takes technology from	. . . sells technology to	x_{433}	y_{433}	z_{433}
	. . . takes capital from	. . . gives capital to	x_{444}	y_{444}	z_{444}
5. Share distribution channels	. . . takes materials from	. . . sells outputs to	x_{511}	y_{511}	z_{511}
	. . . takes personnel from	. . . gives personnel to	x_{522}	y_{522}	z_{522}
	. . . takes technology from	. . . sells technology to	x_{533}	y_{533}	z_{533}
	. . . takes capital from	. . . gives capital to	x_{544}	y_{544}	z_{544}
6. Share laboratories, personnel	. . . takes materials from	. . . sells outputs to	x_{611}	y_{611}	z_{611}
	. . . takes personnel from	. . . gives personnel to	x_{622}	y_{622}	z_{622}
	. . . takes technology from	. . . sells technology to	x_{633}	y_{633}	z_{633}
	. . . takes capital from	. . . gives capital to	x_{644}	y_{644}	z_{644}
7. Supply materials, components	. . . takes materials from	. . . sells outputs to	x_{711}	y_{711}	z_{711}
	. . . takes personnel from	. . . gives personnel to	x_{722}	y_{722}	z_{722}
	. . . takes technology from	. . . sells technology to	x_{733}	y_{733}	z_{733}
	. . . takes capital from	. . . gives capital to	x_{744}	y_{744}	z_{744}
8. Supply technology, services	. . . takes materials from	. . . sells outputs to	x_{811}	y_{811}	z_{811}
	. . . takes personnel from	. . . gives personnel to	x_{822}	y_{822}	z_{822}
	. . . takes technology from	. . . sells technology to	x_{833}	y_{833}	z_{833}
	. . . takes capital from	. . . gives capital to	x_{844}	y_{844}	z_{844}
9. Purchase products, services	. . . takes materials from	. . . sells outputs to	x_{911}	y_{911}	z_{911}
	. . . takes personnel from	. . . gives personnel to	x_{922}	y_{922}	z_{922}
	. . . takes technology from	. . . sells technology to	x_{933}	y_{933}	z_{933}
	. . . takes capital from	. . . gives capital to	x_{944}	y_{944}	z_{944}

[a]The matrix depicts terms of the joint-venture agreement. Its values reflect the interests of its owners.

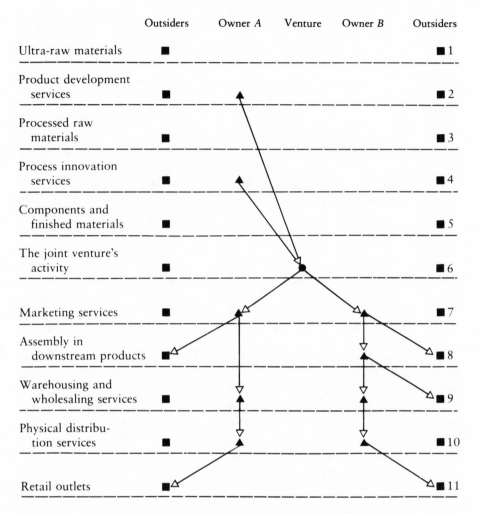

Figure 4–3. Example of Vertical Relationships between Owners and Venture

them through their respective (7) distribution channels or sell them to outsiders that use the outputs in subsequent (8) assembly operations. The venture operates *upstream* from its owners (at processing stage 6 in figure 4–3) and is *vertically related* to them. Note also in figure 4–3 that the venture does *not* sell its outputs to outsiders; the venture is a *captive* supplier to its owners in this illustration of vertical reltionships. But the larger the value of z_{ijk} in table 4–1 (the greater the proportion of outputs the venture sells to outsiders, for example), the greater the venture's need for *independence* from its owners in its operating decisions. The greater the value of the x_{ijk}s or y_{ijk}s, by contrast (the more dependent the venture is on owners as suppliers of inputs or as customers of its outputs), the greater the need for *close coordination* between owner and venture operations in order to maximize vertical integration economies.[2]

Many joint ventures in metals fabrication were vertically related to one or more of their owners and initially served as captive suppliers or distributors. If they thrived, they subsequently served outside markets also. Survival and satisfaction were higher among joint ventures in the metals fabrication industry, perhaps because capital requirements and technological risks seemed lower than in other capital-intensive industries. Greater use was also made of cooperative agreements and licensing arrangements in metals fabrication activities than in mining and metals processing. Alternatively, these joint ventures may have seemed longer-lived because some of them were, in fact, incremental divestitures of assets and goodwill by one of their owners to outsiders seeking entry.

The venture uses *market prices* as a reference point in most of its vertical dealings with multiple owners to ensure that vertical transfer arrangements are economically justified as well as equitable to them. (If a vertical relationship exists between partners to a joint venture, care must be taken that discontent and inequities do not develop when each firm realizes what the other's profit margins have been.) Forcing the venture to take its full requirements from owners (or to sell them all of its outputs) cuts firms off from a useful source of intelligence. For example, using outside vendors' prices to police in-house buyer–seller relationships reduces the heights of vertical integration-related exit barriers when the need for the joint venture's activities ends.[3] The venture will face obsolescence if it is not permitted to advise its owners concerning when the products it merchandizes for them are less in demand. Since a forward-integrated venture is closer to the demand of ultimate consumers, it would know more quickly than its owners whether its existence is still economically justified.

Technology Transfer. Chapter 3 notes that technological prowess is a strength in a potential partner's bargaining position only as long as it is not easily appropriated. Given the perishable nature of this resource, it is scarcely surprising that partners devote substantial attention to devising technology transfer schemes to *protect* their respective competitive advantages, especially when effective joint ventures will require ongoing technical relationships between owners and venture. Mechanisms must be created to nurture those relationships and allay owners' fears that their competitive advantages will be appropriated if their partnership is to thrive. If patent protection is weak, and owners cannot protect their property rights for the technology that will be used in a joint venture, fewer transfers of knowledge will occur, the difficulties associated with preventing technological bleedthrough will be exacerbated, and the joint-venture relationships will be unstable.

The *proprietary* elements of many owners' resources will probably be sold within ventures at arm's-length arrangements that protect their respective property rights. However, for some technologies, even that precaution is insufficient. Because any information that is transferred to the joint venture is no longer fully under the control of the sponsoring firm (and no knowledge can be protected adequately once it is shared), the venture will often receive the proprietary portions of its owner's technologies (and other resources that gives a firm relative bargaining power) just before the technology is superseded, if a joint venture is formed at all. Technology leaders will provide their venture with *incremental* pieces of technology as the knowledge becomes less proprietary or as the firm gains confidence in working with its partners in the joint venture. This is done because firms have no other satisfactory way to protect the appropriable knowledge that gives them bargaining power.

For example, marketing agreements, licenses, and cross-licensing agreements abound in precision controls and robotics, yet there are relatively few joint ventures. Cooperation is necessary in parts of the precision controls, factory automation, and robotics industries because of the long payback periods required to prove experimental technologies. The drain on sponsoring firms' resources is immense and industry leaders take partners to broaden their product lines with less risk.

Owners differ in how they control technology developed within their venture. Ownership is a nettlesome problem because all of the venture's technology originally comes from its owners. Many patterns of coordination exist. Some firms let the venture be the royalty-collecting intermediary when they seek permission to license technology that may have been contributed by another partner. Other firms prohibit any ownership of technology by the venture. Some owners insist only on a licensing right-of-first-access for technology developed by their venture and allow the venture to license technology to others, as well. Still other owners do not allow their venture to license any of its knowledge to outsiders.

Having a high technology venture as both supplier and customer to its owners is an especially complex situation because simply holding transactions to arm's-length relationships does not suffice in situations where quick responses are needed. Several rounds of negotiation between owners often are necessary to resolve which actions their venture should undertake in the face of competition.

Balanced ownership shares in high technology joint ventures are considered desirable by owners in order to ensure that partners remain interested in and involved with the venture's technological development. Innovation is enhanced by reciprocal trading of one owner's laboratory to another's, by frequent visits of technical personnel to partners' plants, and by online computer communications links. Owners who are closer to the market tend to control the venture's operations, and selling tasks usually are performed by the marketing owner's own sales force. By contrast technology owners are involved with customer responses primarily when product modifications are required, and the venture's managers are often granted substantial day-to-day autonomy in manufacturing activities, but closely coordinate design and other technical details with the venture's technology parent.

Market Access. Chapter 3 notes that the most enduring strength that a firm can control usually is *market access,* and partners' negotiations in forming ventures often acknowledge that this advantage endures longer than others. Owners are more likely to sell their venture's outputs through their respective distribution channels (or to consume them in-house) than to pool distribution facilities and permit the venture to develop facilities to interface with their ultimate customers.

Sometimes partners join forces to circumvent powerful distributors that act like a bottleneck, as in the example of the many joint ventures by entertainment producers that were inspired by a desire for vertical integration to create countervailing bargaining power against programming packagers like Home Box Office. (By 1983, Home Box Office had 12.5 million subscribers compared with a combined total of 6 million subscribers for Showtime and The Movie Channel. Its bargaining power over the motion picture studios was immense.) Much like the nonintegrated oil exploration firms during periods of excess crude oil supply, the movie studios found that they had to accept the terms that programming packagers dictated to them until they could find a way of changing the balance of power.

Some motion picture joint ventures were motivated by a need to create more and better programming. During the 1960s and 1970s, theatrical films had been a staple of network television. Firms such as Universal Studios controlled over eleven thousand motion picture titles, but newer films (and "blockbusters") commanded the largest audiences. By 1982, these movies were becoming overexposed and theatrical films began doing so poorly on the commercial networks that their ratings no longer justified their costs. Distribution channels were cannibalizing each other as satellites, pay-per-view, dish antennas, and videocasettes all competed for viewers by offering exclusive programming. As the costs of good programming skyrocketed, the need for film-makers to capture greater value-added margins became acute. Moreover, resentment of their treatment at the hands of the new distribution technologies caused some movie studios to jump into joint ventures in cable-TV, home video, and other distribution systems that they scarcely understood. The movie studios engaged in many ventures because they were hedging their bets. (If any of them had possessed clear insights as to how the industry would evolve, they would have invested alone.) As the motion picture studios were pressed for more good programming, more limited partnership financing ventures were created, even among firms such as Universal Studios, which historically had financed its own movies.

Joint ventures frequently are formed between foreign firms and local competitors to penetrate domestic markets. When such arrangements involve a U.S. partner, the foreign firm often contributes products that the U.S. partner sells. Although the foreign firm may intend for its venture to evolve one day into a stand-alone entity that serves its own distinct group of customers, it will find that it is exceedingly difficult to realize such development plans if its U.S. marketing partner has already established relationships with local customers under its own brand names and will not let the joint venture deal with these customers. Owners' wholly owned business units, in particular, will not appreciate that a new competitor has been created in the venture, and are unlikely to give the venture their full cooperation unless they are encouraged to do so.

Shared Facilities

Shared facilities attain scale economies by pooling firms' individually smaller requirements for manufacturing operations, R&D, or other resources into one facility that enjoys greater economies when operating at a larger, fully utilized scale. Shared facilities are like a bottleneck in the sense that they represent a stage of processing where fewer firms may be operating, but this shortfall of competitors represents an opportunity to exploit technological scale advantages. Briefly, it is *more efficient* for firms to share that stage of processing's outputs than it is to duplicate its facilities to *prevent* the jealousies created by sharing.

In figure 4–4, the vertical stages of processing are numbered consecutively to facilitate discussion of resource-sharing. In figure 4–4, owner *B* and the venture share (5) a components and finished materials facility. Also, the venture has (1) mineral extraction operations to procure ultra-raw materials and (6) operations midway down the vertical chain of processing. In order to enjoy scale economies, the venture in figure 4–4 and owner *A* share (3) a processed raw materials facility and (8) a downstream assembly plant. Their upstream, shared (3) processing plant has a very large minimum efficient scale because the combined inputs of owner and venture (1) facilities are insufficient to satisfy its productive capacity; (3) the processing plant also purchases (1) ultra-raw materials from outsiders.

The heavy horizontal line at the level of (6) the joint venture's activity (and the triangles representing its owners, firm *A* and firm *B*) suggest that the venture in figure 4–4 is *horizontally* as well as *vertically* related to its

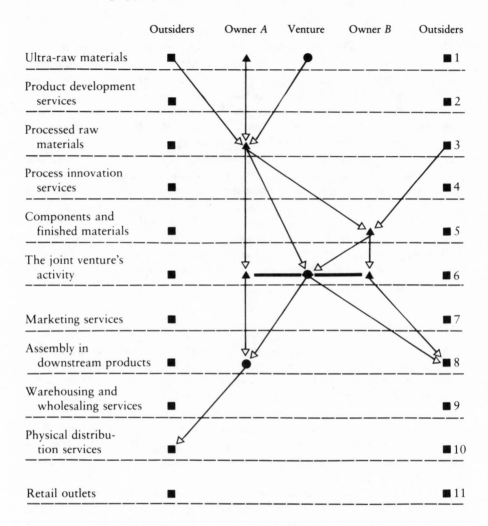

Figure 4–4. Example of Shared Resources between Owners and Venture

owners. The venture could be a *competitor* of its owners for customers, raw materials, personnel and capital resources. Also, the venture in figure 4–4 sells some of its outputs (x_{ijk}s) to (8) owner A and the remainder of its outputs (z_{ijk}s) to outsiders' (8) downstream assembly operations; the joint venture in figure 4–4 is *not* a captive vendor to its owners because it deals with outsiders.

Owners will share facilities with their venture to create synergies when they need to protect their technology, their distribution systems, or other resources that give them competitive advantage. Referring to the synergistic matrix of table 4–1, it can be predicted that owners' needs for control over their venture's activities will increase as its products $(_k)$ are more closely intertwined with their own products $(x_{ijk}s)$.

Horizontal Relationships. *Horizontally related* ventures compete in the same industries as their owners. Given the arguments concerning the sources of bargaining power and competitive advantage of chapter 3, it is unlikely that fearsome owners will create duplicate facilities for their venture in areas of strategic importance to them. Their fears of losing competitive advantage to outsiders would lead them to deprive their venture of the capabilities in question; owners would instead perform these tasks in-house and share the outputs with ventures. Scale economies would accrue from production pooling, and wholly owned business units would enjoy peace of mind because no competitor has been created.

Synergies. Shared resources create synergies if horizontal relationships between owners and venture are managed conscientiously. Wholly owned business units that share resources and facilities can enjoy the synergistic benefits of scheduling advantages, high levels of capacity utilizations, new applications of technological approaches, and other shared knowledge advantages. However, synergies between owner and partially owned venture are difficult to attain without surrendering some knowledge of owners' competitive advantages. To guard against the dangers of bleedthrough of proprietary knowledge into unauthorized hands, firms are more likely to provide their venture with *parallel facilities* that duplicate their ongoing activities or they are likely to deal only on a buyer–supplier basis at that level of processing rather than allowing their venture ready access to certain kinds of information.

Whether the relationship between owner and venture will be horizontal, vertical, or related (or unrelated) in some other manner, care must be taken to prepare the firm's organization for the notion that resources must be *shared* with the venture in order to enjoy synergies. Special care must be given to the reality that firms' true competitive advantages in successful joint ventures are often their people and that such resources can be highly mobile. Consequently, the control mechanisms used to coordinate these relationships (discussed below) must be clear in terms of which patterns of loyalties (to the joint venture or to its owners) will be reinforced by the management systems that firms use to control their relationships with their venture.

If the venture's activities will be coordinated with one or more of its owners, the focal point for coordination will have to be on the resources they share. Where owner and venture address the same customer needs, for example, synergies will be maximized if sales organizations can share innovations and disseminate knowledge. To attain this benefit, programs and centralized responsibilities for information dissemination (for example, a clearinghouse for materials purchasing, scheduling of available managerial talents, customer information, or other common resources, services or experiences) are needed to increase opportunities for owner and venture to enjoy synergies.

Managers who can devise the most effective means of exploiting relationships between owner and venture organizations will have the greatest opportunity to gain a competitive advantage in their venture's industry. An effective integration of owner's and venture's respective strengths will make the venture more than just a new industry entrant. If effective, the synergies they create will require the venture's competitors to seek joint-venture relationships, as well.

In summary, cooperative strategies represent an exciting theory, but they are difficult to implement in practice. The venture's viability may be undermined through the relationships its owners desire and the control mechanisms they impose on their ventures. If undermined, one of the strongest dimensions of the venture as a strategic weapon—the opportunity to realize synergies for its owners—will be negated.

However, in order for joint-venture synergies to be realized, owners must reduce the tensions created by parallel facilities, either by placing all of their activities in a particular industry (or market segment) into the venture organization (as at level [3] in figure 4–6) or by designing other mechanisms for reducing sibling rivalry. The stability of a joint-venture relationship between owners will be eroded by their respective failures to reduce inter-strategic business unit (SBU) rivalries, but will be enhanced by their need for the activities performed by their venture, especially if cost advantages are available from such pooling arrangements.

Parallel Facilities

Owners may create parallel facilities for their venture to ameliorate some of the jealousies the venture will encounter from its wholly owned, sister business units. In figure 4–5, the vertical chain of processing is numbered consecutively to facilitate discussion, and the joint venture is engaged in three vertically related activities: (5) components and finished materials, its (6) core activity, and (8) downstream assembly operations. At each of these stages of vertically related processing, owner *A* and owner *B* *also* operate facilities that duplicate the venture's facilities. These are *parallel facilities*.

The schema illustrated in figure 4–5 would appear to offer great promise for scale economies, logistical synergies, and other benefits because owner *A* and the venture *share* (2) product development and (4) process innovation services from owner *A*'s centralized R&D facilities. The joint venture is *taper-integrated* to obtain its (3) processed raw materials inputs from both owner

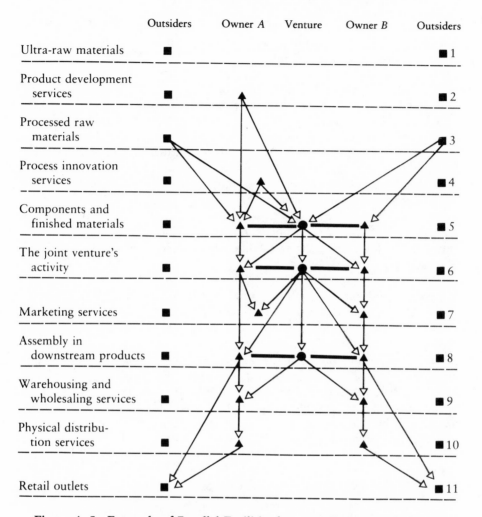

	Outsiders	Owner *A*	Venture	Owner *B*	Outsiders

Ultra-raw materials

Product development
  services

Processed raw
  materials

Process innovation
  services

Components and
  finished materials

The joint venture's
  activity

Marketing services

Assembly in
  downstream products

Warehousing and
  wholesaling services

Physical distribu-
  tion services

Retail outlets

Figure 4–5. Example of Parallel Facilities between Owners and Venture

A and from outsiders. It sells (5) components and finished materials to owner
A, owner *B, and* to in-house (6) processing units of its own. The venture's
core manufacturing activity is *fully integrated,* selling its (6) outputs on (7) a
merchant basis to outsiders as well as incorporating the venture's outputs into
owners' respective (8) downstream assembly operations, and into the venture's own (8) downstream assembly operations. The venture's (8) assembly
operations, in turn, are fully integrated downstream, selling outputs only to
owner *A*'s and owner *B*'s (9) warehousing and wholesaling facilities at the
next stage of processing.

If the joint venture described above had enjoyed greater (but not full) *autonomy* with respect to its buyer—seller relationships, the schema representing the vertical chain of processing would resemble that in figure 4–6, where the vertical chain of processing has also been numbered consecutively to facilitate discussion. In figure 4–6, the joint venture purchases (1) ultra-raw materials from its owners (firms *A* and *B*) *and* from outsiders, and the venture purchases (2) product development services from outsiders. It sells its (3) processed raw materials to its owners, to its own (5) downstream processed components and finished materials operations, *and* to outsiders. The venture's business unit at level (5), in turn, purchases (4) process innovation services from outsiders and sells its (5) outputs to both owners and to its own (6) core operations. The venture's (6) core products unit buys (5) components only from insiders, but it sells (6) outputs to both owners' (8) downstream assembly operations *and* to outsiders. Some of the reasons for creating an autonomous joint venture with facilities that parallel those of its owners are discussed below.

Autonomy and Parallel Facilities. Owners may create parallel facilities for their venture when that venture matures to an experience level that would enable it to issue securities in its own right. Parallel facilities may also be needed if the venture (1) sells similar products to market segments that are *different* from those of its owners; (2) pursues different technological avenues to attain results similar to those of its owners; or (3) must own the property rights for the products and processes it develops. Finally, parallel facilities may be necessary if the venture must move quickly in response to competitive needs in technology or marketing areas where its owners have been sluggish to react to change in the past. (These points are developed below.)

Independent facilities are appropriate for the venture when its activities are *not parallel* to its owners' activities, where firms have pooled their respective resources and facilities in the venture, or the venture is far from the strategic core of its owners. Stand-alone, autonomous facilities are also appropriate where no vertical relationships exist between owner and venture.

If the venture is to have a life of its own—one in which it may evolve from a loosely structured agreement among partners to work together into an entity with its own in-house facilities—it will require assets that either parallel or supplement its owners' capabilities. The venture may even evolve into an incorporated entity with facilities to invent, make, and sell products in its own right. By the time the joint venture has developed to that level of maturity, many of the problems regarding synergies and parallel facilities that may hamstring partners' abilities to work together in their early phases of cooperation must be resolved. Indeed, vertical (buyer—seller) relationships that once may have existed between owner and venture may be terminated later as they become uneconomic, for optimal vertical integration relationships are dynamic, as well.

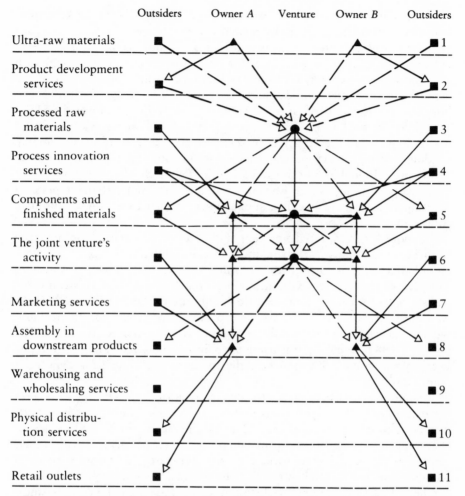

Figure 4–6. Example of Joint-Venture Autonomy vis-á-vis Buyer-Seller Relationships

Moreover, the venture's operations cannot be integrated closely with those of horizontally related owners if partners fear that too much knowledge bleedthrough will occur. If it is necessary to design control mechanisms to protect owners' assets or knowledge, this poses a dilemma.

Reducing Tensions. Venture facilities that parallel the activities of horizontally related owners will be inherently destabilizing to their joint venture agreements because of the inter-SBU jealousies such facilities engender, *but a viable venture will fare poorly without either parallel facilities or operating autonomy.*

The venture's capabilities (if it is permitted any) will have to be kept apart from the core of its horizontally related owner's competitive advantage, yet creating parallel facilities could mean that a potential competitor has been created. Synergies will *not* accrue in the latter case because, even though firm A is the venture's owner, relationships among personnel within owner and venture organizations will be strained over time. For example, in 1980 Ransburg Inc. and Renault Industries Aquitementes et Techniques formed a 51%–49% joint venture, Cybotech, to develop, make, sell, and service industrial robots. Cybotech offered a line of several heavy duty servo robots for arc welding, cutting, heavy part and transport loading, among other uses, all highly programmable. In the United States, Cybotech specialized in serving the aerospace industry for Ransburg; at the same time, Renault pursued painting and resistance-welding applications through Cybotech to automate American Motors Corp. (AMC).

Cybotech had captured 5 percent of the general U.S. market for industrial robots by 1984 and was thriving in its specialized markets. However, by the end of that year, majority ownership in Cybotech had shifted to Ransburg (90 percent) because of Renault's substantial losses in AMC. Meanwhile, Ransburg had formed a joint venture in painting robots with Tokiko to take Ransburg's technology to Tokyo. That partnership thrived and the technology they developed surpassed the technology developed by Cybotech for Renault. By 1984, Ransburg was using the painting robot technology developed with Tokiko in its U.S. products, rather than that developed for Cybotech's painting robot.

In summary, owners' needs for diverse relationships with their ventures are determined by competitive conditions within the industries where partners hope to use them effectively. Many of these conditions are discussed in chapter 5. In all cases where firms find a need to create facilities within their venture that parallel their own, they risk generating animosities between wholly owned and partially owned business units. Sometimes these jealousies can be reduced by dividing marketing territories among competing business units. But if the venture develops parallel facilities, it will frequently begin to think (and perhaps act) like a competitor of its owners *unless its domain is restricted*. Thus owners must also devote attention to issues concerning *when* the competitive challenges that the venture faces merit high operating autonomy and *when* the synergistic objectives of owners require that the venture be reined in by a program of close coordination with its wholly owned, sister business units.

Integrating Owners and Venture

If a venture is managed by an entrepreneurial executive, owners may find that it is straining at its tethers. The venture's management team may wish to exploit opportunities faster than owners' managers had intended them to move. Alternatively, if the venture's manager is not permitted to exercise any initiative, the venture will be ill-suited to move quickly and effectively should owners call on it for assistance. In either case, attention must be devoted to ensuring that the venture enjoys an appropriate mix of autonomy from and coordination with its owners' activities. That mix will depend on the venture's strategic mission and how its activities will be integrated with the business activities of owners' wholly owned units.

Trade-offs between Autonomy and Coordination

As the preceding section notes, the bargaining agreement between partners must reflect their strategic missions and expectations concerning the benefits they seek from their alliance. Using the synergistic matrix notations of table 4–1 to illustrate these tensions from the venture's perspective, the preceding section argues that owners must provide for the relationships they will enjoy with their venture in order to realize the benefits $(_i)$ that motivated them as firms to cooperate. Thus, owners will seek to increase their control over the venture's activities as their internal consumption of the venture's outputs (x_{ijk} and y_{ijk}, for example) increases. As the venture's competitive strategy drives it in directions that diverge from those of its owners and as it sells more to outsiders (z_{ijk}), the venture's managers will agitate for more operating freedoms. If firms strived to protect technological knowledge that was shared with their venture (x_{633}, for example) from bleedthrough to unauthorized third parties (z_{633} or z_{833}), they would increase their control over the venture. If they sought to protect other shared information that comprised their strategic core $(_j)$, they would bind their venture closer through their management systems and other control mechanisms (discussed below), as well as through their control over the flow of materials, personnel, technology, and capital $(_{jk})$ between owner and venture.

Tighter controls will be needed when the activities of owner $(_j)$ and venture $(_k)$ are *similar*. When the venture develops its own distinctive competences $(_k)$ that differ from those of its owners $(_j)$, fewer synergies $(_i)$ will be enjoyed because fewer resources will be shared. But superior operating performance will be enjoyed by firms as owners of (and investors in) the successful venture.

Range of Needs for Owners' Control over the Venture

Owners' need to intervene in the joint venture's decisions increases (1) as the venture's strategic importance to the firm increases; (2) as the value and scope of resources shared with the firm increases; and (3) as the degree of resource transfers between owner and venture (vertical integration) increases. The venture's need for autonomy increases as the *speed* of competitive response needed increases (competitive conditions requiring such autonomy are covered in chapter 5) but will decrease as similarities between owners' and venture's strategic missions increase or as the value and scope of resources shared among them increase.

Figure 4–7, which juxtaposes the intervention needs of owners against the autonomy needs of their ventures, suggests that in some cases, successful competitive strategies require the venture to coordinate its activities closely with one or more of its owners. Figure 4–7 also notes that ventures will be highly unstable when these opposing needs for coordination are both high. Yet owners are likely to seek ways of coordinating closely with their venture, even where the venture would prefer more autonomy to compete as it sees fit.

Need for Tight Controls. The key to determining whether owners must exert strong controls over their venture's activities will be in how much interaction with their ongoing business units is needed to achieve the venture's purpose. The need for owners to exert substantial control over their venture's activities is greatest when they hope to capture internal benefits for their ongoing units, such as to share outputs of large minimum efficient-scale plants, avoid wasteful duplication of facilities, utilize by-product and processes, or share brands, distribution channels, wide product lines, and so forth. Relationships between owners and their venture are more likely to be either horizontal or vertical when internal strengths are sought; the pattern will be less clear when other benefits are sought. For example, joint ventures in the programming and programming–packaging businesses were closely coordinated with their horizontally and vertically related owners, respectively. Because their venture's activities were important to owners, they kept a relatively tight rein over their venture's decisions, not permitting some of them to buy the rights to a movie, for example. Not infrequently, owners' personnel managed the venture's activities as well as their own responsibilities. In the example of ABC Video, anchor personnel were taken from commercial broadcasting assignments to revitalize the cable services.

For many sponsoring firms, the manufacture of videodisc players represented a risky activity that was significantly different from their core of activities. Only *marketing* activities for their videodisc joint ventures were coordinated closely with owners' ongoing activities because control of distribution was close to their strategic cores.

Since the technological configuration that dominated the videotape recorder market had been developed overseas, there was little need for U. S. joint ventures except in the area of programming, and this activity was of strategic importance to the firms that formed these ventures. Not surprisingly, these ventures were coordinated closely with their owners' activities, leaving joint-venture managers little autonomy in decision making. Videodisc players

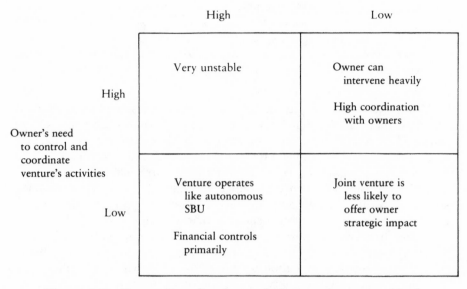

Figure 4–7. **Owner Coordination and Venture Autonomy Needs**

were especially conducive to joint ventures. No one partner controlled all aspects of the technology, manufacturing, and marketing skills needed to make the venture succeed. The technology was risky and costly to start up alone. A global partnership was desirable in order to penetrate several key markets simultaneously (and attain breakeven economies).

When competitive benefits are sought through ventures (to strengthen firms' current strategic positions) in response to blurring industry boundaries and globalization, *close* ties to its owners are needed to ease political tensions with host nations (to overcome local trade barriers) and gain access to global networks. Close ties are also needed in order to create more effective competitors by making them into hybrid entities that possess their owners' respective strengths, or by making fewer, but more efficient, firms. (*Looser* ties will be appropriate if the joint venture buffers dissimilar partners.)

The *closest* ties between owner and venture will be needed to obtain strategic benefits (by augmenting their strategic positions) when it is necessary to create synergies through vertical integration or horizontal linkages. Even where the venture will pursue activities that are not related to firms' competitive advantages, they will want their linkages with the venture to be tight if its activities are of strategic importance to them. For example, firms exerted substantial control over their venture's activities in oil exploration through terms of their partnership agreement. But because the daily operating expenses of oil exploration were so high, delays created by decision-making stalemates among partners were unacceptable. "Side payments" were made to disgruntled partners (as covered in terms of their partnership agreement) when they disagreed with actions taken by the venture's managers. This provision for autonomy was created so that exploratory drilling activities could proceed without costly delays.

Need for Intermediate Controls. Owners must ensure some links with their venture if they seek intelligence, either to obtain a window on new technologies and customers by gaining superior methods of information exchange or by technological personnel interactions. If firms formed ventures to retain entrepreneurial employees, controls over the venture's activities (beyond financial controls) would be needed only if it shared resources with an ongoing unit of the owner and needed to interact with personnel of that partner.

The nature of the strategic benefit sought will suggest how tight the cooperation arrangement must be. Some interaction of the venture with their ongoing organizations will be necessary, where partners hope to (1) influence an industry structure's evolution by pioneering ideas when it is still young; (2) reduce competitive volatility when it becomes too bloody; or (3) rationalize mature industries in the face of excess capacity. If firms seek to preempt competitors' integrations, to link up with the best partners first, a looser arrangement that ties owner to venture may be more appropriate. If one of the strategic benefits sought through the joint venture is technology transfer, owner and venture must have some interactions, but their integrating mechanisms need not be as tight as those used where facilities are shared.

Need for Low Controls. There will be less need to exert control over the venture's activities when partners seek the internal benefits of cost and risk sharing (uncertainty reduction) or seek to obtain resources where there is no market. If strategic benefits such as diversification are sought from ventures, the links between owner and venture need not be as tight, particularly if the venture's purpose is to gain a toehold entry into new markets, products, or skills that are unrelated to firms' ongoing activities or if the venture is for rationalization (or divestiture) of firms' investments.

Some technologies, like aluminum smelting or mineral exploration, change so slowly that owners need not intervene frequently in the operations of their ventures. Coordination between owners and ventures in mining and minerals extraction need not be close (even if the parties are vertically related) because the technology of such activities is highly predictable. Partners in mining joint ventures typically met quarterly to give guidance to their ventures. Since these ventures usually had their own facilities and dealt in an arm's-length manner with the owners that purchased their outputs, few synergies were realized between owner and venture, a further reason for low controls by the venture's owners.

Range of Needs for Venture Autonomy and Coordination

The venture's needs for autonomy from owners' interference arise from competitive requirements within its industry. The venture's autonomy needs are mitigated by its needs for certain types of interaction with its owners' business units in order to compete effectively. Before the influence of industry structure on owner–venture relationships is traced in chapter 5, the tensions between the venture's needs for coordination and autonomy must be identified, particularly as these opposing pressures will affect owners' abilities to satisfy the strategy needs of their venture.

The venture will need to coordinate its activities closely with those of its owners when it shares facilities, personnel, or resources with them, when it is captive in its owners' vertical chains of processing, or when competitive needs for owners' advice, services, and resources are great. As the discussion (below) concerning the sheltered venture will suggest, however, tying the venture too closely to owners will ultimately be disadvantageous for them because doing so harms the venture's ability to compete.

The venture's needs to coordinate with its owners are greatest, other factors held constant, when technology changes rapidly and prices change erratically, requiring owners' help in modifying products or technologies. Coordination with owners will be important when the venture's products are differentiable, markets can be standardized, or excess capacity must be rationalized, due to the scale economies that can be exploited if they work together. If demand grows slowly (or is declining) close coordination will be needed to serve the most promising customers while closing the most appropriate facilities. In this manner, owner and venture can be most profitable while keeping capacity in line with demand. If the venture is physically interconnected, its activities must be coordinated closely with its owners' activities, since a vertical relationship probably exists. (These points are developed further in chapter 5 and are sketched below.)

Briefly, success within certain types of industry environments requires great strategic flexibility. Where these competitive conditions are present, ventures need substantial autonomy to make their own competitive decisions. Certain strategies require close coordination between the venture and the owner that provides those resources that are crucial for success. The most difficult owner–venture interface problems arise where autonomy needs and coordination needs are both high.

The venture's needs for autonomy will be greatest, other factors held constant, when competition is volatile, requiring a rapid response to change. Timing advantages will be lost if its decisions must be approved by owners in a cumbersome process of ratification. The venture must be autonomous where the resources crucial for competitive success are people-intensive, so that owners will not sap the motivation of the venture's personnel and thereby undercut a differentiation strategy based on service, for example. The venture needs autonomy when the industry's infrastructure is yet embryonic (hence changeable) in order to adopt alternative product standards, processes, and suppliers (or channels of distribution) that prove to be superior to the approach taken initially. Autonomy to subcontract with outsiders will be needed when demand is growing rapidly. The venture can also be autonomous from its owners when the exit barriers associated with its strategic posture are low. (The reasons for these relationships are developed in chapter 5.)

The "Sheltered" Venture. Using their venture as a guaranteed resource supplier or channel of distribution may seem attractive to firms, but they must beware of "sheltering" it too much from contact with outsiders. Tying the venture to them more closely than is necessary will be disadvantageous because outsiders may be reluctant to deal with a venture that is too closely identified with firms that are their competitors. Firms' wholly owned business units may become complacent without pressures to innovate or lower costs if their venture lacks the autonomy to find outside suppliers or customers.

Without the prod of outside competition, the venture's technology may become obsolete or lose cost advantages. Managers' motivations may be sapped if the venture is sheltered because their entrepreneurial efforts to innovate or lower costs are not rewarded. As their enthusiasm wanes, the brightest personnel will abandon positions that are little more than those of caretakers.

The "Boisterous" Venture. Unbridled joint-venture managers often wish to expand the venture's scope of activities into areas that its owners had intended to reserve for their respective, wholly owned business units. The "boisterous" venture may even be continually waging turf battles with its owners' managers in an effort to gain autonomy where it is not truly necessary for competitive success. Therefore, owners must study the success requirements of various competitive environments carefully to determine whether autonomy should be granted in some areas at a rate faster than they had intended, or whether the venture's managers are too boisterous.

Summary of Autonomy Needs. In summary, the venture needs autonomy when competition is volatile, but it will also need to coordinate its efforts for rapid competitive response with the owner that contributes crucial inputs to it. For example, when technology changes rapidly in the venture's industry, it will need to work closely with its technology owner; if customers are exerting their bargaining power by demanding more features, services, or other product features, the venture must work closely with the owner that contributes product styling and marketing services to respond effectively. (High coordination with its marketing owner will be especially important, other factors held constant, when products are marketed to sophisticated consumers.) When managers evaluate the specifics of a joint venture's needs for autonomy and for coordination with one or more of its owners, they must also weigh (1) the distribution of partners' equity investments; (2) the joint venture's success in its chosen strategy; and (3) the actions of competitors, for reasons explained below. The dynamics of owner–venture relationships must anticipate changes in the respective strategic needs, capabilities, and successes of the other parties to the joint venture if it is to realize its full potential.

Control Mechanisms

The joint venture is governed by terms of a bargaining agreement between partners that specifies the (1) nature of information sharing; (2) personnel contacts; (3) representation by owners in the venture's performance; (4) reporting mechanisms; and (5) other details of the management system created to support owners' strategy objectives. If the purpose of the venture includes innovation and technology transfer, special attention must be devoted to control mechanisms that protect the venture's proprietary knowledge and property rights, as well as those of its owners. The bargaining agreement provides for control mechanisms to ensure that owners' objectives are attained.

Joint-Venture Management Systems

In theory, the bargaining contract that forms the venture will contain the details of the management system that will bind the venture to each respective owner. In fact, it is unreasonable to expect owners (or their lawyers) to foresee and provide for all of the conditions that could make joint-venture relationships evolve. Many effective firms are in a constant state of fine-tuning with respect to their own management systems. It is unreasonable for these same firms, as owners, to expect their venture's system to be cast in concrete. Therefore, adaptive systems are needed to provide for the changes that may occur in the relationships between joint-venture partners, between owner and venture, or within the venture's domain (discussed in Chapter 5).

Ownership Shares

Earlier studies of ventures devoted a disproportionate emphasis to questions concerning the need for the balance (or imbalance) of equity ownership. They have asserted, for example, that evenly divided ownership of the venture (that is, 50%–50% ventures) often encourages deadlocks in decision making, unless one partner is willing to trust the decisions of the other partner on minor issues.[4] For this reason, asymmetric equity controls (such as 51%–49% ownership splits) have been touted as being more effective than ventures where ownership (and veto power) is evenly distributed to accommodate managers' desires for equal proportions of equity ownership.

This issue is a red herring; arguments about the division of ownership have erroneously assumed that ownership is equivalent to management control. The correct balance of managerial controls and autonomy, *not* ownership shares, are the key to effective management of the venture. Some firms will take a slight minority *ownership* position so long as they can obtain a clear majority position in *managerial* authority. Firms are most likely to concede a larger share of profits to partners in this manner if the venture's activities are of high strategic importance to them in other ways. For example, in 1974, AMAX and Mitsui & Co. formed a 50%–50% joint venture in aluminum fabrication that was more successful than many wholly owned aluminum fabricating companies. ALUMAX gave AMAX an investment tax credit when it was fully owned, but this benefit could not be tax-consolidated when AMAX owned but 50 percent of the venture. AMAX and Mitsui restructured their joint venture in 1984 to provide AMAX with 80 percent ownership for tax purposes. Mitsui received slightly more than 50 percent of ALUMAX's profits as compensation for this concession. The venture continued to operate as before.

Thus, the distribution of equity control, profit splits, board representation, and other forms of managerial control will not necessarily be symmetrical because some partners will accept a lesser degree of control to obtain something they seek. It is important to recall that when a decision must be reviewed by all partners, they can become deadlocked whether one particular firm has majority ownership or not. If partners cannot agree, their cooperation simply cannot work. Mechanisms to encourage continued cooperation among partners must not be overlooked in negotiations concerning how to structure the joint venture deal.

Executive Boards of Directors

Board composition provides owners with a unique opportunity to guide the activities of their venture. But instead of placing managers who could help the venture to compete more effectively on the executive boards that govern ventures, some firms make board directorships an honorary position occupied by managers with experiences far removed from those activities that would be salient to their venture. The best candidates for joint-venture boards are often managers operating so far down within owner firms' hierarchies that they would never be considered for similar honors within their own organizations. Yet their skills and insights may be more compatible with the needs of ventures, especially in the early years of a venture's start-up, than higher-ranking executives that are more accustomed to dealing with firms' external environments and the complexities of multibusiness enterprise.

A combination of rotation and continuity is needed in selecting board members. Because different operating needs may require closer attentions as the venture develops its own capabilities, some of the managers selected to guide the joint venture through the board should rotate in a pattern that reflects these changing needs. For example, as the venture graduates into an ongoing entity that issues equity securities in its own right, a different type of board composition will be appropriate than when the venture was a struggling start-up venture that emphasized product design questions. As the venture acquires more activities that make it tantamount to a stand-alone entity, more general management guidance will be needed, for example, than when owners limited the venture merely to manufacturing or research activities.

To maintain some continuity in partners' dealings with each other, however, some board members must remain in their positions as others rotate off the board. No number of codicils can overcome the benefits of prolonged exposure by the permanent members of partners' delegations to each other. The longer they work together harmoniously, the less need they will feel for recourse to legal documents to establish a homogeneity of vision concerning their venture's purpose.

Personnel Rotation

Staffing decisions whereby owners send managers to work within their venture will be complicated by an unwillingness to let go. Too many firms permit restive employees to use the "revolving door" back to headquarters and the security of the owner's organization. Because it is not possible for the best interests of the venture to be served by managers with unclearly focused loyalties and attentions, the venture's managers may have to be recruited from outside. Key positions, in particular, must have unswerving loyalties to the well-being of the venture.

The revolving-door policy encourages the bleedthrough of ideas. In some cases, this may be *desirable*. If employees from the venture's owners are frequently rotated through the venture, there is a good chance that they will disseminate knowledge of the venture back to their respective firms' laboratories. Revolving doors are useful if owners seek to create their own in-house technological capabilities by repatriating knowledge to their factories and laboratories. Some aggressive owners will even build parallel facilities and hold in-house seminars to emulate each experiment their venture undertakes. Thus, if owners want to *encourage* knowledge bleedthrough, they will *not* give their venture a permanent complement of managers and technical personnel. Owners will treat the assignment of employees to the joint venture as part of their regular career path of experiences and will expect these personnel to disseminate knowledge in both directions.

Trial Marriage

Joint ventures can result in deadlocks if partners have not created equitable mechanisms for resolving day-to-day deadlocks in decision making. For this reason, it is generally more advantageous to draft a *team* of operating managers that can maximize the tradeoffs between synergies (from shared resources) and economies (from centralized facilities) during the courtship stage. The team should be taken from both owner's personnel and should work together during the "trial marriage" era.

Joint ventures that hope to maximize synergies by sharing assets, managers, and capabilities with owners increase their abilities to do so by looking at both firms' respective positions within the industries the joint ventures will cover *before* the marriage is consummated. The trial marriage management team should create a proposal for the best use of *all* owners' facilities that would be contributed to the joint venture, without preconceived notions of equitable schedules concerning which plants will be shut down, what political solutions are needed for layoffs, and so forth. Briefly, the trial marriage managers should be placed in charge of *all* contributed facilities and required to develop the most economic plan for combining these facilities, without knowing *who* will be chosen to run the venture's operations after the trial marriage period. During the trial marriage, teams of managers from all owners work together to implement the best plans for combining operations, adding capabilities, and rationalizing the venture. Finally, when the trial marriage organization evolves into a full-fledged joint venture entity, the venture's management team is selected on the basis of which managers best solved problems together.

Review Points and Venture Autonomy

Although the management systems that link owners to their venture should provide for the ways in which the venture's capital requests and budgeting cycle will mesh with that of its owners' planning cycles, firms must be wary of overburdening their ventures with excessive reporting obligations. Paradoxically, the management systems used to govern ventures are often *more* detailed than the systems of either owner because the venture must bridge the cultural differences between partners. The paperwork involved in doing so can stifle creativity within the venture.

Earlier studies indicate, for example, that autonomous ventures were more innovative than those that were tethered closely to the review of their owners' board.[5] Yet, because performance measures, review procedures, reward systems, and other mechanisms used to delegate responsibilities to the joint venture must be designed in a manner that will be consistent with the needs of each owner, a complex management system and organization design (often embodying some version of a matrix organization) has often been embraced.[6] Such management burdens quickly cancel the expected benefits of cooperation and slow down the venture when it must move quickly, as in volatile industry settings (discussed in chapter 5).

Russian Roulette Buy-outs

The fragile nature of cooperative strategies requires mechanisms that will ensure that parity among partners is protected. If the relative value of partners' contributions changes, the management systems that govern the venture should (in theory) revalue owners' contributions regularly and adjust ownerships (and managerial) shares to reflect current market values. Such valuations may be difficult to implement in practice, however, unless a reference point for pricing assets is readily available, as in the example of crude oil. Where there is no market, partners could become deadlocked regarding valuation methods. To overcome such stalemates, partners may have to agree on unorthodox ways of resolving such disputes. Russian roulette buy-outs, for example, are schemes some partners use whereby one firm evaluates the venture and proposes a price for the equity of the venture to its partners who choose, in turn, whether to be buyers of the evaluating firm's interest or sellers of their own joint-venture interests.

Changes in the Bargaining Agreement

As the joint-venture framework has noted, a bargaining agreement will specify the markets where the venture will operate, the outputs it is authorized to produce, and which of its inputs, if any, owners will provide. It should also provide for a means of adjusting the joint-venture relationship to change in the venture's environment.

Joint ventures must revitalize themselves as do other ongoing organizations. Because the industries where joint ventures operate will change over time to accommodate the effects of competition, the manner in which owners integrate the activities of the venture with their own must change also. As explained above, synergies will not accrue between owner and venture unless they are consciously managed. Buyer–seller relationships and shared resources where they exist, must be reinforced by compatible management systems and should not be perpetuated beyond the time when these linkages make sense.

The termination of a joint venture does not always mean the end of a synergistic relationship. RTE sold its 50-percent interest in their power transformer venture back to ASEA in early 1984 because ASEA had several other electrical equipment products it wanted to sell in the United States (such as high-voltage circuit breakers, power transformer bushings, and other components which ASEA had formerly sold to its venture). ASEA continued to use RTE Corp.'s sales force to distribute its products after the joint venture ended. As a result of this arrangement, RTE offered a wider product line to its customers (and to firms that were once its competitors).

If firms expect to enjoy synergies by interacting with their venture, they must foster good relationships between their organizations. To do so requires diplomatic skills as well as patience on the part of the managers who represent the venture's *owners* as well as on the part of the managers who protect the *venture's* interests. Relationships between employees of the venture and its owners must be managed to ameliorate feelings of envy or excessive competition. Owners' employees may envy the success of the venture if it outperforms wholly owned, sister units. Owners' employees may even *sabotage* the venture's operations in some manner if they perceive that their future is too dependent on uncontrollable revenues from the joint venture. Scientists in firms' wholly owned laboratories may perceive that excessive rewards are given to innovators within the venture's laboratories or that the most interesting projects are farmed out to the joint venture.

Effective management of ventures will depend on trust, mutual respect, and a willingness among partners to negotiate any dispute. A policy of open and enhanced communications is necessary in order to air the perceived inequities that could develop within owner–venture relationships. These precautions will be particularly important where legal voting control of the joint venture is distributed in a manner that could produce a stalemate, especially if no partner possesses the bargaining power needed to break the impasse.

Where a joint venture has been formed to marry dissimilar cultures, there is always a risk that the arrangement will fail because partners are too dissimilar and unwilling to compromise. This impasse is most likely to occur where executives are of dissimilar ages, educational backgrounds, and work experience, if they seek differing personal goals, enjoy differing socioeconomic roots, and aspire to diverse levels of security, or if their concept of the role of the venture differs from that of partners.[7] (If the personalities and styles of two companies are totally different, a successful joint venture between them is doubtful. It may be possible for such parties to cooperate contractually instead.)

For example, the terms of joint-venture agreements in the oil and gas exploration industry were strongly influenced by (1) decades of experience in using joint ventures; and (2) homogeneity of interests among partners. Firms often created a web of "offset" joint ventures where partners alternated acting as the venture's "operator"—the partner whose managers made day-to-day operating decisions on behalf of other partners—in a series of joint ventures. Because partners had often been both operators and nonoperators in the past, they saw each other's perspectives more easily.

Today's partners could become tomorrow's competitors because ventures are often reconfigured when partners have gained knowledge of markets and skills that they previously did not understand.[8] Providing for joint-venture disposition is important, or firms may encounter difficulties in recovering the value of their investments in their venture. Although a market usually exists for the resources owners have committed, their ability to exit can be better ensured if firms have managed for this important contingency.

It is important for owners not to lose sight of their motivations for co-operating. Their management systems and other ways of integrating the venture with their ongoing operations must continually test and retest the assumption that motivated them to work with partners originally. By the mid-1980s the only certainty that owners could rely on was that competition in the venture's industry—as well as in their own industries—would be more trying than it had ever been before. In the midst of such confusion, owners tried to anticipate how industries might evolve when they provided for their joint-venture relationships with other firms.

When firms do form joint ventures, their ventures can represent important structural changes in an industry's profitability potential because the resources and capabilities of diverse owners can be treated as though they were one. Their venture's presence can change the basis for successful competition to the disadvantage of other firms that have no ventures. But the severity of the actual threat represented by their venture will vary (from the perspective of the venture's competitors), depending on whether the venture links owners horizontally, vertically, or in a related (or unrelated) pattern of diversification. Firms create a credible threat to competitors through their joint venture *only* if owners can bring their respective powers to bear on competitors through their venture's activities.

Effective use of those powers requires partners to tap the strengths that gave them bargaining power in forming their joint venture. It requires owners to update the role of their venture in their respective strategic missions. It requires owners continually to question the need to provide inputs to their venture or to absorb its outputs as they may have done in the past. It requires owners to be willing to wean their venture and send it out on its own when the venture's need to coordinate closely with its owners has diminished. Industry differences will suggest how quickly ventures should evolve from loose cooperation to partnerships to stand-alone entities, if at all. Volatile competitive conditions will require shorter-lived and more informal liaisons, for example. Demand uncertainty will necessitate tentative affiliations, modest funding, and pilot plants or test situations. These and other specifics concerning industry differences are covered in chapter 5, which adds the third leg to the joint-venture framework's strategic triangle, the consideration of the venture's domain.

5
Viability of the Venture

T his chapter covers the venture's relationship to its competitive environment as these pressures affect owners' cooperative strategy choices. Industry analysis represents the third leg in the joint-venture strategy model, as is shown by the heavy arrows in figure 5–1. The construction and content of chapter 5 is dramatically different in its specificity and analytical approach from the chapters treating partners' private weightings of the cost-benefit agreement and how the venture coordinates activities with its owners with respect to horizontal or vertical relationships, synergistic resource sharing, and operating autonomy (for performance maximization).

Relating the Venture's Competitive Environment to Owners' Cooperative Strategies

Most of the arguments contained in chapter 3 and 4 concerning firms' cost-benefit analyses, partners' bargaining agreements, and tradeoffs between coordination and autonomy in relationships between owner and venture have been intentionally basic because they generally can be applied to many situations. Only the final discussions of chapter 4 concerning how competitive forces might augment the highly coordinated relationship between owner and venture have foreshadowed the influences of industry traits on the range of cooperative strategy options that firms might embrace. Chapter 5 demonstrates how specific industry forces will affect applications of the basic concepts presented in chapters 3 and 4. It suggests that owners will face fewer cooperative strategy options in some competitive environments than in others and that industry traits will make a difference in the likelihood of joint venture success.

Chapter 5 is presented last in the sequence of chapters that describe the joint-venture framework for two reasons. First, a full appreciation of the issues motivating partners to cooperate with specific partners and to relate their ventures to their wholly owned business units in a particular way was

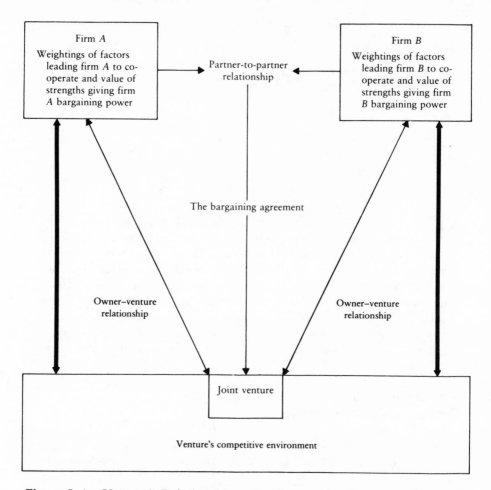

Figure 5–1. Venture's Relationship to Its Competitive Environment as It Affects Owner's Joint-Venture Strategy

needed in order to understand how industry traits affect these fundamental issues. Chapter 5 revives the debate of chapter 3 concerning whether firms should form jointly owned ventures as a means to build new strengths, gain a timing advantage over competitors, enter new markets, gain new products or process, or otherwise diversify from their ongoing scope of activities. It also suggests that close coordination with the activities of owners' business units, when using some of the control mechanisms described in chapter 4, will prove to be stultifying to the venture's ability to thrive within particular types of competitive environments. Second, chapter 5 tracks closely the specifics of situations where ventures have been used with varying degrees of success. The joint-venture framework was tested using industry-specific data because the effects of competitive environments are recognized as being important in defining the range of feasible strategies sponsoring firms might pursue.

The Venture's Domain

The tensions between owner and venture come to a boiling point in matters of competitive strategy. Determining the venture's success requirements involves issues of autonomy and of resources that will evolve as the nature of competition changes. If the venture's managers are entrepreneurial and aggressive, they will see opportunities where the venture should move *preemptively* to improve its strategic position. As the venture's industry evolves, the strengths and resources needed by it may be available from a different owner than the one that supplied those resources in the past. Or the best resources may be available from outsiders. Yet venture managers (or managers of sponsoring firms) may cling erroneously to the notion that the old linkages between the venture and its owners must be maintained instead.

The result being hampered by such inertia barriers could be disastrous for reasons explained here. Briefly, competition within many industries has become more demanding due to the effects of evolutionary forces that include: maturation of U.S., European and Japanese economies, leaps in communications technology, shorter product lives (but larger capital requirements for innovation), globalization of industries (where competition was previously constrained to geographic boundaries), and entry by new players (supported by their respective governments), among others. Chapters 1 and 2 argue that cooperative strategies and, in particular, joint ventures offer one way of coping with these tensions. The examples that follow suggest how sponsoring firms' cooperative strategies must adjust to competitive forces if they expect their ventures to be viable players in their respective industries.

Analysis of these issues asks how the use of cooperative ventures differs where demand is uncertain or where competitors have differing expectations concerning product viability. It asks how joint ventures might best serve both customers and the venture's owners. It considers how attractive joint ventures will be when competition becomes volatile, and it asks how autonomy and coordination needs will change when the boundaries separating industries erode?

Domain refers to the industry within which a venture competes and the type of competition it encounters therein. The profitability potential of any venture—jointly owned or not—will be determined by its industry structure and by how firms behave therein. The venture's strategy determines whether it will exploit the full potential of its environment, and the venture's performance will be determined by its effectiveness, and the venture's performance will be determined by its effectiveness in implementing that strategy. Owners will judge performance according to the venture's delivery of value to them.

Analysis of the venture's domain considers the nature of the markets (and customers) it will serve, the products that competitors might offer to satisfy anticipated demand, differences in the strategic postures firms could embrace to serve attractive market segments, and how firms will protect their competitive advantages from rivals. The key *demand* traits that determine how joint ventures are best used include: customer attributes (including product differentiability, buyer sophistication, and hence bargaining power), supplier expectations, and whether products may be standardized to serve diverse market segments. These relationships hold true whether a venture is jointly owned or not.

The key *competitor* traits that determine how joint ventures will best be used include: how competitors cope with the technological attributes of products (particularly with respect to capital intensity and rates of technological change), as well as the kinds of competitive advantages that firms can carve from an industry and protect over time. Effective cooperative strategies should enable ventures to hurdle entry barriers with greater ease while maintaining their abilities to adapt to changing competitive conditions within their industries with greater flexibility (assuming the venture's managers can tap into the relevant strengths of its owners effectively).

Demand Traits: Customers and Uncertainty

Two key demand traits that affect joint-venture success are *demand uncertainty* and *customer bargaining power.* Unless cooperative strategies are being forged to permit firms to phase *out* of an industry, demand must be attractive enough to justify a firm's investment, whether through a joint venture or by going it alone. Analysis of customer traits will suggest how long a market opportunity may be expected to remain attractive. The windows of opportunity in some markets may be so short-lived that firms must use joint ventures (or similar cooperative alliances) to leap frog into such growing markets to exploit them before their luster fades.

Analysis of *market attractiveness* is based on the study of customers' attributes, particularly on their sophistication in evaluating products and their propensity to exercise their bargaining power in negotiating with vendors. There is a constant tug-of-war between customers and vendors because vendors seek to reduce operating costs by standardizing as many products as possible, especially where profit margins are low. Customers, however, want as much product customization as they can extract from vendors without paying higher prices. In an effort to spread the overhead costs associated with satisfying demanding clients, some firms form cooperative ventures by pooling certain types of orders in one factory. The more attractive the perceived reward of serving such customers, the more tempting cooperative strategies will be, particularly where the costs of entry seem too high or the payback period on investment seems too long for one firm to undertake the venture alone. The more attractive the market, the *more autonomy* the venture's managers may require.

Demand Uncertainty. As chapter 2 suggests, when demand uncertainty is high, investments to enter (or shift from one strategic posture to another) will be too risky for one firm to undertake alone. More joint ventures will be formed when the combined resources of sponsoring firms would make seemingly uneconomic investments become acceptable. This risk-return relationship will hold true whether joint ventures are used to enter industries where demand is growing rapidly, as in the communications services industry, or to consolidate excess capacity within industries experiencing mature (or stagnant) demand, as in farm and industrial equipment. The differences in how they are managed depends on demand uncertainty and the rate of sales growth (or decline). As figure 5–2 indicates, joint ventures will be used more frequently where demand is uncertain or business risks are high, particularly when demand is growing rapidly or is declining. Joint ventures could enable firms to be more responsive to variations in customer demands, provided owners design their alliances effectively. Joint ventures may be used to ease a firm out of a declining or troubled industry such as steel where excess capacity will plague all ongoing firms. One partner to a joint venture may buy out the other, or a firm that previously owned a business outright may create a joint venture as a means of passing ownership to an interim partner.

When demand is growing rapidly, other factors held constant, the joint venture's managers need freedom to subcontract production or make other accommodations to satisfy customers. When demand is declining, the joint venture must coordinate its endgame strategy closely with its owners' activities in order to serve the most attractive customer niches without disrupting industrywide price levels.

Rapidly Growing Demand. Vertical ventures, where owners share their venture's outputs or use their venture to absorb their respective outputs, are particularly useful in settings where demand is growing rapidly as a means of utilizing large plants economically (perhaps by sharing a supplying plant with a customer, initially) or by reaching target customers to alleviate their fears concerning the new product's or process's viability, as in the postwar years of the petrochemical industry.[1] Firms use horizontal arrangements later to consolidate excess capacity and focus competitors' attentions (to alleviate wasteful price cutting when demand growth slows). Horizontal ventures are em-

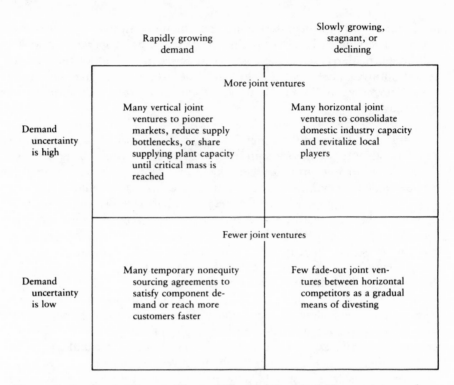

Figure 5–2. Single-Firm Analysis: Effect of Demand Uncertainty and Industry Evolution on Joint-Venture Formation (Assuming Firms Will Cooperate, Ceteris Paribus)

braced when firms would otherwise battle for market share at each other's expense because demand has become saturated or is primarily for replacement purposes.

PETROCHEMICALS. Vertical joint ventures were used to build infrastructures in the petrochemicals industry in the 1940s and 1950s when demand was uncertain and product standards were not yet established. When the Federal Trade Commission reported in the mid-1950s that 15 of the 1,000 largest U.S. corporations were joint ventures, petrochemical firms comprised the bulk of these ventures. Although partners were often horizontally related, owners were often *vertically related* to their joint ventures. This pattern may be explained by the minimum efficient scale (MES) differences of upstream and downstream stages of processing in the technologies of the petrochemical industry. Outputs from supplying plants were shared by partners. Risk- and cost-sharing also motivated the use of joint ventures.

Horizontally related competitors were often partners in the rearing of their vertically related venture in the then-embryonic chemical industry because the costs of creating distribution channels, transportation systems, and other supporting activities were substantial and demand was growing rapidly. Owners shared their venture's outputs until demand reached volumes that permitted firms to build wholly owned plants.

Slowly Growing Demand. Demand uncertainty is lower where demand is growing more slowly, and joint ventures are particularly appropriate in such settings if significant scale economies are available at large production volumes, particularly if cost reduction is becoming the key to effective competition as in mining and other extractive industries. (This often is the time when domestic firms will be most vulnerable to foreign competition; this point will be developed further in the section discussing market standardization.) Joint ventures allow firms who were formerly rivals to retain the most efficient parts of their assets in building a new, world-scale competitive entity. Joint ventures may also be used by firms to divest their assets incrementally in situations where they face such high exit barriers that no buyer could afford to purchase them outright, as in metals processing, heavy machinery, or other capital-intensive industries.

As demand slows, stagnates, or declines it will become necessary for some firms to cooperate in order to prevent destructive price wars. Joint ventures are preferred over nonequity arrangements in such settings if businesses are of high strategic importance because they facilitate divestitures (as well as diversifications) when firms must adapt to changing industry conditions. Firms seek to acquire partners' shares (or use *fade-in ventures*)[2] later to increase their control over joint activities and destroy excess capacity to ensure that assets will not be resurrected by new firms and continue to plague their troubled industry in the future.

PETROCHEMICALS. In 1983, there was substantial excess capacity in the declining Japanese petrochemicals industry. Cutbacks were being coordinated by Japanese Parliament under its antimonopoly law, which encouraged cartels and joint ventures to eliminate an industry's excess capacity and make it more competitive. Twelve Japanese ethylene producers and six ethylene derivate makers were grouped into three consortia, each with its own joint marketing company. Although the agreements were voluntary, each Japanese consortium was required to trim production capacity by 36 percent.

The Japanese industrial policies reflected a major transformation that was occurring throughout the world in the petrochemicals industry in 1984, as oil producing nations (such as Mexico, Saudi Arabia, and Canada), which at one time had flared the natural gas that occurs in nature with crude oil, began using this natural gas to make ammonia or methanol. Similarly, their excess crude oil was used to make ethylene or other petrochemicals.

In the United States, firms responded to this excess capacity by forming joint ventures to divest petrochemical businesses when they exited the industry (as Hercules had done), or by shutting down plants if they merely wanted to bring supply in line with demand. The changes in joint-venture formation in the petrochemicals industry reflected a significantly different pattern from the dominant motivations of an earlier era. The key to petrochemical joint-venture formation had always been access to cheap raw materials. Since U.S. feedstocks were no longer the lowest in cost, joint-venture formation for that reason was no longer justified. Although U.S. antitrust agency opposition to joint ventures was expected to occur initially, the need to reduce industrywide excess capacity eventually forced these economic regulation policies to be amended. The realities of global competition motivated the use of joint ventures in a manner similar to that of the U.S. steel industry.

STEEL. Prior to 1940, U.S. firms produced 33 percent of the world's steel, but they became net importers of steel in 1959 and by 1980 produced only 15 percent of the world's steel. Nations with lower labor costs, such as South Korea and Brazil, rose to prominence in steelmaking in the 1980s when even Japanese steel firms suffered from the effects of excess capacity brought about by their enthusiastic overexpansion in the previous decade. But stagnant consumption and a shift to electric furnace steelmaking—a process where scrap steel was recycled, thereby eliminating the need for iron ore—left the industry with overcapacity in iron ore mining that greatly exceeded its excess of steel mills.

As U.S. protectionism intensified to include quotas and other restrictions while laws to protect environmental quality undermined domestic plant efficiency, the use of joint ventures as a means for outsiders to partake in the large U.S. market for steel became inevitable. United States joint ventures in steel in the 1980s were used to transfer cost-effective technology and to rationalize outmoded and inefficient excess capacity in both steelmaking and in iron ore mines. This was necessary because during the 1950s and 1960s, U.S. steel firms had formed joint ventures to build processing plants for low-grade taconite ore from the Mesabi Range to supplement their dwindling pure iron-ore reserves. Forty such iron ore joint ventures were operating in 1957, and take-or-pay contracts secured partners' investments in the taconite reduction facilities and bound steelmakers to cover taconite production expenses even if they could not use the output.

Writing off these investments later required steelmakers to recognize debts from joint venture obligations that did not appear on their consolidated balance sheets. Whenever steel plant capacity was retired due to declining demand in the 1980s, steelmakers' iron ore mines also had to reduce capacity.

But since many ore mines were created through a complex maze of joint venture agreements, firms were reluctant to face the exit barriers of closing ore mines until they also faced the pressures of steel plant shutdowns.

Customer Traits. Whether or not cooperative strategies are appropriate depends on how well the product can be differentiated, how sensitive service is to the product offering, and whether the market is global. Analyses of these forces may be combined to suggest the relative stability of profits. As long as firms can offer products that retain some dimension of uniqueness for which customers will pay a price premium, their profit margins will be higher. If their product's uniqueness can be eroded easily, their profits will be less stable.

Where markets are standardized and coordination needs in serving them are high, joint ventures or other arrangements that impede a firm's strategic flexibility are less attractive than when customers' requirements are varied. As figure 5–3 indicates, firms prefer to control more of their activities through in-house facilities where many markets can be served by similar product configurations, as in global industries. This preference is intensified where customers are sophisticated in their abilities to discern differences among vendors' products. Therefore, joint ventures are more likely to be tolerated where customer bargaining power is low but customers' product requirements, nevertheless, cannot be standardized with those of other markets. If cooperative strategies are forged where product configurations *could* be standardized across markets, global partners tend to seek control over the venture's activities in order to coordinate them closely with the rest of their networks of facilities, as in the electronic components, pharmaceuticals, and automobile industries. Customer sophistication (especially in terms of costs) is a destabilizing force on the duration of joint-venture relationships, particularly where product configurations change rapidly.

The more demanding the customer, the more autonomy a venture requires in responding to such demands. But close coordination with the venture's marketing owner also may be needed to satisfy some sophisticated customers. And if the products in question are complex and require precision in manufacturing, as in robotics and precision controls, close coordination with the venture's technology owner is also needed.

The greater the bargaining power of customers over the venture (by virtue of customers' large purchase volumes affecting owners' other business units), the more important those customers are to the venture's owners. Coordination of customer accounts is particularly important if owner and venture are both facing the same purchasing agents. The greater the percentage of total purchases an important customer makes through a centralized purchasing agent, the closer sponsoring firms will need to work with their joint ventures in satisfying customers' demands, other factors held constant. Although they need not be customers of their ventures themselves, access of

	Product configurations cannot be standardized across markets	Product configurations can be standardized across markets
Customer sophistication and bargaining power is high	Spider's web of cooperative strategies for cost reduction styling Many short-term cross-licensing arrangements for new product features, cost reductions	Few joint ventures, except as required to enter High coordination control by global partner to keep costs lowest
Customer sophistication and bargaining power is low	More longer-term joint ventures (depends on competitors' activities), primarily for new product features	Few joint ventures, except as required to enter (local partner allowed some coordination controls)

Figure 5–3. Single-Firm Analysis: Effect of Customer Bargaining Power and Market Standardization on Joint-Venture Formation and Use (Assuming Firms Will Cooperate, Ceteris Paribus)

viable customers (or autonomy to create channels of distribution to reach outsiders) is one of the provisions sponsoring firms must anticipate in forging their joint-venture strategy if that venture is to be effective.

Product Differentiation. Even products that might ordinarily be considered to be commoditylike can be made unique or *differentiated* in the minds of buyers through vendors' attentions to services, uniform quality, or other dimensions. Joint ventures are less risky when products have the long-term potential to remain differentiated, but their durations are affected by the conflicts that could arise among owners concerning control of the basis for differentiation, access to markets, and product presentation. Briefly, when firms enter ventures to make differentiated products, the production tasks that owners entrust to ventures are not ordinarily the most sophisticated or complex ones, lest outsiders gain control over sponsoring firms' sources of competitive advantage. Moreover, firms possessing differentiated products often want *complete control* over marketing activities, even if a local partner's personnel perform the venture's selling tasks.

Conflicts concerning which owner maintains marketing control are destabilizing unless domestic partners can use their knowledge of local customers to increase their bargaining power over non-domestic partners and thereby compensate for product attribute changes that may undermine their relative bargaining power. Frequent changes in product attributes are also destabilizing to ventures because, although profitability potential may be higher (because firms emphasize nonprice competition), such changes increase the likelihood that partners may become mismatched. To hedge these risks, strong firms form a spiders' web of alliances that are individually easy to dissolve. Joint ventures quickly become too inflexible if the basis for competitive advantage changes frequently, unless sponsoring firms agree that their affiliations must be temporary in nature.

Commoditylike Products. If sellers cannot effectively differentiate their products from those of other firms, and price is their major dimension for competition, joint ventures will still be formed. However, because firms need the lowest-cost technologies to succeed, their ventures tend to emphasize process innovations. Briefly, when ventures occur where products are commoditylike (like many basic chemical products), they are often the types of arrangements that fill underutilized plants and increase productivity. Such ventures last *longer* because product traits change less frequently and because the large capital investments entailed in cost-reduction ventures increase owners' exit barriers. High exit barriers may increase joint-venture stability, but they also decrease profitability potential (because high exit barriers exacerbate competitive volatility) unless owners work with their ventures to reduce their barriers.

Figure 5–4, which combines the effects of demand uncertainty and product differentiability, indicates that firms seek sourcing arrangements and other temporary ways of obtaining access to new technology and marketing channels if they cannot adequately satisfy the rapidly growing demand they face by relying on in-house facilities alone, as in the example of new financial services. But as demand growth slows, firms need fewer ventures because they can move more on their manufacturing responsibilities in-house and develop their own generations of technology. Eventually, ventures flourish again, but this time as a means of consolidating excess capacity due to declining demand or import competition, as in the example of metals processing operations.

While products are highly differentiable, joint ventures are undertaken primarily to gain access to unique product features as well as new channels of distribution. When products become commoditylike, joint ventures often emphasize process innovations to reduce unit costs rather than marketing attributes.

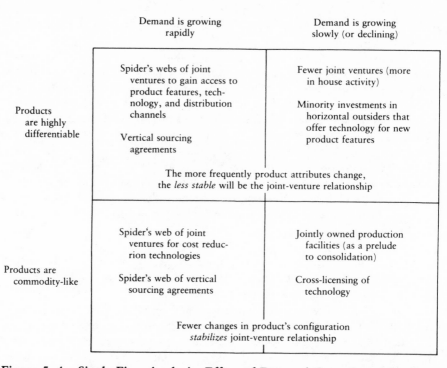

Figure 5–4. Single-Firm Analysis: Effect of Demand Growth and Product Differentiability on Joint-Venture Formation and Use (Assuming Firms Will Cooperate, Ceteris Paribus)

If products can be differentiated in the minds of customers and if both owner and venture will offer the products in question, their need to coordinate decisions concerning product features, supporting services, and other attributes increases, other factors held constant. If they do not share products, the venture's need for *autonomy* in differentiating its products in the minds of customers increases.

Highly Differentiable Products. When cooperative stategies involving highly differentiated products sold to retail consumers and to sophisticated industrial customers, respectively, were examined, many cooperative arrangements were found. Patterns regarding the use of joint ventures differed significantly between the consumer and industrial businesses, however. For example, there were many joint ventures in the programming, programming packaging, and home video entertainment businesses, but there were relatively few joint ventures in the high technology precision control businesses.

Figure 5–4 predicts that fewer joint ventures will be formed in precision controls, factory automation, and robotics than in cable and home video entertainment because the industrial products did not possess the potential to remain differentiated as long as those in the consumer industries. In fact, more equity joint ventures were found in the consumer products industries. Firms cross-licensed technology, marketed outsiders' products through their respective distribution channels, and cooperated in a flurry of nonequity ventures in the industrial products industries, but they created few joint ventures. Figure 5–4 also predicts that firms will form a spider's web of alliances, as they did in cable-TV programming, videotape programming, and programming packaging, to hedge the risks that one configuration will win out over another. This pattern was indeed observed.

Close coordination between owner and venture was necessary within the industries involving differentiable products that were examined because (1) no firm could ensure that competitors would not enter their market niche and erode their competitive advantage; (2) the venture shared facilities with owners, as in the programming and programming packaging joint ventures; (3) technology was changing rapidly; and (4) prices were lower than many firms' costs. Although the cable-TV programming packaging, home video, and robotics industries were embryonic (and the joint-venture framework predicts such ventures require high operating autonomy), the effects of high product differentiability and rapid technological change made the need to coordinate activities with owners relatively greater.

MOTION PICTURE PRODUCTION. In 1982, CBS, Columbia Pictures, and HBO formed a film company and motion picture studio, TriStar Pictures, with an initial investment of $300 million. Through TriStar, HBO was guaranteed an additional source of feature films. CBS obtained a toehold in cable TV services (and gained a source of feature films for commercial broadcasting). Columbia Pictures obtained a new source for its films and an extra studio when space was scarce. Joint ventures were commonplace in the motion picture production industry, but several features of the TriStar agreement made the venture unusual.

TriStar leased its motion picture studio, which it had acquired from Warner Brothers Studios, to outsiders when it was not filming its own feature length films. Unike most movie-making ventures that dissolved when a motion picture was completed, TriStar endured. Although TriStar operated completely separate from its owners, it did *not* have its own distribution system. (Historically, the most important function of the motion picture companies had been the distribution of films. If they lost control of distribution, they lost control of their raison d'etre.) TriStar's sponsoring firms distributed its films through their respective distribution systems. Finally, TriStar Pictures was notable because the venture was preparing to issue securities in its own right as a stand-alone entity in 1984. (After the public offering, TriStar's sponsors would each own a 25 percent interest in the studio.)

HOME-VIDEO HARDWARE AND SOFTWARE. The home video entertainment hardware and software industries were developed through teamwork. Japanese firms cooperated to establish standards for videotape recorder products; they formed joint ventures to introduce the riskier videodisc players. Programming for videotape and videodisc players was provided by joint ventures and other alliances in the 1970s because the home video entertainment industry was still developing. Technical standards had not yet been established and there was little programming (software) until standards were established because software producers were unwilling to incur the cost of producing disks for three or more different formats. New distribution channels were needed to handle the small-ticket videotapes and videodiscs containing programming. Joint ventures seemed to be the best way to introduce these new products, especially where technical standards differed around the globe.

Market Standardization. If customer tastes can be standardized across several geographic markets, investments in the means of satisfying demand appear to be more attractive than where each pocket of demand wants different product configurations and no market segment is of a size large enough to enjoy scale economies in production or distribution. The greatest critical mass exists when customers' tastes are homogeneous throughout the world. Such customers are highly attractive because they enable firms to pursue global strategies.[3]

Global competitors can enjoy significant cost advantages because they possess supply networks that span their many factory locations, assembly plants, warehouses, and distribution systems within several countries. In their quest for *access* to the most desirable locations for the components of their interconnected network of facilities, global firms may offer local partners generous terms in a joint-venture agreement, *provided* the global partner can retain managerial control over logistics to maintain maximum flexibility in its international system of operations.

But it is unreasonable to expect that firms that have devised an efficient means of serving standardized markets will abandon their traditional networking policies by accommodating cumbersome joint-venture arrangements, unless their expected payoff for doing so is great. While local firms control market access, they possess a bargaining chip that they forfeit when foreign competitors have established rival distribution channels in their home markets. One way that local firms can delay the establishment of outsiders' own marketing systems is by offering the use of their marketing networks to global competitors. The advantage of such cooperation yields only short-term gains, however, unless firms use their time together in a partnership with global firms to exploit the *other* benefits of joint ventures.

GLOBAL PARTNERS. In those cases where global firms took local firms as partners in the industries I examined, they often maintained close controls over their many plant locations, assembly plants, warehouses,and distribution facilities within their global systems. They frequently treated their venture as an extension of their corporate system of business units and integrated their partners' products into their global product lines.

Rather than form joint ventures—and cope with the unwieldiness of shared decision-making—global firms preferred to use licenses, cross-marketing agreements, and other informal ways of cooperation. Even where alliances were announced as being "joint ventures," their arrangements proved to be agreements to work together in bidding for a contract, sharing research findings, or serving as OEM vendors in many cases. Where joint ventures were formed to satisfy local governmental requirements, these units were rarely given tasks that created competitive advantage for the rest of the global system. They were merely a means of implementing part of a global strategy that had been forged for other parts of the owner's global system. The ideas, innovations, and suggestions of the joint venture diffused infrequently through that system. Instead the flow of information tended to be one-way, reflecting the lack of autonomy that global strategies afforded the managers of local business units.

PHARMACEUTICALS. Competition in the global ethical pharmaceuticals industry centered on R&D for new product innovation. Joint ventures and licensing agreements were used to flesh out product lines when the cost of bringing new drugs to market began to skyrocket. Successful inventors of new medical products needed help from established marketers because selling costs were substantial and knowledgeable sales representatives scarce, making marketing-oriented joint ventures commonplace. However, few firms pursued joint R&D ventures (except in the area of genetic engineering), since patents were the stronger source of competitive advantage.

Autonomy was rare when joint ventures were part of a global pharmaceutical firm. Such ventures were primarily *marketing arms* of their global owners, and this pattern was supported by the competitive advantage afforded by patents in the pharmaceutical industry. Few partners formed joint ventures for basic research. Instead, joint ventures (and other forms of cooperative strategy) enabled firms that were standardizing their products globally to overcome local variations in market conditions.

FINANCIAL SERVICES. The financial services industry was also global by 1984. In order to succeed in this industry, firms needed an image of leadership that could only be established through decades of customer contact. Because there were no economies in serving many small and diversified accounts, successful firms marketed their products aggressively but selectively to attain scale economies in processing. A large distribution network was required for success to take advantage of scale economies in serving desired customers. Telecommunications assets could be used to reach some customers, but customer access was nevertheless the key resource to control. (Software capabilities were important, but these could be purchased. R&D skills were needed to develop a wide range of new products, but these could also be obtained through cooperation.) Thus, firms used their successes in serving local markets to expand globally and to supplement their product lines by offering the products of others.

Impediments to Global Flexibility. If customers in diverse geographic markets will accept standardized products, firms must move faster to exploit the temporary advantages of joint ventures because it will be more difficult to erect effective entry barriers against competitors where markets are homogeneous. Coordinating the logistical aspects of a firm's cooperative strategy grows more important and timing in execution becomes crucial due to the rapid dissemination of ideas with homogeneous markets. Care is needed to ensure that local partners' needs in joint ventures do not become impediments to future strategic flexibility. There is some evidence suggesting that global firms are divesting those business units that no longer fit their coordination strategies for serving homogeneous markets. Instead of loosely coupled international diversification strategies, for example, global firms instead appear to be consolidating their holdings to focus on rationalization and cost reduction.[4]

Competitor Traits, Industry Structures, and Technological Opportunity

Analysis of the venture's domain also considers how a firm elects to satisfy demand. A key determinant of joint-venture stability is the venture's effectiveness in coping with the demands of sophisticated customers and tough competitors, and this relationship is dynamic. The key structural changes in industries are precipitated by technological innovations in manufacturing, although innovations in the product's configuration, in channels of distribution, or in other activities could also cause the relationships between buyers and sellers to evolve. These structural changes affect whether an industry's profitability potential will remain attractive for joint ventures.

Industry Structures. Joint ventures represent a significant change in industry structures and in competitive behavior. Owner firms embrace ventures because they are ways to implement changes in their strategic postures or to defend current strategic postures against forces too strong for one firm to withstand alone. Joint ventures permit firms to create new strengths, perhaps by sharing in the use of technologies they could never afford to explore alone. The combinations of talents that effective joint ventures can create have the potential to introduce new competitive vigor into lethargic industries as well as to let embryonic industries develop useful products faster.

Joint ventures are transitional strategies. They can be used for entry into, repositioning within, or exit from an industry. Joint ventures can be used to test the waters for entry into mature industries when firms cannot enter alone because they cannot afford to match the accumulated experience curve advantages of early entrants.

ENGINES. Large engines (and other complex propulsion devices) are capital- and labor-intensive products. Although key engine features can be standardized, customers usually want minor customization. Because a centralized engine-making facility could produce all but the finishing steps when customized features were added in order to exploit scale economy advantages, the engine industry should have evolved into a concentrated structure of a few firms operating centralized plants. Instead, it evolved into one composed of rival consortia with many subcontractors operating in many geographically dispersed locations. This structural evolution was due to government requirements regarding local content.

Engines and other propulsion devices primarily were sold to governments or other large and sophisticated customers (such as airlines) that both realized and exercised their inherent bargaining power over their vendors. Most frequently, customer bargaining power was exercised in the form of demands for a greater proportion of local labor content as a percentage of the total costs of the very expensive engines. This request aided government employment objectives and gave the government a more favorable balance of trade.

Vendors of large engines tried to satisfy the government's demands that local suppliers, artisans, and workers be employed, but because the components and skills needed to produce high quality engines were not always available in local economies, a complex system of credits awarded for purchases of *other* locally produced goods and services was developed to permit vendors of engines to offset the sales price of their products by their purchases from local manufacturers. Frequently, this practice evolved into a series of quasi-barter transactions that were orchestrated by the partners themselves or by a trading company.

Unexpected combinations of firms occurred as customer requirements grew more sophisticated, and vendors learned to cooperate on a project-by-project basis with partners who were previously tough competitors. While firms cooperated as partners to make engines on one project, they competed intensely against each other on other aerospace projects where they were not partners.

AUTOMOBILES. The automotive industry has evolved from one where firms preferred to export complete vehicles during the 1910s and 1920s to one that exploits the advantages of a global organization. By 1984, the automotive industry had become global due to improved computer power and computer-communications capabilities, which enable automobile manufacturers to track lower materials costs, labor productivities, and other sources of comparative advantage and to exploit these opportunities in a program of world-wide sourcing.

As local governments increased their trade barriers against imported products by demanding greater local content, automobile manufacturers formed joint ventures, built assembly plants, and changed their logistics patterns by importing knockdown kits composed of parts manufactured in lower-cost environments. Whenever possible, automobile manufacturers procured only the cheap, easy-to-make components locally, unless governments intervened to prevent such practices. If local restrictions concerning imports of lower-cost components became too stringent, automobile manufacturers could not include those plants in their closely coordinated global strategies. Instead, local competitors banded together to make their respective plants economic in sourcing agreements to provide standardized designs for axles and other common components. The designs of major automobile manufacturers became more standardized throughout the world as major parts suppliers, like Dana and Rockwell, worked with major automobile manufacturers to design components that could be interchanged locally across companies.

As the pressures for fuel economy required the development of more sophisticated vehicles, the task of incorporating another firm's components into one's own vehicles became an astronomical engineering feat. Long-term alliances became more attractive than loose cooperative agreements because technologically complex vehicles required close coordination on all aspects of automobile components. Yet automobile manufacturers were reluctant to bind themselves in relationships that limited their day-to-day operating autonomy. Consequently, firms participated in design consortiums, but they tolerated few cooperative strategies that required shared decision-making activities. The NUMMI joint venture between General Motors and Toyota was a pioneering effort in an industry that needed more consolidation joint ventures (as in the steel industry) as well as innovation joint ventures (as in electronics) in order to succeed.

Late Entry. Joint ventures may be the only way to match the ongoing intelligence advantages of established firms when entering *late*. Such ventures can be important change agents for launching new products, legitimizing new technologies, and rationalizing capacity as industries evolve. Vertical joint ventures are used to stabilize demand and to introduce new products within young industries, whereas horizontal ventures are used in mature settings to keep abreast of technological improvements and control excess capacity.

Joint ventures to facilitate learning new skills are likely if products are differentiable, particularly if this knowledge fills gaps in a firm's abilities, such as quality-control techniques in the automobile industry. If firms cannot focus on standard configurations or other stabilizing points of cooperation, however, joint ventures may be short-lived, since they are too risky for most firms to tolerate within volatile industries. In their efforts to hedge risks within unstable, fragmented, or volatile industries, firms who possess adequate bargaining power forge a pattern of spider's-web alliances, if they decide to cooperate at all.

Thus, volatile competitive environments—those with fragmented structures, commoditylike products, powerful suppliers (or customers), and other attributes that erode profitability potential—diminish the amount of equity partners would be willing to expose through joint ventures. If the environment is volatile and the activity is not of strategic importance to them, partners will not waste their efforts on cooperative strategies, as figure 5–5 indicates. In environments where competition is not volatile, firms are more willing to use cooperative strategies, but they still favor greater control over those activities that are of strategic importance to them. Thus ventures could become the agent that *stabilizes* industry conditions by introducing standard product configurations, creating lowest-cost production processes, or facilitating improved competitive intelligence, if used effectively.

Embryonic Industries. When an industry is embryonic, demand is uncertain and product standards are not yet established. Frequently infrastructures must be built within embryonic industries. Firms use joint ventures to forge vertical arrangements in such settings to build infrastructures, legitimize new products, and educate customers. Often these vertical arrangements are jointly owned by horizontally related partners, especially if the costs of creating distribution channels, transportation systems, or other supporting activities are substantial.[5] Vertical joint ventures will provide these partners with market access and are most appropriate as a means of joining industries when basic relationships between buyers and sellers are evolving. A presence within at least two stages of a vertical chain of processing gives partners a "listening post" to assess and communicate competitive intelligence back to the venture's owners if the joint venture is structured effectively. (This sort of intelligence is necessary in order for firms to respond quickly to changes in demand, to develop new technologies, and to incorporate innovations into their products.)

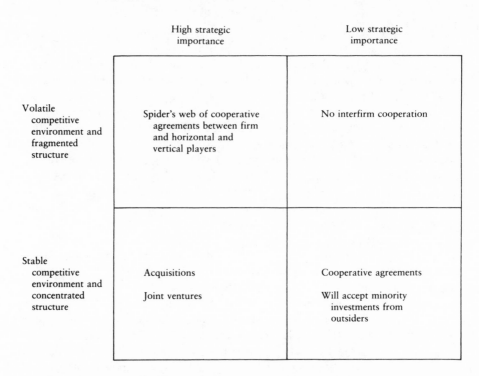

Figure 5–5. Single-Firm Analysis: Relationship between Competitive Conditions and Strategic Importance in Joint-Venture Formation (Assuming Firms Will Cooperate, Ceteris Paribus)

Embryonic industries pose a potential source of conflict between owner and venture concerning risk-taking. If an industry is embryonic, great uncertainty remains concerning which competitive approaches will be most successful. Product and marketing standards are not established; neither are relationships between suppliers and customers. Until successful strategies become evident, some firms hedge their bets by trying several approaches, each in a different venture. But managers within a "boisterous" venture often want the freedom to move in directions that seem more promising as uncertainty is reduced. If the venture's owners have hedged their bets concerning which approach will prove most successful by creating a spider's web of ventures, owners will expect the managers of each respective joint venture to act as champions of their respective strategies until another is proven to be superior rather than to diversify (in technologies or product configurations) to a strategy that looks better to them. If an industry is embryonic and the best technologies (products features, styling, means of distributing a product) are yet unknown, the venture needs autonomy to move in the directions that seems most promising. But since technologies are most frequently obtained from one or more owners, close coordination with technology owners will be necessary in order to modify the venture's activities to suit the evolving demands of its owners.

COMMUNICATIONS SERVICES. Product life cycles were shorter and competition was becoming keener in the communications services industry in 1984, partly due to deregulation and partly due to success in marrying telecommunications with data processing. Joint ventures were necessary in telecommunications because of (1) the convergence of computers and telecommunications; (2) shorter product lives driven by rapid technological improvements; (3) huge R&D expenditures made by ongoing and new competitors; (4) intensification of global competition; (5) deregulation of telecommunications; (6) expectations concerning a boom in the office automation equipment industry; and (7) a potential breakdown of trade barriers as a result of technological changes and political activities. A record number of joint ventures were announced at this time.

Established Industries. Tensions concerning infrastructure uncertainty are reduced when an industry matures, other factors held constant. If the joint venture shares no resources with its owners, its managers can act autonomously in matters of competitive strategy, subject to the financial controls imposed by the venture's owners. When the venture shares resources with or parallels those of its owners, other industry factors may make close coordination necessary.

Joint ventures are useful in slowly growing, established industries such as satellite-communications equipment or oil extraction. As projects grow large and more risky, as technologies become too expensive to afford alone, and as the challenges of global competition increase, it becomes more difficult for numerous firms to survive independently. Joint ventures are one means of accommodating new competitors within markets where capacity has been overbuilt and demand is growing slowly, at best. Under these circumstances, firms must either shrink capacity themselves or through marriages in order to avoid debilitating price wars. The recent burst of U.S. ventures in industries such as steel and farm and industrial equipment suggests, in part, that managers would prefer to enter into ventures *voluntarily* (rather than follow federally directed policies of industry rationalization) because such strategies permit them to decide which portions of a business unit to divest.

PETROCHEMICALS. The changing purpose of joint ventures can be traced to the changing relationships among partners in petrochemical ventures that occurred over time. Prior to the 1970s, petrochemical joint ventures linked horizontally related owners upstream to a vertically related venture. The energy crisis created feedstock scarcities and skimpy profit margins. Supply uncertainty made a firm's venture play a critical role in its value-added chains. A firm's desire to participate in markets that offered it higher value-added margins brought together vertically related partners, which performed upstream and downstream processing activities. These firms became linked in the vertical chain of processing through their joint ventures.

Owners controlled market access for their venture's outputs. Chemicals were sold by the carload or pipeline, and one sales force could handle a wide range of chemical products. The venture's outputs were usually consumed internally by its owners or marketed on a merchant basis by the owners' sales representatives. Thus, petrochemical joint ventures often operated in close coordination with one or more of their owners due to their physical proximity and the highly interconnected nature of petrochemical technology. Linkages between owner and venture were simply a matter of laying a pipeline from one plant to another. Some owners transferred all relevant assets for a line of petrochemicals to their joint venture and gave it complete autonomy to manufacture chemicals for in-house consumption, but owners usually marketed the outputs they did not consume.

ETHICAL PHARMACEUTICALS. Because drugs are a necessity and most competition among patented drugs is on the basis of innovation, new patentable drugs are needed at a rate faster than most pharmaceutical laboratories can satisfy demand. Hence, cross-licensing arrangements and joint ventures frequently are undertaken in the pharmaceuticals industry to increase the rate of technological change.

The ethical pharmaceutical industry provides an exception to the argument that control of market access is more important than control of technology because patent protection is strong and gives patent holders an irreplicable competitive advantage. The ethical pharmaceuticals industry was prolific in the number of new chemical entities discovered and certified during the 1960s. However, the 1970s and early 1980s were characterized by low R&D productivity. To counter this slump, joint venture in genetic-engineering technologies and other innovations were formed to increase the number of new chemical entities entering the U.S. pharmaceutical market in the 1990s.

STEEL. The steel industry's experiences with joint ventures illustrate how a venture's role changes over time. In the early years of the steel industry's development, horizontally related partners formed vertically related joint ventures in iron-ore mining to develop their industry by procuring stable sources of raw materials. When cheaper sources of ore and pig-iron were developed overseas, steel firms' obligations to their joint ventures encumbered their strategic flexibility. Unike the petrochemicals firms that shut down their joint ventures when those ventures no longer served their needs, steel firms delayed disentangling their iron-ore coalitions until they loomed as significant exit barriers.

By 1984, steel joint venture linked horizontally related partners in horizontal fade-outs. This pattern was consistent with the behavior expected of firms in mature (or declining) industries with high exit barriers. The rules of steel competition had changed radically and required drastic actions to amend its problems.

FARM AND INDUSTRIAL EQUIPMENT. Joint ventures in the farm and industrial equipment industries were needed to rationalize excess capacity, consolidate product lines and widen product offerings, transfer manufacturing technology, provide sources of lower-cost production, and forge global distribution channels. Many cooperative agreements were used to obtain products to fill out a firm's product lines after it had shut down its underutilized plants. The joint ventures used in the farm and industrial equipment industry in many ways paralleled those in the automotive industry. Prior to the conditions that depressed U.S. demand for farm and industrial equipment, joint ventures in this industry primarily were formed by U.S. firms overseas as a means of entering protected markets.

Timing of Joint Ventures. Because small but timely investments made early in an industry's development could give firms important leadership positions later on, joint ventures are frequently used when industries are embryonic to gain first-mover advantages. Pioneering investments in research are also appropriate reasons to form joint ventures in embryonic industries, particularly where expectations of commercial success are low and firms are reluctant to invest heavily until uncertainties regarding product standards, commercial viability, or other factors have been reduced.[6] Joint ventures spread the costs of innovation when the risks of obsolescence are high due to rapid rates of technological change. Pioneering strategies are often risky, however, because more powerful late entrants could make the product configurations, standards, and other attributes of early entrants obsolete. Accordingly, firms engage in a mutual spider's web of alliances to test many alternative technologies while an industry is still young.

Strong and highly determined competitors can piggy-back on the infrastructures built by early entrants if pioneers have not created standard product configurations for the industry or sustained other first-mover advantages. But if effective pioneers can defend their early investments from the incursions of late entrants, joint ventures within embryonic industries would be well justified. Moreover, if firms could effectively move their industries in directions that late entrants would find difficult to match, joint ventures may be their best means of acquiring the skills and resources needed to precipitate these changes.

As industry structures evolve and the nature of competition changes, the capabilities that firms will need to compete effectively will change.[7] When the structure of an industry is well established, less uncertainty will exist concerning the most successful product standards, buyer–seller relationships, and other means of competing. Structural relationships between buyers and suppliers will be better established. Although new competitors could still enter mature industries, their behaviors will be more predictable in such settings.[8] Fewer joint ventures will be necessary, but those that endure will assume greater importance in a firm's corporate strategy.

When competition is volatile and prices fluctuate erratically, the venture needs autonomy and yet it also needs to coordinate closely with the owner that provides its marketing support, if either form does so. When competition is not volatile, and nonprice competition prevails, the venture's autonomy and coordination needs are lower, other factors held constant.

Success within changeable environments demands rapid responses and high strategic flexibility. A joint venture's flexibility can be greater when exit barriers are lower if owners grant it the autonomy needed to respond to pricing, product feature, or technological changes quickly. But if pioneering (by taking a position early in the development of an industry) does not provide strong competitive advantages, the joint venture's response need not be as rapid, nor must its autonomy from owners' activities and intervention be as high as when pioneering strategies provide competitive advantages to joint venture partners.

Technologies. Joint ventures enable firms to capture more profits than they would enjoy if they merely licensed their technologies. Moreover, joint ventures provide more control over how a firm's resources will be used. But technology leaders will not readily share those kernels of knowledge that are central to their competitive advantage, and partners would be unwise to transfer their technological expertise to their ventures (since knowledge is highly appropriable and joint ventures do pose problems of bleedthrough), unless they must exploit their highly perishable knowledge rapidly and can fine-tune their pace of technology sharing more easily through joint ventures than nonequity arrangements.

When industries are people intensive rather than capital intensive, the forces driving firms to exploit their perishable technological advantages are subdued by the reality that their competitive advantages reside in highly mobile assets. Short of chaining these people resources to their desks, firms protect their rights to intangible assets gained by developing new processes, taking risks as pioneers, or setting product standards by forming joint ventures *with their entrepreneurial employees.* More cooperative strategies of shorter duration are pursued to restrict outsiders' personnel to one generation of knowledge per agreement, if technologies are people-intensive. In cases where owners might have contributed critical technological knowledge earlier to their venture in capital-intensive industries, they will withhold such knowledge longer in people-intensive settings. Instead, owners will use more arm's-length licensing agreements to exploit perishable competitive advantages.

When outside suppliers are powerful, by virtue of the importance of their products to the joint venture or the lack of alternative vendors, the venture's need for close coordination with its owners' purchasing activities increases, other factors held constant, in order to mitigate this power. Although they need not be suppliers themselves, access to an economic source of raw materials or components (or autonomy to negotiate for them from outsiders) is one of the provisions owners must anticipate in their joint-venture strategy if it is to be effective.

If firms wish to seize a competitive advantage, they must be prepared to take risks. Technological innovation is a major way to change an industry's structure to a firm's advantage, but many processes that firms invest in are very expensive failures. Joint ventures permit firms to share those risks by hedging their bets concerning which products, processes, or configurations will become industry standards. Moreover, joint ventures permit firms to keep abreast of technological innovations by providing a means of sharing development costs. But firms must exert care in their use of joint ventures for technology acquisition. Although technology is one of the major bargaining chips that firms possess in forging cooperative strategies, it is a more perishable advantage than market access and is a particularly fragile asset where technologies are people intensive. Accordingly, firms share less knowledge of this bargaining advantage with outsiders (through their venture) if they cannot replenish this strength, as chapter 4 suggests.

Rates of Technological Change. Technological joint ventures enable pioneers to capture more of the value added by their research efforts where knowledge quickly becomes obsolete. Joint ventures help technological followers also because they spread risk and bring an infusion of new ideas from innovative partners. Rapid technological change often increases a firm's need to cooperate, but it may also create an arrangement that is too inflexible to adapt to the volatile competitive environment if structured incorrectly.

Joint ventures are formed among technology leaders in environments of rapid technological change such as robotics, medical products, and software. Because volatile competitive settings may squeeze down profit margins and prevent such firms from reinvesting in the R&D needed to sustain a competitive rate of innovation, they need a means of producing the cash needed to fund their next generation of discoveries. Technologies are obsolesced so quickly in some industries that paybacks cannot be earned on a single generation of products. This means that even when firms might prefer the greater control of wholly owned ventures, they team up with a strange collection of bedfellows (including foreign competitors) if other desirable objectives can be attained.[9]

During periods of scarce resources and rapid technological change, technological leaders should be interested in using cooperative strategies to gain competitive advantages or to sustain leadership. The magnitude of harm created by choosing the wrong cooperative strategy depends on how rapidly a firm's advantages might be eroded by a competitor's innovations if the firm did not engage in some program of cooperative strategies. If the magnitude of harm is substantial, then the form of cooperation matters less.

TECHNOLOGY LEADERS. In settings where technological strengths could rapidly become obsolete, innovating firms must exploit their discoveries as quickly as possible. When technologies change rapidly, technology leaders who fear that their investments will be obsolesced before the costs of developing them can be recovered will license many firms and share technology with their joint venture faster in order to exploit their resources rapidly. (If technologies change slowly, by contrast, firms will not share their cutting-edge, proprietary knowledge with their venture until they have developed a new generation of technology to hold in reserve as a competitive advantage.) Furthermore, technology leaders will seek market access in exchange for their technology in settings where rapid exploitation of their resources is not imperative. Even where technology changes rapidly, leaders may be choosy concerning which firms they will allow to use their newest processes and designs in a partnership.

TECHNOLOGY FOLLOWERS. Technological followers seek a spider's web of partnerships, where available, to supplement their obsolescing technology. (Since they have little strength to bargain from, however, technological followers are rarely at the hub of any webs of cooperation. Instead they link with others' spider's webs of ventures.) Since their bargaining positions as technology followers are not strong but their needs for new generations of technology are substantial, followers hedge their bets to reduce uncertainties regarding which technologies will eventually become industry standards, especially within volatile settings where technologies are changing rapidly, by forming several joint ventures. If followers cannot offer coveted assets (such as market access) in exchange for needed technology, they will not keep pace with competitors, especially in environments of rapid technological change.

COMMUNICATIONS EQUIPMENT. By 1984 many electronics, information processing, and telecommunications firms were teaming up to develop new technologies and products. Some firms formed joint ventures because a self-centered, vertically integrated approach to the communications business did not seem appropriate any longer. Moreover, because no firm could develop in-house every product needed to compete effectively in 1984, firms were moving swiftly to find appropriate partners. Collaboration had become so important to the interface between communications and data processing that some companies were even investing in partners to cement their relationships and alleviate their fears of being left behind.

Many firms feared that if they did not team up, they would lose their market position to foreign competitors for whom cooperation was nothing new. Some firms formed joint ventures for survival, especially smaller, younger firms that specialized in information processing technologies. Affiliation with larger telecommunications firms gave them access to much-needed management experience as well as to sales and service capabilities they could not afford on their own.

The communications equipment industry was characterized by substantial capital requirements, pressures to reduce costs (by exploiting scale economies), and increasing sophistication of products in the data transmission industry. Excess capacity was a continual threat as the telecommunications industry was deregulated and vendors strived to offer complete, compatible network systems.

New technologies were constantly being developed and as each generation of equipment appeared on the market older versions were rendered obsolete. In order to succeed, firms needed: (1) technological expertise; (2) large amounts of capital; (3) the ability to adapt technology to customers' needs and partners' configurations; (4) distribution networks (or ways to access others' networks); (5) cost structures that permitted firms to offer attractive pricing and acceptable quality; and (6) willingness to hook up with other vendors, among other traits.

ELECTRONIC COMPONENTS. Capital required to introduce a new generation of electronic components was large even in the 1970s, and risks of failure or premature obsolescence were great. Patent protection was insignificant, and firms enjoyed a brief window of advantage (eighteen months or so at best) before their designs were incorporated into another's products. Technology changed rapidly and successes were quickly outmoded. Profit margins on electronic components were thin because prices dropped rapidly as unit volumes accumulated and firms pressed their cost advantages. Yet firms felt obliged to participate in each technological generation to apply their experience to the next iteration of product designs. They typically obtained next-generation knowledge through *cross-licensing agreements,* if not through internal development. Second-source vendor licenses frequently were used to assure customers that each product was available from at least two vendors. Thus, electronic components quickly lost their differentiated status and became standardized (hence, commoditylike) products that could best be made by large, global competitors. There were few joint ventures but many other types of cooperative agreements. Close affiliations with partners often meant that firms "borrowed" each others' ideas, and this practice contributed to the electronic component industry's volatility. No firm could hope to exploit a position of advantage for long alone.

Capital Intensity and Scale Economies. Some industry technological scales, such as those in metals processing and communications equipment, are so large that smaller firms could exploit those scale economies only by sharing a plant's outputs. Schemes to share large-scale plants have a stabilizing effect on competition because they bring industry capacity more closely in line with demand. In this manner, joint ventures can be used to increase industry concentration by rationalizing capacity, neutralizing disruptive players, or introducing other structural changes. The opportunities to exploit these information- and asset-sharing economies will occur with less frequency, however, if an industry is people intensive, as figure 5–6 indicates.

PETROCHEMICALS. Petrochemical firms frequently developed new products and tested new processes through joint ventures in order to minimize individual losses. Frequently, the feedstocks for the venture were provided by the refineries of one partner and the chemical processes used in production were provided by the other partner. Such cooperative arrangements accelerated innovation and facilitated the testing of new materials and methods. The shared risks of these ventures enabled petrochemical firms to participate in larger write-offs if these ventures failed.

The oil shocks of the 1970s modified the historical pattern of petrochemical venture partner relationships. Chemical firms seeking stable acesss to petrochemical feedstocks integrated vertically or formed joint ventures with oil firms seeking higher value-added margins through further processing of their feedstocks. When the oil firms brought their knowledge of joint ventures to bear on the petrochemicals industry, joint ventures became larger and more global in scope.

SERVICE VENTURES. The experiences of firms that formed joint ventures in the software, database, computer-assisted management services, communications services, financial services, entertainment programming, and programming packaging industries suggest patterns for the use of joint ventures in service businesses. Key among these patterns is the suggestion that the uses of joint ventures in service businesses are similar to those in other types of industries, *except where the industry's technology is labor intensive.* When the key strategic asset is people, different patterns of joint venture strategy will be found.

	People-intensive technology	Capital-intensive technology
	Spider's webs of cooperative strategies Objective: hedge bets, exploit many avenues quickly	
Embryonic industry structure	Venture capital arrangements Many cooperative (nonequity) agreements Many short-lived arrangements to recognize asset mobility	Many short-term "project-basis" ventures to spread risks Many partners in capacity sharing to scale economies
	Fewer, but larger cooperative strategies	
Well-established industry structure	More in-house venturing with entrepreneurs taking equity More development of technology in-house Less sharing of critical kernels of knowledge with venture Slow technology transfer to venture	More acquisitions as critical mass sales volume is attained Longer-duration joint ventures Equity transfer ventures to consolidate industry capacity and keep abreast of technological innovations

Figure 5–6. Single-Firm Analysis: Relationship between Industry Evolution and Capital Structure in Joint-Venture Formation (Assuming Firms Will Cooperate, Ceteris Paribus)

Fewer equity joint ventures are used when the key asset needed for success is human resources. When joint activities are used, they are more likely to be personal service contracts of limited durations than equity joint ventures. There are several reasons for these patterns. First, contractual relationships reduce the cultural friction between potential partners. Creative talent generally does not mix well with the management systems needed to run the activities of most complex corporate entities.

Second, the high mobility of labor resources make it more difficult to transfer the key technological assets necessary for success without danger of appropriation in service businesses. Licenses and other protections of intellectual property are inadequate where human resources make the difference between success and failure in the provision of services.

Third, scale economies can be exploited in the provision of communications services (especially in satellite communications) and other automated activities where capital requirements are high. Joint ventures in services with capital-intensive assets are motivated by risk- and cost-sharing advantages, as they are in the other capital-intensive industries. However, scale economies are more elusive where the fixed costs of salaries must be spread over production volume while *also* maintaining high service quality.

Thus, there are fewer joint ventures in activities where services are provided by technologies that are truly labor intensive, particularly where the knowledge in question cannot be protected adequately and the rate of technological change is rapid. A spider's web of joint ventures developed among the players in the entertainment programming and programming packaging industries because critical resources (film libraries) were owned by sponsoring firms and securely protected under licensing provisions. Close coordination was necessary between owner and venture in the entertainment programming, programming-packaging, databases, communications services and financial services industries because facilities were shared among them. Coordination with owners was also important when the venture tried to differentiate its products from those of competitors in service businesses. But efforts to differentiate services often created frictions between owner and venture because people-intensive ventures preferred to be autonomous. The heavy hand of owners that tried to draw their ventures more closely to their own activities could sap the motivations of key personnel—thereby undercutting differentiation strategies that were based on service. Owner intervention in venture activities can be so potentially harmful to the venture's strategic success where critical resources are people intensive that arm's length dealings should be used if joint ventures are created at all.

When service joint ventures are highly labor intensive and can be differentiated in the perceptions of customers through the efforts of personnel (particularly as they interact with customers), scale economies can be attained to the extent that certain tasks can be routinized or due to the spreading of fixed costs of tangible assets used in providing services. Services often are customized to a class of customers, depending on their sophistication and bargaining power over the vendors of the services. Software customers tend to be more sophisticated, for example, in evaluating products than retail financial customers.

Joint ventures are a way to offer new services faster. This motivation is illustrated most graphically in the example of joint ventures to provide communication services, where the effects of deregulation on communications services are dramatic. Prior to 1983, joint ventures were used infrequently to provide communications services. As the window for offering communications systems and services opened, firms rushed in to exploit this opportunity before it evaporated. For many firms, joint ventures were the only way they could achieve rapid entry into the communications services industry.

But if an industry is people intensive, fewer opportunities exist to exploit asset-sharing economies. Instead, more opportunities exist to exploit *information-sharing* advantages. It is necessary to move faster when competing in service industries because the forces driving firms to exploit their competitive advantages are highly perishable and mobile. Thus, joint ventures are needed to pioneer new service offerings and to more quickly pool knowledge in response to the innovations of others.

The highly mobile nature of assets in service businesses significantly affects owner–ventures relationships. Coordination between owner and venture is higher when competitive advantages reside in highly mobile assets but is lower when *proprietary* information has to be shared among them. Instead, owners either pool their capabilities in their venture (to team up against stronger competitors) and give their venture full autonomy for the activity in question or use cooperative strategies that do not create a separate entity. Critical technological knowledge does not pass to ventures as quickly in service industries, and the venture is reluctant to pass knowledge back to its corporate owners. Lawsuits and employee contracts are an imperfect way to safeguard an owner's intellectual property rights in service businesses, especially where employees frequently walk out on employers.

It is sometimes necessary to inculcate a culture within the venture that is substantially different from that of its owners. When owner and venture develop different cultures, interactions among them inevitably grate on each other's organizational nerves. Shared resources, for example, can provoke such cultural clashes between owner and venture. If the cultural differences between potential partners is dramatic, contractual links supplant their equity ties. If their cultures are similar, firms are more willing to enter joint ventures rather than some other form of cooperative strategy.

Finally, joint ventures to provide services are formed to prevent a firm's brightest employees from going elsewhere. However, if these employees are culturally dissimilar to their employers the resulting ventures will reflect these differences. The relationship between venture partners (the firm and its former employee) is uneasy and functions more like that in minority investments where owners cannot *directly* influence their venture's activities.

Software, Databases, and Computer-based Management Services. Scale economy advantages are enjoyed by services that depend on computer hardware. However, as the cost of software outpaced that of hardware and as the technology of data communications improved, the distributed data-processing concept grew *less* economic for larger customers as a way to provide these services in-house when compared with vertical integration arrangements. Moreover, as hardware became a relatively less-expensive part of the total package, programmers started their own firms with increasing frequency.

Many database joint ventures were established at a time when technologies were risky and demand was so uncertain that partners were needed to share costs and risks. By 1984, communications links and costs were the most expensive portion of many computer-based services, and links with partners possessing communications facilities became more desirable.

Thus, a new motivation for joint ventures had developed. In the past, computer companies had sold hardware, and their customers (or third parties) wrote the applications software. By 1984, customers wanted computer vendors to supply them with software as well as hardware. The ability of computer manufacturers to respond to this demand depended on their R&D capabilities, the personnel they could hire, and their ability to fund scale-up campaigns during compressed time periods. Cooperative strategies provided firms with rapid access to these needed skills.

ENTERTAINMENT PROGRAMMING AND PROGRAMMING–PACKAGING. Motion pictures are distributed to satellite communications firms and cable system operators by "programming packagers" such as Home Box Office (HBO). The capital costs of entering the entertainment programming–packaging business in the 1970s were not so high that a large firm could not afford to go in alone but the capital costs of entertainment programming (movie making) were large. Nevertheless, there were many joint ventures in the entertainment programming–packaging part of the industry in the late 1970s because of the many changes that the industry was going through. The programming–packaging industry was new and still developing. Firms believed that they needed partners to share losses and other risks while they experimented with the new kinds of distribution channels that might experience growing demand. Like firms in the oil industry, even large players preferred to invest in several projects to hedge their bets concerning which distribution channel would be successful and to lower their exposure to "dry holes." There were many crossover relationships as the composition of partnerships changed in entertainment programming. This pattern later carried over to entertainment programming–packaging. Thus, many firms were engaged in spider's webs of joint ventures in both industries.

Entry Barriers, Mobility, and Cooperation. Joint ventures can be a potent evolutionary force on industry structures because they provide a means for firms to enter industries (or adopt strategic postures) where ongoing competitors previously were protected by high entry (or mobility) barriers. Because potential entrants do not have to enter de novo and surmount the barriers that might deter stand-alone firms, the old concept of entry barriers must be updated when discussing ventures to take into account the changing structural traits and competitive dynamics such alliances create. Internally, the management systems used to guide joint ventures must adapt quickly to the dynamics of the venture's industry, or they may act as exit barriers by impeding its ability to reposition its strategy with respect to customers or vertical linkages with its owners.

Consideration of the effects of joint ventures on ease of entry (and exit) suggests that a new type of entry barrier will be created. When it is operative, an astute and timely joint venture could preempt competitors from linking up with those entrants that are most likely to succeed. For entering firms, competitive advantage is also gained by allying with the best local partners first (provided the early joint venture is a mutually exclusive one). Thus, the need to cooperate is especially acute—on both sides—if entry is inevitable, as in the the example of industries where technological or economic forces are eroding old industry boundaries and forcing firms that were never previously competitors to compete.

If entry barriers protect the venture's strategic posture from easy emulation by outsiders, its need for close coordination with its owners increases, other factors held constant. But if entry barriers are high, the joint venture may need to coordinate its entry-deterring responses closely with owners (particularly if they share facilities), or it may injure their respective strategic postures.

A New Concept of Entry Barriers. For foreign firms seeking cooperative strategies with ongoing domestic firms, the price of admission is embodied in the terms of their joint-venture bargaining agreement, not in the strong brand name, high capital costs, access to channels of distribution, control of scarce resources, or other attributes that comprise entry barriers when firms enter an industry alone. Instead, many of the relevant entry barriers surrounding ventures are mental. They exist in a manager's outlook—his way of conceptualizing market demand, his way of competing, and his way of working with suppliers and distributors.

Owner needs represent the salient entry barriers for analysis of industry attractiveness. If all potential entrants seek the same capabilities from potential partners, those capabilities are the barriers that best protect ongoing firms from entry by new players or best prevent easy emulation of their strategic postures by competitors.[11]

Maintaining Flexibility. Firms must guard against inflexibility created by joint ventures, particularly if their strategic postures require rapid modification. Being flexible means being willing to create flexible systems where people (an important differentiating factor in joint venture success) are given autonomy to make economic decisions for the venture's well-being. Venture flexibility is exacerbated by changing attributes in a venture's customer base, by changes in buyer knowledge and hence by changing heights of customer-switching cost barriers, as in embryonic industries where demand uncertainty is high.

In settings where structural traits are not yet established, a firm's posture must remain flexible. As chapter 4 notes, that means that the management system accompanying a joint venture must not become an exit barrier.[12]

Changing technology can increase interdependencies between activities that were previously conceptualized as being separate. For example, changing technologies and factor costs coupled with the information technology revolution have resulted in more industries becoming global. If the success requirements of competition change so quickly that there is less tolerance for error, then perhaps the "true" barriers to mobility or exit in joint ventures are in systems, management, and people. If a wrong control system emphasizes wrong targets, then owners will have the wrong means of mobilizing resources in their ventures. If the terms of the bargaining agreement do not provide adequately for decisions regarding these mobility barriers, then partners will be impeded from diversifying out of stagnant industries or from modifying an ineffective cooperative strategy as competitive conditions change.

Evolutionary Changes in Competitive Advantage

As chapter 3 indicates when it introduces the joint-venture framework, a joint-venture's *stability* depends on whether changes in terms of the bargaining agreement are necessary before its objectives are attained, and the stability of joint ventures is determined, in part, by the attractiveness of the market opportunities that ventures are created to exploit. Some ventures will be of short duration because owners can attain their objectives after only a brief period of cooperation. Other ventures will be short-lived because market conditions were (or have become) so unattractive that renegotiation (including termination of terms of the joint-venture agreement become necessary.

Changes in a firm's mission alter their needs for joint ventures, just as industry evolution alters the need for firms to cooperate in a particular way. Joint ventures can better fulfill some missions *later* in an industry's development than when demand uncertainties or other risks are high. Technological change will be particularly germane to the role that joint ventures may play in a firm's competitive strategies at varying times during an industry's evolution because technological changes may accelerate the pace by which product standards change, customers become more sophisticated and assets become obsolete. Because it is particularly difficult for numerous firms to survive independently as industry structures evolve rapidly, joint ventures are often used to shrink capacity and avoid price wars. However, even in this example, the tensions that make partners' interests and abilities diverge will exert a destabilizing force on shared ownership arrangements. If the joint venture no longer provides its owners with competitive advantages, it has outlived its usefulness. Even within the most stable competitive environment, shared ownership and management inputs are difficult to sustain after they have served their purpose.

Joint Ventures and Industry Evolution. Even when their effects on industry structure are most dramatic, the time when particular types of cooperative strategies are appropriate is brief. The many, short-lived ventures created when demand fluctuated erratically are replaced by a few, larger ventures of greater permanence as demand slows and stabilizes. The vertically related capacity that owners once shared becomes insufficient even to satisfy the throughput requirements of one partner later.

As customers become more discerning in their ability to distinguish among products, the number of joint ventures that firms can maintain decreases, and those that remain tend to emphasize price reductions and processes for adding value to products without increasing their prices. As customers become *more alike* around the globe, the need for joint ventures *becomes less* if firms are pursuing global strategies (unless one owner is willing to play a passive role in coordinating the venture's activities with its own). But if customers' preferences cannot be standardized and they become evermore demanding in their expectations, more *short-term arrangements* such as licensing agreements or sourcing arrangements will supplant a firm's preference for jointly owned ventures.

Briefly, the more volatile the competitive environment, the less attractive joint ventures become over time. The more flexible the assets that provide firms with competitive advantage, the more transitory are owners' uses of cooperative strategies with a particular partner. Firms continue to forge joint ventures and other arrangements for pooling skills, intelligence, and resources, but they become more fickle in their alliances. The more experienced a firm becomes in the use of cooperative strategies, the greater the advantage it can carve for itself when negotiating joint ventures because it understands when shared ownership ventures no longer meet the competitive requirements of an industry better than going it alone.

Therefore, if joint ventures provide firms with competitive advantages, they will be continued. If the use of joint ventures can stabilize an industry's structure, standardize the products that customers accept, or create scale economies (or other means of cost reduction), they will become a part of the strategy that successful firms embrace. If the need for risk-sharing activities does not abate, joint ventures will be a durable strategy for all phases of an industry's development, however, the identities of partners may change over time as one firm gives up its ownership position to another.

Joint ventures are an important structural trait of industries where firms embrace them to explore technologies they could never afford to use alone. Cooperative strategies introduce new vigor into lethargic industries as well as help embryonic industries develop useful products more quickly. Joint ventures are used in embryonic industries to gain "first mover" advantages, and spider's webs of joint ventures are used to test many technologies when the "best" technology is not yet known.

As projects grow larger and more risky, as technologies become too expensive to afford alone, and as the challenges of global competition increase, joint ventures enable firms to survive together where they could not do so independently. Horizontally related ventures rationalize overbuilt industry capacity and accommodated new players in slow growth settings. As customers become more alike around the globe, the need for joint ventures falls unless partners are willing to give their venture full autonomy and assets to pursue global strategies.

AUTOMOBILES. For example, in 1980 General Motors and Toyota began discussions concerning a 50%–50% joint venture to manufacture a family of Toyota-designed cars in the United States. By 1983, their negotiating teams had created a twelve-year, jointly owned venture called New United Motor Manufacturing, Inc. (NUMMI) to produce a version of Toyota's subcompact Corolla model in a formerly shut-down General Motors plant in Fremont, California. Toyota was chosen as operating manager of the joint venture, and it used Japanese-supplied automotive components until Toyota could teach U.S. suppliers how to meet its quality standards. Initially, NUMMI's cars were sold under the Chevrolet name. Partners split profits from the joint venture, but, as the car's designer, Toyota received design and engineering royalties based on unit sales. (Toyota's U.S. marketing and distribution activities were already adequate prior to its liaison with General Motors. It did *not* need General Motor's market access to penetrate the U.S. automobile market.)

Toyota hoped to learn about the U.S. labor environment through the joint venture. The venture also was a response to U.S. critics, especially the United Auto Workers (UAW) union, who had called for federal action against the rising tide of Japanese imports. The Japanese automobile industry's interest in a production base in the United States paralleled the Japanese response to informal quotas on steel exports to the United States. "Voluntary" quotas on cars were established in the face of mounting U.S. criticism of Japanese car imports. Under these pressures, Honda Motor Co. had built a plant in Ohio, and Nissan Motor Co. had built a plant in Tennessee.

General Motors was curious as to whether Japanese management techniques could be applied successfuly to a U.S. unionized labor force. Consequently, Toyota was given maximum freedom in the agreement to bring in their manufacturing programs and their Japanese work methods. Toyota insisted on hiring autonomy and freedom to use its own work rules, including the flexibility to move employees from one task to another. (At most, Toyota wanted three work categories. The typical U.S. automobile manufacturer has 25 work categories and has enjoyed substantially less flexibility in redeploying workers to even out work flows than Toyota was requesting.) The UAW acquiesced in this matter.

There was great interest in 1984 concerning how General Motors and Toyota would integrate their venture's activities with their own. NUMMI operated with substantial autonomy from General Motors as it adopted the customs of Toyota. For example, NUMMI ran pre-employment training programs to teach potential employees Japanese employment fundamentals, as did Nissan Motor Corp. NUMMI planned to hire only those workers that could adapt to Japanese-style management practices. Conflicts between partners were not expected to be substantial, due to the way in which the venture had been structured and due to similarities concerning management styles. Indeed, the partners' cultures were *more similar* than those of General Motors to other U.S. automakers. For example, until 1982 Toyota sold its automobiles in Japan through a separate company, Toyota Motor Sales, that was managed by Japanese who had learned their marketing techniques from General Motors Japan during the 1930s. Many of the principles of Toyota marketing and distribution were *more* similar to those of General Motors than they were to those of Japanese competitors such as Nissan, for example.

Since the activities of joint ventures such as NUMMI often share facilities with those of their global owners, they have to be coordinated closely with those of their owners' wholly owned business units. The principal role for local partners in such situations is often (1) to cope with local regulations concerning product standards and efficacy; (2) to represent the global firm's activities as those of a local firm within protected markets; and (3) to provide products to round out partners' offerings to global customers. Close coordination with an owner's activities is especially important when the venture's products do not have to be differentiated in a special way for local customers because the image of the product, its quality, and other attributes that customers value are similar from market to market.

Many global firms use cross-licensing agreements to move quickly in exploiting new technologies within diverse geographic markets. They keep close control over R&D activities, using their venture as a way of extending their reach into diverse markets. Licensing is a first step for some global firms in their efforts to gain a toehold into new markets; they often import products made in offshore facilities. In some cases, liaisons with local partners give way to acquisitions, particularly as global partners find their relationships with local partners to be unwieldy.

ENGINES AND AIRCRAFT. In the 1980s, protectionism, trade balance offsets, and requirements for local co-production detracted from the implicit efficiencies of global strategy because they required firms to make investments in facilities that otherwise would not have been justified by the needs of the system. Government policies concerning national security and the need to sustain local employment levels made manufacturers of diesel engines, jet engines, and aircraft include more local content. This pressure pulled against the forces that made the diesel engine, jet engine, and aircraft industries global. Close coordination was needed between partners in order to design pieces of engines and other complex and capital-intensive products. What were called joint ventures were often loosely formed alliances that had been formed to coordinate projects when bidding teams were successful.

Almost every government required some form of offset arrangment when overseas vendors tried to sell the many military products. Some governments required co-production arrangements as well as offsets. In those situations, pieces of military products are subcontracted to manufacturers in customer nations. Partnerships in military products were also necessary in cases where governments prohibited the resale of domestic technological products in products assembled overseas. Thus, a U.S. firm took a British firm as partner to provide engines when aircraft were to be sold to countries that were on the U.S. government's technology restriction list.

Summary

The arguments given above suggest that demand traits are important when assessing whether joint ventures are needed. Customer attributes affect a firm's ability to differentiate its product offerings from those of competitors while standardizing its respective product configurations across markets. The actions suppliers take by relying on their expectations concerning future demand traits determine an industry's competitive environment. Taken together, these forces determine the attractiveness of the domain for the formation of joint ventures.

Firms use cooperative ventures when products are first introduced to share in the risk that customer acceptance may never materialize. Later, they use joint ventures as a means of divesting their facilities to others that may be better suited to compete in environments of mature, stagnant, or declining demand. Market access, a major source of bargaining power when forging terms of joint-venture agreements, is less critical to obtain through ventures when customer's attributes enable firms to standardize their products across market boundaries.

These arguments suggest that fragmented industries are less attractive settings for joint ventures than concentrated ones because firms within fragmented settings focus on short paybacks for quick profits. The industry examples also suggest that concentrated settings are more attractive for joint ventures because firms operating within oligopolies can focus on mutually desirable goals with greater ease. The ability to identify such focal points permits owners to accept longer paybacks in testing new products, undertaking research, or making other expenditures because competition takes forms that firms can predict with greater ease. If joint ventures can consolidate a fragmented industry, price competition is replaced with rivalry in new product features, services, and other nonprice dimensions. These traits make industries more attractive, but price wars (or activities that change a firm's competitive standings rapidly) increase competitive uncertainty and exacerbate the political pressures that already divide partners with dissimilar backgrounds, motivations, and values. Instability is greatest when a joint venture links firms that are *not* competitors because such partners have different outlooks concerning how to compete. Moreover, joint ventures between dissimilar partners are difficult for owners to monitor and even more difficult to evaluate.[13]

Therefore, joint ventures with *horizontally related* partners reduce some forms of price-cutting pressures because firms that have served the same markets with similar products find it easier to focus on other ways of alleviating volatile competition. This ability to agree is important because change in the structural relationships within the venture's industry and in the nature of competition affect the joint venture's stability as well as its profitability potential. If the venture's initial strategic posture no longer addresses customer needs adequately, change is necessary. Joint ventures that face high mobility barriers due to their owners' abilities to agree are unable to augment their strategies to fit new competitive realities. They are more likely to use price as their primary dimension for competiton, and such actions make their industry less attractive for all players, whether jointly or wholly owned.

Conclusions Regarding Importance of Venture's Domain on Owners' Cooperative Strategies

In summary, joint ventures are assuming greater importance because product lives are shorter, cost advantages are becoming more pronounced, and greater numbers of firms who served only domestic markets are now becoming global competitors. These changes in competition have ominous ramifications for a manager who is likely to be offered a partnership in ventures by others who covet his firm's strengths (transitory though they may be). A timely analysis of how ventures fit the interests of their firms could help managers to forge configurations that leave their firms better off.

In the past, joint ventures have often been read as a signal of lesser corporate commitment to the project in question (unless firms purposely signaled high commitment to the markets in question in other ways). Firms have been particularly loath to use joint ventures where local governments did not require them as a condition of entry for domain-expanding multinational players. In environments of scarce resources, rapid rates of technological change, and massive capital requirements, however, joint ventures may be the best way for some firms to attain better positions in businesses they deem to be of great strategic importance. As long as managers recognize the dangers and limitations of cooperation and manage these shortcomings, their firms can use cooperative strategies effectively.

6
Joint Ventures and Adaptation

T his chapter along with chapters 7 and 8 summarizes managers' comments concerning the usefulness of joint ventures as a means of adapting to changing competitive conditions. It evaluates the robustness of the arguments presented in chapters, 3, 4, and 5 concerning the creation of competitive advantage through joint-venture strategies. In particular, chapter 6 compares findings concerning (1) partners' bargaining power; (2) owner–venture relationships; and (3) the venture's needs for autonomy with respect to its competitive environment. Thus, it evaluates the points concerning joint-venture strategies that were presented in figure 3–2. Chapter 7 devotes attention to findings concerning the use of ventures as technological change agents. Chapter 8 suggests how managers might best form and guide their ventures.

Using Joint Ventures

Firms vary substantially in their uses of joint ventures both within particular industries and across industries. Firms such as Control Data Corp. use ventures frequently because doing so has become part of their corporate culture. Other firms form ventures because they face too much risk in their competitive environments and possess too few skills internally to cope with these challenges alone. Firms accommodate the objectives of their partners in ventures only where those objectives do not clash with their own. Therefore, the best ventures match firms possessing particular strengths that *complement* those of their partners and objectives that are compatible. Usually these objectives are related to strategies to obtain resources and skills that cooperating firms lack internally.

Supplementing Resources and Capabilities

Managers were unanimous in noting that joint ventures are harder to manage than wholly owned business units but that cooperative ventures are undertaken with increasing frequency when the need to do so is substantial. Since there is no need for firms to form joint ventures if they can do everything themselves and since firms will rarely use cooperative ventures without considerable incentive to do so, it is reasonable to conclude that firms intended to use joint ventures to expand their competitive capabilities and create new strengths.

Firms obtained relatively easy access to expertise and distribution outlets through joint ventures and they moved faster in securing market positions than they would have done if they had had to develop assets and carve out a market position on their own. By pooling facilities, they were able to keep their costs low until their internally generated sales volumes reached critical masses that justified investments in their own plant, equipment, sales force, and other facilities. Thus, joint ventures were a means of supplementing a firm's resources and capabilities.

Accelerated Competitive Response

There are limits to the widespread efficacy of ventures, however, and firms must adjust their cooperative strategies to the special problems of certain types of competitive environments. In particular, learning to work together sometimes slows down the speed with which firms move into promising markets or respond to competitive maneuvers. In embryonic industries, for example, where great uncertainty looms concerning which marketing approach will be most successful or which technological standards customers will embrace, *more liaisons of shorter durations* result from successful firms' unions. In order to avoid long entanglements in arrangements that later could prove to be wrong, firms adopt less binding partnership arrangements in embryonic settings. Firms do not remain for long in ventures with any particular partner in environments of high uncertainty. Indeed, some firms even concluded that alliances that last for shorter durations, such as those used when technology changes rapidly, should *not* be bound by shared-equity agreements. Instead, firms create nonequity entities on a project-by-project basis for such projects. They do so because, when partners' interests change, ventures must end in a nondisruptive fashion as each partner moves on to its next dancing partner. To facilitate easy transitions, agreements are formed to last for only a few months at a time and proceed on the basis of a handshake rather than a voluminous legal document. These ventures are easily terminated with verbal notification from one partner to the other.

Remaining Flexible

Flexibility is necessary because some market opportunities evaporate within months if they are not exploited quickly. High technology products, in particular, need to accomplish faster market penetration in order to place them into distribution channels and consumers' hands before they become obsolete or are copied by others. When it is important to maneuver fast, nonequity partnerships (which do not create a venture) are used to accelerate a firm's product introductions.

Shorter Product Lives

It is especially important to have access to international linkages in industries where technology changes rapidly. It is increasingly expensive to reach key markets in global industries quickly when the half-life of a technology is very short because firms can scarcely recapture their development costs by going it alone. When firms recognize that their competitive advantages constitute only a fleeting strength, loose partnerships are combined with licensing agreements and other speedy ways of disseminating and exploiting whatever transitory competitive advantage firms possess. These informal alliances save time and keep firms from being preempted by competitors. For many firms, these cooperative arrangements are the best way to penetrate international markets quickly and to build up significant market shares.

Stable Industry Environments

Joint ventures are more likely to result when partners join forces in the early stages of industry maturity, when technology changes less rapidly and product standards have at last been established. As demand uncertainty—concerning the nature of customer tastes, price sensitivities, product features, and other market traits—lessens and firms become more concerned with how to forge effective strategies to satisfy demand, such as whether to use lowest-cost technologies or other tactics to protect their turf, they begin to seek the talents of accomplished partners and form joint ventures with greater longevities.

Joint ventures are also more likely to be formed as industries mature and competitive advantage is gained through higher-scale economies. Joint ventures are used to rationalize smaller, inefficient plants and to replace them with more efficient ones without creating floods of excess capacity. Many such ventures are actually *disguised divestitures* in cases where one partner no longer wishes to invest in a particular market or in the industry and is selling its assets incrementally to another firm.

In summary, different cooperative strategies of differing durations and involving different types of progeny are used in industries of different ages and infrastructure stability. Where there is still *great uncertainty* concerning the efficacy of technologies, customers' tastes, and other structural traits that affect the attractiveness of profit-making opportunities within an industry, partners keep their joint activities *informal and brief*. When industries mature—as more competitors enter and technological standards are better accepted—there are fewer ventures per firm, and each venture encompasses a larger-sized investment or broader market scope.

Building Strengths

All cooperative strategies—joint ventures, minority investments, cross-licensing agreements, and so forth—are a means of extending a firm's domains with relatively lower investment stakes than if it went into a similar venture alone. As such, cooperative strategies permit a firm to develop new competencies, gather more competitive intelligence, and engage in activities it cannot otherwise justify economically. The ideal objective in choosing a joint-venture partner is to offset each other's strengths; successful partnerships enhance the complementary nature of partners' assets and strengths. Therefore, marketing firms would choose a partner that offers technology, innovation, management experience, or funds, and technology partners would seek a partner to help penetrate markets quickly.

Joint ventures provide an excellent way for firms to strengthen their competitive postures by expanding their product lines. In such cases, partners with good products (or manufacturing technology) but poor marketing skills can obtain better market coverage by sharing the benefits of their experience curve advantages in manufacturing with potential entrants possessing the very strengths they lack.

Managing an Illusion. Whether these strengths are realized or not, the 1980s are a time for dazzling Wall Street with the illusion that firms are building strengths through cooperative strategies. Valuation problems are rampant for financial analysts as firms' stock prices enjoy speculative gains when joint ventures and other cooperative strategies are announced, especially when they try to evaluate technology transfers.

For example, if a firm overvalues its partner's technology contributions, such valuation errors are *never* admitted to outsiders, due to the image of wealth creation that the firm is trying to project to the financial community during this time period. If the firm later encounters start-up problems or if its partner's technological contributions are not as promised, these realities frequently are masked by the speculative stock price increases generated by investors' beliefs that (1) small firms are bettering their technological positions (by allying with big firms); or (2) that big firms, which were not doing anything impressive in a particular line of research, have found a promising way to catch up.

Protecting Strategic Turf. Results from field interviews are somewhat contrary to the prediction that joint ventures are a middle ground—a compromise—for firms in need of assistance in areas of strategic importance. By 1984, more U.S. firms were trying to use cooperative strategies, but most firms were not yet willing to compromise on the use of ventures in areas of great importance to them. If they cooperated at all in many areas of high strategic importance, it was only through relationships of exclusivity where they were strongly in control of their venture.

The higher a product line or area of technology is in strategic importance to its sponsors, the more reluctant firms are to use cooperative strategies to leverage their competitive positions further. Joint ventures are formed to supplement some firms' strengths; but *other* forms of cooperation are used more frequently in those areas that constitute a firm's strategic core. One explanation for a firm's reticence to trust partners in areas of great strategic importance may be that it is reluctant to rely on the successes of others for survival. Joint ventures are considered by many managers to be appropriate to gain new and related strengths; but some knowledge is considered to be too sensitive for their firms to share through cooperative ventures. Managers prefer to acquire the strengths they need rather than barter for it by sharing critical knowledge. If managers cooperate at all in sensitive areas, they make certain that they protect their competitive advantages, often through restrictive policies discussed in chapter 7.

Bargaining Power

An attractive firm's bargaining power is based on *what it knows and can do* as well as what it possesses. Although firms that are considered to be most attractive as partners possess great relative bargaining power and firms do not want to form ventures with partners weaker than themselves, most ventures are formed among industry underdogs. This pattern of cooperation persists because firms that are dissatisfied with their marketing skills or their product lines have to accept equally hungry (but deficient) firms as partners. Together, the underdogs try to create stronger competitive entities. But if one of the partners is notably stronger than the other with respect to the relative assets, skills, resources, or other attributes that give it greater bargaining power, the stronger eventually extracts compensation from its partner for its relatively greater strengths. Thus, alliances tend to be more costly in the long run for relatively weaker firms.

Balance of Power. This scenario of asymmetric strengths should not be a surprising one. Joint ventures are readily recognized as being a way for firms to acquire strengths and resources that they lack. In order for this bargain to work—in order for the other firm to desire a joint venture also—partners must be *unable* to utilize their own strengths fully. In addition to pooling their assets, effective partners add know-how that allows firms to build on each other's basic strengths in a way that they cannot do effectively alone.

Some agreements create bargaining power *for the venture* because each partner uses the venture as a stable source of raw materials. Using this guaranteed demand (secured by owners' take-or-pay contracts), ventures can penetrate new markets to dispose of excess outputs. If they are not constrained by their owners in the markets they can serve (after satisfying supply commitments to their owners), enterprising ventures are able to prosper (1) more than competitors that have no sponsors to absorb a base level of their outputs; and (2) more than other ventures that are prohibited by their owners from dealing with outsiders.

In sum, autonomous ventures have the best of both worlds. Their contracts with their owners give ventures a base of stable demand that creates bargaining power to offset downside risks and to resist customers' urgings to cut prices merely to fill ventures' plants to break-even levels.

More Cooperation. Even making minority investments in suppliers gives firms some bargaining power because they can block competitors from acquiring suppliers that can better serve industrywide demand by remaining independent. Firms are frequently suspicious of buying from the vertically integrated business units of their competitors. For this reason Ethyl Corp., the joint venture of Exxon and General Motors, created an arm's-length distancing from its owners to persuade Exxon's competitors to purchase its tetraethyl lead catalyst. A similar passive linkage strengthens independent suppliers without capturing them. (Antitrust fears concerning vertical joint ventures are unfounded because little *downstream* blocking occurs. By contrast, upstream blocking is increasingly condoned under the guise of an informal national industrial policy.)

In summary, findings suggest that ventures and other forms of cooperative strategy are used with increasing frequency by weak firms to create stronger market positions. Despite skepticism expressed by some managers, a plethora of minority investments, joint R&D projects, and ventures were announced in 1984 by firms that had never jointly ventured before. This pattern suggests that searches for sources of competitive advantage have led firms to discover that joint venture can be a way to build strengths from weaknesses.

Creating Synergies

If synergies are created through ventures, they accrue from vertical relationships between owner and venture or from resources shared among them. The coordination difficulties of ventures make it most likely that synergies are enjoyed among *horizontally related partners* with horizontally or vertically related ventures. Horizontally related partners are frequently more homogeneous and, accordingly, such partners enjoy greater synergies, because it is easier for them to agree on how to correct operating problems in their venture and how to coordinate its activities with theirs.

Vertically related ventures enable owners to avert the jealousies that frequently erupt between wholly owned business units that compete for the same customers that the venture serves because vertical joint ventures are less likely to be competitors of their owners' business units. In either case (horizontally or vertically related joint ventures), the benefits of cooperation are not automatic. The coordination problems associated with attaining joint venture synergies are substantial because synergies rarely accrue unless relationships between ventures and owners are consciously managed. Effective management of synergies requires owners to make appropriate tradeoffs concerning the benefits of venture autonomy and desirability of tight owner coordination. The struggle between these extremes is frequently a difficult one.

Vertical Relationships

A major issue examined in this book concerns whether ventures can thrive without access to the means to function as a stand-alone entity. Based on results from field studies, it appears that it is *not* necessary for the joint venture to have any downstream facilities of its own, provided the venture is not penalized for its failure to sell outputs that are not consumed by its owners. This amendment to the framework of chapters 3, 4, and 5 reflects firms' diverse motives for forming ventures, as well as the different missions owners give to their ventures.

For example, if a joint venture is formed to be a supplier to horizontally related owners, they will not want their venture to sell its excess outputs to other competitors, especially not at prices reflecting their marginal costs of production. Owners sometimes restrict their joint venture's customer list because they can pool their internal needs for components in order to exploit scale economies and do not want to share this significant cost advantage with outsiders.

Managers, except for those in the pharmaceuticals industry, concurred that market access is a very important (if not the single most important) competitive resource that U.S. partners control in joint-venture negotiations to form domestic ventures (because technology changes so quickly that competitive advantages based on it are less durable than those based on market access). However, many U.S. firms value access to partners' technologies more highly than they value their own sales organizations and accumulated goodwill with the trade. They readily help foreign partners learn how to market products effectively in the United States. In one case, a foreign partner sent its personnel on calls with the local partner's sales force in order to make customer contacts and observe U.S. marketing practices.

Boisterous Ventures. When ventures market outputs using their own sales forces, frictions result unless the venture's owners define specific geographic sales territories that become the venture's exclusive responsibility. Failure to circumscribe the joint venture's market domain frequently results in boisterous ventures going into competition against their owners and, when this occurs, few vertical synergies are realized because the venture's activities become counterproductive.

Some joint ventures develop their own marketing and sales forces when their owners cannot consume the venture's total outputs in quantities that will use the venture's plant capacity efficiently. For example, when Texaco's need for ethanol declined (as oil prices dropped) and it could no longer absorb the volumes it was obliged to purchase under a take-or-pay contract it had given its partner, CPC International, in their Pekin ethanol joint venture, the managers of the Pekin venture began to look for substitute customers. Although it may not have been the intention of Pekin's owners to give it a sales force, the oil industry's reversal forced Pekin to sell ethanol on a merchant basis in order to remain economically viable, and Pekin did so with great zest. Similarly, in the motion picture industry, joint ventures were forced to develop their own marketing and sales forces in cases where owners' business units refused to market their products.

Sheltered Ventures. Although they offer synergies, vertically related ventures pose unique problems if the joint venture is restricted from dealing with outsiders by right-of-first-refusal arrangements or by outright prohibitions that are imposed by its owners. Ventures' problems are similar to those problems that excessive vertical integration of the wrong type creates for wholly owned business units. For example, most joint ventures are most likely to become sickly if they are required to rely on owners for more than 50 percent of their sales or purchases. In consumer products, in particular, ventures that rely on owners to take more than 50 percent of their outputs often lack the discipline of outside markets to reflect consumer preferences. Such ventures are more likely to make products that the market does not want and its owners are more likely to be subsequently locked into purchases that are out of fashion with what end users desire. In summary, careful management of the buyer–supplier relationship between owners and their venture is needed in order for the benefits of vertical synergies to offset the *dangers created by strategic inflexibility.*

Overreliance by the venture on its owners as customers can injure sponsoring firms' strategic flexibility as well as their venture's longevity, as in situations where one owner wants to change its historic supplier–buyer relationship with the venture while its partners are content with their old allocations of the venture's outputs (or purchases). Without that owner as customer, the venture's plant becomes uneconomic. It must go to the outside market. Many owners do not relish partial ownership of a vertically related merchant unit, and at this point they terminate their venture instead. Alternatively, some firms never fall into the strategic flexibility trap of giving long-term take-or-pay contracts to their joint-venture partners and never agree to totally open-ended technology-sharing arrangements that cannot be truncated without penalties.

Jealousies among Partners. Joint ventures among vertically related partners pose particular problems when firms know each others' costs, especially when the payback cycles for various stages of processing are asynchronous. Thus, firms that finally enjoy better economics after making large expenditures for several years (with no return) face resentment from partners downstream that are on different cash-flow cycles. For example, mining ventures require substantial rates of return to justify years of development expenditures, but steel companies forget by the time their mine proves to be commercializable that their partners have starved for years to develop the mine. All the steel firms notice is the high returns that are enjoyed once a mine comes in and the low returns they face in their own core businesses. *Corporate memories are short* in supplier–buyer relationships, and partners that believe they are on the short end of a joint venture want to renegotiate their agreements, especially when they perceive that partners' profit margins are too wide or believe that other perceived inequities exist. Partners' displeasure at discovering suppliers' profit margins often make them forget that the venture is earning a fortune for them as well as for prospering partners.

Conscious effort is required to exploit the potential for vertical synergies between owner and venture when several partners have buyer–supplier relationships with their venture. All partners must be treated equitably, and the venture's future viability must be protected in managing those synergies. Transfer pricing mechanisms are designed to ensure that no party benefits to the detriment of the others. Product development must be coordinated to reduce internecine jealousies should owner and venture become competitors. The venture needs autonomy to purchase inputs from outsider suppliers (or to sell to outside customers) when they are willing to offer better prices than those by its owners. When ventures are only development-and-manufacturing companies for their owners, it is more difficult to determine whether their outputs are cost-competitive with those of outsiders (since owners are their only customers). If the joint venture cannot match the prices of outside suppliers, it is often terminated. But if owners are willing to tolerate periods of underused capacity, ventures can provide them with helpful back-up sources of supply.

Horizontal Relationships

Synergies are best exploited in vertical ventures when owners agree not to undermine their venture's ability to attain break-even levels of capacity by maintaining internal business units that parallel the joint venture's activities. Managers agreed that activity duplications create conflicts of interest between owner and venture when they possess buyer–seller relationships, as well. Owners' purchases of components from in-house, wholly owned business units frequently undermine their venture's economics to the detriment of its other owners.

Parallel Facilities. Parallel facilities were a major impediment to the continuation of software-writing joint venture relationships, for example, especially when firms refused to market outsiders' software that competed with their own products. This jealousy was compounded when market access became highly important to the commercial success of software products. Few firms that possessed this crucial access wished to share it with rival products, or with duplicate products developed by their ventures.

Joint ventures in software-writing were given authority to package hardware and software provided by owners. Arm's length buyer–seller relationships ascertained the economic viability of their joint ventures, and many of them were shortlived, given these marketing jealousies. But the highly competitive, marketing-intensive business environment of 1984 changed all this. Even IBM was forming a spider's web of joint ventures in software by then.

Stand-Alone Ventures. By contrast, joint ventures in the oil industry were done on a project-by-project basis. Because they were structured as stand-alone units, there were relatively few opportunities for shared resource synergies between the venture and organizational units of its owners within the oil exploration industry. Seismic information (which was close to the strategic core of sponsoring firms) was shared between owner and venture, but other resources were less likely to be shared due to the coordination difficulties that were created.

Protecting Competitive Advantage. There are fewer horizontal synergies from most R&D ventures. As in the example of ethical pharmaceuticals ventures, basic R&D is usually not performed in jointly owned business units in industries where technological innovation is the key to competitive advantage, with the exception of the genetic-engineering experiments. (Basic research activities are too close to pharmaceutical firms' strategic cores to share them with partially owned ventures.) The Microelectronics & Computer Technology consortium of 20 firms set up to explore product and process technologies in electronic components, software, and computers is unique in its focus on basic research, since its sponsors' survival depends on successes in basic research.

As chapter 7 explains, innovation activities are especially difficult to manage successfully within R&D ventures because owners' jealousies are difficult to overcome in those areas closest to the owners' strategic cores. In consumer products, survival depends on a firm's ability to sustain a differentiated image. While products are highly differentiable, joint ventures are undertaken to gain access to unique product features as well as to new channels of distribution. (Cost reduction concerns become more important motivations as customer bargaining power increases.)

Coordinating Activities. Owner and venture must closely coordinate decisions concerning product features, supporting services, and other attributes when both firms intend to offer the same products, lest the venture's activities in some manner harm the goodwill and image its owner has created. If they are not sharing products, promotional campaigns, channels, and so forth, the venture's need for operating *autonomy* in decisions pertaining to how it differentiates its products increases.

Similarly, there are few successful marketing ventures in consumer products industries for the purposes of creating new marketing activities and sales forces (unless these are to penetrate new markets such as cable television, home video, or other outlets where owners had no existing stakes). Owners are less likely to create a venture for the purpose of replicating activities on which they depend for strategic survival.

Most of the communications services joint ventures are closely coordinated with their owners' operations. Coordination among the joint ventures in cable communications, for example, is necessary from a capital- and risk-sharing perspective, but as the case of Warner-Amex illustrates too vividly, such ventures incur large losses when the venture's managers become too boisterous. In the Warner-Amex example, neither owner possessed the wherewithal to assess whether the venture was running out of control.

There are many more joint ventures in the area of videotex communications where demand is dubious or will take a long time to realize than in teletext communications where the commercial viability of the offering is more uncertain. The videotex ventures do not seem to be as closely coordinated with their owners' activities. A key difference that may explain this pattern is the *differences* between the owners' activities and those of their ventures in the videotex examples, as contrasted with the teletext examples.

Sharing Resources

Shared resources provide the potential for synergies between owner and venture (or between partners) when a means is devised to ameliorate scheduling jealousies and other inevitable problems, such as learning how to cooperate where entities are accustomed to competing. Firms face the same problem inhouse among their wholly owned business units when their cultures have emphasized competition. When business units are accustomed to bargaining aggressively during intrafirm transfers of resources and usually compete for capital from corporate funding sources, resource sharing poses a difficult challenge for affected business units.

Access to a desirable customer base is the key competitive advantage needed for success in the financial services industry. The assets used to supply financial services in joint venture are often the same assets used by owners to supply financial services. Consequently, joint ventures are more often organizations *on paper* than in fact. Personnel from owner and venture might be the same, but their product lines are wider as a result of the venture and they are trained to offer new services to the same customer base.

Expanding Scope of Activities. The effective provision of financial services often requires significant investments in computer systems and paper processing facilities. Systems shortfalls are often rectified through acquisitions, but problems concerning how to teach both new and existing personnel to sell each others' products remains. Consequently, synergy increases between owner and venture are realized slowly (if at all) since another sales force is often added to the original one, and both organizations are expected to sell the products of their combined owners. Computer systems also must be wed if personnel are expected to increase their product line breadth, whether new products are acquired through mergers or joint ventures. Thus close coordination between owner and venture is needed in the financial service business. The joint venture enjoys little (if any) autonomy in developing or marketing products since it must coordinate its activities so closely with owners' ongoing activities in most cases.

Reducing Conflicts. In a well-coordinated joint venture, partners consciously share their venture's outputs and depend on their joint venture to satisfy their needs for as long as it continues to be a cost-competitive vendor. Owners do not maintain parallel facilities in-house so as not to undermine the joint venture's success by creating rivalries or reducing the scale economies all partners share in. When Sperry joined the Magnetic Peripherals, Inc. (MPI) joint venture, it had its own magnetic peripherals business unit, ISI. The Sperry facilities, people, and talent were transferred to MPI. During the transition period, Sperry customers were serviced until noncompatible products could be phased out in favor of MPI common products.

Owners share marketing and sales resources with their venture when joint ventures are formed to supplement firms' product lines. Owners share upstream processing facilities with their venture when joint ventures are formed to expand firms' market coverage.

The petrochemical industry is a literal web of interconnected processing units that share feedstocks, intermediaries, and facilities regardless of ownership, and it has been successful with this structure for over twenty years.

Their use of joint ventures forced managers of petrochemical operations to address the problems of sharing selling facilities—as well as processing facilities and other resources—earlier than managers in most other industries. It is useful to review why this pattern of sharing facilities evolved as it did.

When most ventures share inputs, distribution facilities, or other resources with the business units of their owners, friction results from the internal competition for suppliers' (or distributors') attentions for their respective plants (or products), especially if negotiations or selling activities are needed subsequent to the decision to build the initial plant. For many firms, the costs of arbitrating among business units that share supplying or distributing facilities are *not* offset adequately by the synergies they realize. Petrochemical firms avoid these conflicts by creating self-contained activity centers. Since there is only one place within an owner's organization where any particular activity is done, this arrangement reduces internecine warfare. (Some of the side payments used to reduce the problems that shared resources create are recounted in chapter 8, which provides guidelines for forming and managing cooperative strategies.)

Breaking Loose. Two pressures accelerate the transition of the venture into an autonomous business unit in industries where its activities are conducive to stand-alone facilities. First, the managers of ventures are as boisterous as those in charge of other internal venturing units. If the venture is successful, they press for more autonomy, often in the form of the venture's own capabilities and facilities. Managers also press for a larger share of corporate funding in competition with the wholly owned business units of its sponsoring firms. (The latter source of intrafirm jealousy accelerates some ventures' entries into the capital markets in their own right to obtain supplemental financing.) Second, as chapter 8 explains, loyalties to the venture develop that lead managers to advocate actions that are inimical to owners' interests.

Venture Autonomy

This section summarizes additional findings concerning the boisterous venture—the joint venture that evolves (sometimes too quickly to suit its owners) into an autonomous entity that is allowed to choose whether to purchase from (or sell to) outsiders.

Too Much Freedom

Autonomy creates problems on the other end of the continuum. Too much autonomy often results in a strong venture that is terminated by bringing it inside one of the owners' organizations (one partner purchases the interests of the other), or by spinning it off into a stand-alone corporation (like the Corning family of ventures), or by letting it vie for outside financing (like TriStar Pictures) in arrangements that convert owner interests into minority investments. In this last example, less internal coordination between the organizations of the owners and their former venture occurs over time as each entity pursues its respective business strategy. As several industry examples have illustrated, minority agreements strengthen partners without bringing them too closely into the investing firm's orbit.

Cut-off Points on Resource Allocation. When firms venture into new arenas, they use implicit cut-off points in rationing their capital expenditures for start-up or entrepreneurial ventures. A similar discipline guides owner decisions concerning when they should let their ventures evolve into autonomous units, fold into their own organizations, or liquidate. If owners do not wean their joint venture after its time for nourishment has passed or convert it to another organizational form, it becomes a drag on their performance and morale.

Industry differences suggest how quickly ventures evolve from loose cooperations to partnerships to stand-alone entities (if at all). Volatile competitive conditions require shorter-lived and more informal liaisons. Demand uncertainty requires tentative affiliations, modest funding, and pilot plants or test situations. Some relationships retrogress.

Preparing to Let Go. Owners must anticipate how their venture's industry can evolve if they hope to provide for all contingencies in their joint-venture agreements. As chapter 8 notes, even partners that prefer to negotiate decisions as conflicts develop (rather than setting out divorce settlements in great detail in a legal document ahead of time) find it necessary to agree on the venture's purpose. If the venture is attaining its strategic mission successfully, owners must put up the cash as it becomes necessary or give the joint venture authority to go elsewhere for necessary funding. Recognition of this contingency requires owners to establish ground rules for how their ventures are going to operate—how much autonomy as well as how much cash the venture can claim as it matures and as strategic milestones are attained. This contingency also suggests that the management system—the controls and other management policies for accountability to the joint venture's owners—must be anticipated as much as is possible in advance of the venture's birth.

Experienced owners give their ventures more autonomy in operating decisions (where such autonomy is appropriate for the venture's mission) than do first-time owners. A firm's first joint-venture experience seems to be the most difficult one. Moreover, as their ventures mature, experienced owners wean them from using corporate resources without sharing in such resource costs. Hence, control systems similar to those used in allocating overhead costs to internal start-up ventures (perhaps in the form of a corporate over-head or strategic expenditures account) are maintained by experienced managers to track relevant shared costs until the venture acquires dedicated facilities, personnel, and other resources of its own.

Joint ventures that are eventually to become part of an owner's integrated global system pose a special problem with respect to autonomy (and joint-venture termination). Although the venture's management system initially does not have to resemble that of the surviving owner, the surviving owner will feel more comfortable about integrating the venture into its global system if, with time, the venture's control system becomes more similar to its own. If a high level of coordination with the owner's operation is not required of the joint venture, its management system does not have to evolve beyond what is needed to be helpful to the owner's managers, and these problems are avoided.

Control of Whole Tasks

Unless the venture is allowed to stand on its own—with its own assets, personnel, resources, and self-contained information reporting systems—it cannot hope to operate autonomously. When ventures control everything—marketing, manufacturing, and even research—they make more informed decisions. Many owners find this level of control desirable because it provides a check and balance against their wholly owned organization's prowess. Autonomous ventures are able to focus on competitive issues and make decisions faster because they can control (or acquire) the resources they need. Joint ventures cannot respond to competitive conditions as quickly when there are interface problems between their owners' business units and their own business unit. Moreover, if the joint venture operates in a highly volatile industry, its autonomy to form alliances with outsiders—to use outside manufacturers to get a product quickly, to make licensing and technology agreements, to buy marketing services—is necessary in order for its strategic survival.

Sometimes it is necessary to throw the venture out of the nest for it to gain the competitive resiliency it needs to survive. Furthermore, partners sometimes understand their venture's role more clearly after they cut it loose. In one case, a joint venture was given autonomy when it did not want to be free. Its managers were terrified of being on their own. But when the venture went out and found the resources it needed to make a good product (which if offered to sell through its owners' marketing organizations), it was rebuffed by jealousies inside owners' business units (because its sister units were told that they had to market the venture's products and they did not want to do so). Sadly, the venture offered to sell its new products through a competitors's organization. When the venture's owner realized that its products were good enough to interest rivals, the venture was invited back into the nest. (In fact, it was *ordered* to deal only with family members thereafter.)

In another example, one owner pushed its partner to put more aggressive managers into their venture because its markets were becoming more competitive. Managers of the caliber that the owner wanted from its partner demanded more operating autonomy for the venture, and they received it. The joint venture became a major supplier to both owners over time because it consistently outperformed its owners' wholly owned sisters and other competitors.

Arm's-length Dealings

When ventures have true arm's-length to buy and sell where the best margins can be earned, they maximize their owners' earnings as well as their own. In one example where a seasoned manager was placed in charge of a joint venture and given operating autonomy, he reported back to the venture's owners that his team was making decisions that were best for the venture. That meant that obligations to supply the venture's owners with raw materials were satisfied at competitive prices, and surplus outputs were sold at market prices as well. Had its owners restrained the venture's management team when they moved away from their captive role, its owners would not have enjoyed the profits their venture went on to win. Indeed, with time, the venture's operations would likely have become uneconomic without the sales volumes generated by its sales to outsiders, and its plant probably would have been shut down. (Giving the venture its own marketing capability was not a part of the original scheme in this example, and owner firms were not aware that the venture's managers had researched outside market opportunities until they were *advised* of the management team's decision to sell to outsiders.)

In order for ventures to make informed operating decisions that can increase their owners' returns, vertical relationships with owners' wholly owned business units are encouraged but not required. Experienced managers concluded that the sacrifices made by trying to tie together synergies between owner's and venture's operations are often so debilitating to the venture's management in terms of their abilities to run their own businesses on a profit-and-loss basis that their attentions to such issues are scarcely justified. Managers from sponsoring firms reasoned that if their venture's managers were smart they would realize that it helps owner firms to purchase from their divisions. Such managers expected that wholly owned divisions would be given a preferential chance to sell to the venture provided they matched outsiders' prices. Beyond that, owners obtain better performances from their ventures when they do not force their business units to trade with each other.

Finally, better results are obtained when arm's-length operating autonomy is combined with policies that do not sap the venture's abilities to compete. The entrepreneurial spirit that allows ventures to thrive is fragile. In one large and notable failed joint venture, managers were told that they had operating autonomy to build up a large market share position for the venture. When the venture's sales force responded to its owners' mission with great enthusiasm (and success), jealousies within one owners' organization led it to curb the venture's autonomy and to reserve certain accounts for the owner's in-house development. Many of the venture's best sales representatives resigned. Then the other owner decided that the instructions that had been given to the venture's sales force resulted in the wrong customer mix. The sales force compensation plan was changed, and a new policy of owner review of the venture's contracts was instituted. Slowly the owners pulled their venture closer to their in-house operations. Although owners talked about making their venture more entrepreneurial and about giving the venture's personnel opportunities to compete locally as best they could, the good customers were divided between both owners' wholly owned units. The venture failed.

In summary, if used in an informed manner, ventures can be an attractive response to risky environments, competitors' incursions, and other challenges firms confront. Owners must have realistic expectations for their venture and a clear understanding of the shortfalls arising from confused signals. Owners must also agree among themselves on their venture's mission and how the venture will relate to each of them. Owners must maintain clear understandings with each other—as well as good relationships among managerial counterparts—to keep their ventures under strategic control.

7

Joint Ventures as Technological Change Agents

This chapter summarizes findings from field interviews concerning the use of joint ventures in technology transfer and innovation. It contrasts competitive environments where ventures are appropriate with those settings where licensing or other loose partnership arrangements are more appropriate. It also summarizes findings concerning how firms transfer technology and surmount the "not-invented-here" biases that prevent them from exploiting opportunities to supplement their organization's internal capabilities. Finally, it relates findings concerning the use of parallel facilities and spider's webs of cooperative agreements within settings where exclusive agreements may have been more appropriate.

As chapter 6 notes, few joint R&D partnerships thrive in the area of basic research because that activity is too close to the strategic cores of most firms. Furthermore, technological advantage is becoming increasingly difficult to protect, and firms are reluctant to expose this activity to appropriation. Accordingly, a discussion of findings concerning technology ventures must include some assessment of how firms cope with the threats of obsolescence, piracy, bleedthrough, and other negative forces that reduce the value of competitive advantages. These threats are treated below.

Solving Technological Problems

Although firms engage in few basic R&D partnerships, ventures to exploit knowledge in new applications or markets thrive in the United States. Development ventures enable firms to enter new fields, and assignment of scientific personnel to such challenges revitalizes them by letting them concentrate on novel technology areas. There are several ways that joint activities can help firms solve technological problems that they cannot cope with alone.

Technological prowess is the key to attaining competitive advantage when technologies (1) change frequently; (2) are highly risky; and (3) require extremely high creativity in design and precision in manufacturing. Innovation can change an industry's structure to a firm's advantage (because it affects entry barriers and buyer–seller relations, as well as the number of surviving players), but many processes that firms invest in can be very expensive failures. Joint ventures permit firms to share those risks by hedging their bets concerning which products, processes or configurations will become industry standards. Moreover, they permit firms to keep abreast of technological innovations by providing a means of sharing development costs.

Technology as Competitive Advantage

High technology products are a logical arena for joint ventures because they usually carry worthwhile profit margins if partners can get in and out of them quickly enough. Rapid technological obsolescence is another reason to form joint ventures. Partners can better share the development costs of multiple generations of products, particularly when they are supplanted by competitive technologies before such costs can be recovered.

Cooperation is a fundamental structural trait of many high technology industries. Yet *licenses and informal agreements* are becoming more commonplace than shared-equity ventures in the United States, except where technologies are poorly understood by all partners. Difficulties in managing owner–venture relationships provide one explanation for this pattern of cooperative strategies. For example, because technology leaders want to guard the kernels of knowledge that are central to their competitive advantage, they devise ways to share proprietary knowledge with their venture and their partners while maintaining peace of mind. The very nature of competition in high technology industries makes this sharing activity difficult to manage.

Patents are poor protection for knowledge within high technology businesses, and many firms expect to have only two or three years before competitors copy their products (with or without authorization). Some firms file patents on seemingly commonplace technology to protect themselves lest they be accused of violating another firm's technology, not because they believe patents are a safe way to transfer knowledge between owner and venture.

The implications of this type of environment for joint-venture strategy are straightforward. If knowledge cannot be protected adequately through the cooperative strategies that create a venture, and if information transferred to a joint venture is no longer under the absolute control of the venture's owners, firms pool their knowledge, but they license their intellectual property only where there is mutual trust among players. In high-technology industries, mutual trust among players is sometimes difficult to maintain because reverse-engineering and improvements on pioneers' designs (such as unauthorized borrowing of intellectual property rights) are commonplace. Firms must develop cooperative strategies to cope with these practices while they establish technical standards to persuade customers to adopt their products' configurations. Pragmatic solutions concerning how to transfer technology to joint ventures encompass what information to provide (and when) as well as how owners' personnel interact with those of the venture—assuming a separate organizational entity is created.

Technological Leapfrogging

Some firms must move earlier in forming joint ventures than others because their bargaining power is less than that of their competitors. Other firms form alliances early to set industry standards. But joint ventures rarely last long in industries that are subject to volatile competition. That means that firms must devise arrangements to get in and out of ventures before their knowledge becomes obsolete. Given their need to move quickly and to reposition if they are wrong, firms tend to eschew arrangements that seem to be too inflexible.

If an industry is embryonic and the best technologies (product features, styling, means of distributing a product) are yet unknown, joint ventures must have needed autonomy to move in the directions that seem most promising. But since their technologies are most frequently obtained from one or more parents, close coordination with them is necessary to modify the venture's technology to suit the evolving demands of its markets. Frictions between owner and venture are exacerbated if it is necessary to reject owners' technologies and seek them from outsiders. Few owners are willing to allow their joint ventures that much autonomy in industries characterized by rapid technological change.

Joint ventures are a way to bring some uniformity to a stream of products that are developed through highly uncertain R&D expenditures (with a success rate analogous to striking oil, for example). R&D discoveries often come in bunches followed by long dry spells, if they came at all. Savvy firms recognize that their dependence on in-house R&D efforts alone is often inadequate to remain competitive in some industries, especially as competition within them intensifies.

Firms enter cooperative arrangements in technological areas in order to avoid having to buy assets, replicate laboratories and testing periods, and build up a marketing presence in industries that are subject to rapid rates of obsolescence. Firms also seek licenses as a means to offer new products more rapidly or offer to license other firms with their technology as a means of getting their products into new markets faster without having to build up a special sales force.

Increasing Value-Added Margins

Even firms with vast R&D and technological capabilities use ventures and other cooperative strategies to supplement their in-house capabilities where partners offer (1) the ability to manufacture equivalent products at a reasonable price; or (2) credibility among customers, as is needed to promulgate technological standards.

Joint ventures enable firms to exploit technologies that their own organizations have underutilized. By sharing access to promising materials with entrepreneurial firms, for example, it is often possible to develop new applications for them, new product formulations, or other ways to recover value on products that in-house research personnel has viewed as ugly ducklings.

Retail access is a formidable bargaining chip that enables firms with distribution strengths to choose partners with the best technology (or the most promising technological approach). Firms that control retail access sometimes form ventures to gain technological innovations for their product lines. The joint-venture decision is like a make-or-buy decision for these firms because they can satisfy their needs for innovative products by purchasing them from outside vendors for resale, if they wish to do so. Margins are better for such firms when they manufacture products internally, but since their strategic core is retailing—not R&D or manufacturing—they prefer to take partners, especially in areas of very difficult, high technology products where they lack in-house design capabilities.

Learning about State-of-the-Art Technologies

Joint-venture opportunities are often missed because (1) managers are unwilling to defer to differences in corporate cultures; and (2) partners will not be open with each other. Some U.S. firms tend to believe that their potential partner is trying to take their market away from them. Because they fear that they are creating a competitor in their joint venture, some firms tend not to share information freely. If partners cannot negotiate in an open and flexible way, the strain that the negotiating team places on the partnership reduces the joint venture's progress in forming a good working relationship as well. A right-of-first-refusal licensing agreement or other loosely familiarized liaison is often a preliminary step for firms that desire a more formal relationship but do not know each other very well. Therefore, they must tread carefully.

It is necessary for partners to be well informed on the value of the technologies they offer (or hope to obtain) *before* discussing ventures. Woe be unto managers who skimp on their homework in this area, because it is easy to become misled and confused in discussions of risky and unproven technological approaches. Some of the best technological joint ventures are formed by partners that have each done considerable R&D work on the problem in question prior to their collaboration. Since each partner has done the market research and product development work before discussing a venture, they know from a technical and marketing standpoint whether the approaches proposed in a joint venture will yield commercializable results in the near future.

Technological Foot-Dragging. Technological problems are solved best when partners sustain an amiable relationship. When firms become upset with the course of cooperative agreements to share technology or to market products locally, they begin to drag their feet on the next generation of technology transfer. Legally, it is difficult to assess whether a partner is really holding back on technology that is not covered by a carefully worded document. Sometimes renegotiation is necessary. For example, if a partner believes that its bargaining position has changed with respect to its partners—making its cooperation *more* important to the joint venture's success—it could seize management control over the venture's operations (often without changing the equity arrangement) by taking control of distribution or by holding back on the next generation of technology that should be transferred.

In order for partners to work together productively, a trust relationship must be developed in which partners admit that they share information with their partners, can learn from each other, and are planning to capitalize on their partners' strengths. Open relationships between partners reduce dissatisfactions later on when the agreement must be renewed, renegotiated, or terminated.

For example, in 1984, Genentech and Baxter Travenol Laboratories formed a joint venture, Travenol-Genentech, to develop radioimmunoassay products for the diagnostics market. Baxter Travenol was the majority owner and it contributed the assets of its Clinical Assays Division, which included production facilities, its own U.S. sales force, and access to a worldwide marketing organization. One of the venture's first products was a test for the acquired immune deficiency syndrome (AIDS) virus, which was produced under a license from the Department of Human Services (DHS). Since all of Baxter-Travenol's relevant assets were placed into the joint venture, there were fewer concerns about unauthorized bleedthrough of technological information than in many other joint ventures in the medical products and ethical pharmaceuticals industry. This arrangement gave the joint venture more autonomy to act quickly and enabled the venture to focus its objectives with greater clarity since it did not have to manage conflicts of interest between owner and venture organizations.

Protecting Technological Assets

Many U.S. ventures link horizontally related firms in horizontally related activities. Because such cooperative strategies link potential (if not actual) competitors, special care must be given to protecting partners' strategic cores when they form ventures.

The closer activities are to a firm's strategic core—the higher their importance to the firm's survival—the less likely the firm is to rely on the research success of ventures or other arrangements with outsiders. The closer the research area is to a partner's strategic core, the more concerned the partner is with losing control of knowledge pertaining to those technological applications. In areas of high strategic importance, partners will make deals—licensing, cross-marketing, or other arrangements that they can tightly control—but they are less likely to create joint ventures.

Managers can be as crafty as they please in writing clauses to protect their firms' technology rights, but the joint venture's success depends on trust. Patents are nearly useless in many industries, and technology (which is embodied in firms' personnel) grows legs and walks into competitors' laboratories looking for better compensation, despite employment contracts prohibiting use of a technology for two or more years after employment termination. Although there is really no way to ensure that a particular trade secret will not be lost, if a trusted partner chooses to betray its partner by pirating intellectual property, word goes out in the industry. Reputation is valued among scientists and engineers who take pride in their own solutions to problems. A conscientious scientific community protects some of their firms' most valued technological assets through their own ethical behavior.

Intellectual Property Rights and Patents

If firms are concerned about control of their proprietary knowledge, they have several options. They can use exclusive licensing provisions, right-of-first refusal provisions, noncompetition agreements, and other contractual provisions to protect knowledge from disseminating to unauthorized third parties. But these provisions protect knowledge only to a limited extent because patent transgressions must be litigated to recover damages. Moreover, the harm has already been done. Instead, managers suggest that certain proprietary parts of a firm's core technology should be withheld from its venture and transferred only under stringent licensing provisions or sold on an OEM vendor basis.

Copyright laws protect some software products, and technology licenses that are based on control of patents often provide that certain information cannot be passed on or used in another application (or for another purpose) without the owner's explicit permission. However, it is also difficult to litigate violations of these property rights. Software, in particular, is such a complicated phenomenon that courts are often not adequately equipped to deal with infringements of these rights. Good faith at the top of an organization does not mean that some employee within a firm will not try to steal information concerning software.

Therefore, firms become cautious concerning which customers they will license. They prefer to deal with firms on the basis of personal trust. They rely on their abilities to innovate generation after generation of improved technology to keep them ahead of blatant thieves. They retain design control of crucial components and prohibit licensees from making certain kinds of changes in their products without explicit permission (which they frequently withhold). Consequently, pirated knowledge becomes increasingly obsolete as firms introduce enhancements of their original technology. Above all, managers emphasize that their firms do not deal with potential partners when they feel uncomfortable with their representatives because so much of their joint venture's success depends on activities that cannot be covered adequately by legal documents.

In research ventures, partners often cooperate in developing technology and patents that can be applied to different end uses. If the joint venture develops a novel patentable technology that creates an asset base that is not contributed by its owners, the venture may become the owner of it. As owners move off in diverse directions to develop technology, the joint venture sometimes becomes their licensing repository to keep track of the technology's royalties. In some cases, the venture survives as a paper corporation, solely for the purpose of protecting its owners' technology and licensing it for the benefit of its owners, long after other business activities within the joint venture have ceased and its scientists have moved on to other projects, perhaps within other firms.

Joint-venture contracts often specify that if the partnership is dissolved, the surviving firm (the one that purchases its partner's interest) retains rights to use its partner's technology on a royalty basis if it is not the owner of the technology. Ownership is a nettlesome problem because all of the venture's technology originally comes from its owners. Firms differ in how they control technology developed within their venture. Many firms let their venture be the royalty-collecting intermediary when one of the partners wants permission to license technology that may have been contributed by the other partner. Other firms prohibit any ownership of technology by their venture. Some owners insist only on a licensing right-of-first-access for technology developed by their venture and allow their venture to license technology to others, as well. Other owners do not allow their venture to license its knowledge to outsiders.

Licensing and Control of Technology

Licensing strategies can be used to promulgate a technological standard. Use of licensing strategies requires inventing firms to license all applications and to find partners to endorse these standards in their technical specifications. Royalties tend to be minimal for standard-setting licenses because firms are trying to encourage others to use their designs. By contrast, licensing strategies to exploit patents are usually on an exclusive or narrowly shared basis because the firms that take licenses do so to gain competitive advantage over others.

Licensing is rarely more attractive than a joint venture as a means of *acquiring knowledge* unless, by granting a license, a firm gains access to another license that it desires. Except in unique cases, like the pharmaceuticals industry, simple licensing fees offer lower returns than taking a piece of the action in a joint venture. Licenses enable entrpreneurial firms and inventors to receive advances against royalties with no risk participation, but joint ventures can teach fledgling firms how to exploit a technology, how to enter a new market, or how to market their discoveries appropriately.

First-mover advantages are very important in the ethical pharmaceutical industry, and the first new drug in a therapeutic category to hurdle Federal Drug Administration (FDA) barriers captures the largest market share, regardless of where it was invented. (Note that a sales force does not suffer as severely from the not-invented-here syndrome that discourages scientists from championing outsiders' products enthusiastically. The sales force will sell anything in its line that pays well.) Therefore, if the new product is efficacious (and the first of its kind), it receives more attention than "me-too" products. Unless the U.S. partner is shepherding a direct competitor product through the regulatory maze in ethical pharmaceuticals, it is often interested in expanding its product line through licenses from outsiders.

Technology, market knowledge, and other sensitive information that is transferred to ventures is frequently protected from unauthorized exposure to partners that can become competitors (or to unauthorized parties) by confidentiality agreements and explicit, formal agreements signed at very senior levels within partners' organizations. However, some managers that were interviewed expressed skepticism concerning their lawyers' abilities to prevent technological bleedthrough from occurring, however, especially within the electronics industry, where patents are virtually useless.

Technological Bleedthrough

Bleedthrough is the diffusion of knowledge (not covered by formal agreements) that is gained by working with partners on ventures. Some firms form ventures to gain knowledge, skills, and technology, and they hope to transmit this knowledge back to their own organizations. It is difficult to avoid knowledge bleedthrough when a joint venture is composed of personnel from different research laboratories working together. Successful firms, which know how to exploit *positive bleedthrough*, have developed a science for engineering advantageous arrangements between owners and their ventures in their day-to-day communications and in everything else. This is done with careful attention to detail to ensure that knowledge is returned to the sponsoring firm. It is necessary for managers to design this bleedthrough process carefully, since knowledge of a venture's work methods, managerial practices, and technologies is not accepted readily by owners' in-house research organizations.

Parallel Laboratories. When partners' scientists work together to develop products for the U.S. marketplace, firms frequently devote space to parallel research experiments in their wholly owned laboratories to learn more about their partner's technological approaches. Sometimes, they even move scientists and other technical people through the joint venture and back to their wholly owned laboratories to disseminate information. Doing so is consistent with the principles of science—results from experiments must be replicable—and sometimes these arrangements yielded the additional bonus of new insights obtained from scientists that tried to extend their partners' approaches. As long as intellectual property rights are not abused, firms are not very much concerned by such practices. Indeed many firms do the same with their own in-house laboratories.

Managing the Flow of Information. Special care must be given to designing management systems to alleviate the special tensions of ventures formed with partners that would otherwise be the firm's competitors. For example, the organizational configuration and management systems that a partner firm might prefer to use within its venture may provide too much information about how the firm looks at markets and competition that it would not want to pass through to other firms. Accordingly, firms often design management systems that gather information for in-house laboratories and selling organizations but do not allow much information to flow back to their ventures.

Many managers noted that they do not explicitly consider how to manage positive technological bleedthrough, but there are many informal ways that information could be collected for that purpose. For example, one electronics firm formed a vertical agreement with a semiconductor house for the purpose of keeping up to date on state-of-the-art developments in chip-making technology. In exchange for this information, the electronics firm used the semiconductor firm as a second-source vendor on its products.

Concerns regarding *negative* technological bleedthrough are often unfounded because several firms have not learned to cope with the not-invented-here syndrome among their technical personnel. As one manager noted, bleedthrough is not a problem because its partner's scientists are too jealous to recognize when knowledge from the joint venture should be shared with its owner's laboratories.

Some firms concluded that any knowledge developed in their venture should be usable by all partners. This policy permits partners to pool ideas and information without the need for the many protective mechanisms that ordinarily impede collegiality. Many owners expect their joint venture to receive a monthly entourage of visitors from its partners; they also, regularly send research teams to study their venture's procedures and progress. In this manner, firms reduce the tensions caused by technology bleedthrough by discussing the problem openly with their partners and by recognizing that collegiality is a two-way street.

Managers with several ventures to their credit also concluded that some partners will do almost anything to gain information if they want it badly enough. Recognizing this, managers initiate discussions with their partners' management teams on these points and negotiate training fees as compensation when they take partners' personnel on sales calls or teach them other skills that are highly appropriable.

Finally, when all else fails, concerns about the bleedthrough of shared information to unauthorized third parties motivates firms to segregate their research operations and to exchange information between them carefully. Firms protect information from getting into the hands of potential competitors (which also may have ventures with their partners) by keeping their venture physically removed from contact with other parts of their partners' organizations and by ensuring that proprietary information is not disseminated easily through their venture to unauthorized personnel within their partners' organization. Such precautions require tight legal definitions of what technology is licensed to the venture and of how information developed by the venture is to be returned to its owners. (Precautions also discourage the creation of synergies.) Such procedures are necessary—tedious as they are to implement—because if firms cannot define their technology tightly, they lack a proper basis for ventures. Managers discourage their firms from forming technology agreements without such precautions unless they want to encourage their technology to be disseminated to the rest of their industry. Managers must understand the value of their firms' resources and skills before they venture forth to take partners.

Transferring Knowledge

One of the side benefits of working together in ventures is the cross-pollination process whereby ideas are shared among research, manufacturing, and marketing personnel and thereby transferred to owners' organizations. If firms try consciously to do so, it is almost always possible to benefit from affiliations with partners when facilities can be shared. (Such suggestions are heretical to some U.S. firms because they tend to believe that outsiders' ideas are inferior or because they have already filed patents on potential partners' ideas but never thought to apply them.)

One of the vexing problems associated with technology transfer is that nobody wants to let anything go, yet some knowledge or assets must be traded in order to transfer technology. Solving this problem requires firms to assess the value of partners' contributions. It requires firms to go beyond complaints from their scientists and engineers that partners' technology is as good as either side says it is or other objections concerning why ventures between particular partners will not work.

Experienced managers of joint ventures put scientists, engineers and plant managers on their negotiating teams as well as on their operating teams. They take an open position regarding their desire to acquire technology and manufacturing know-how from potential partners and write strong techno-logical-protection contracts to protect the intellectual property rights of all partners. Finally, experienced managers form ventures in an incremental approach that permits them to see the technology and test it for a right-of-first refusal fee before they form arrangements that commit them more deeply. If partners' products or processes prove to be as good as represented, experienced managers ensure that knowledge flows back to their wholly owned divisions through a variety of management systems and integrating mechanisms.

Not-Invented-Here Syndrome and Parallel Facilities

Rapid technological change and customer diversity forces firms in the electronics, pharmaceutical, factory automation, office equipment, communications, and financial services industries to be polygamous. Competition requires them to form a spider's web of cooperative agreements—often of short durations. But implementing such strategies is difficult until firms have worked through how to accept outsiders' products as readily as they accept their own inventions. Managers cited their firms' not-invented-here problems as being a major impediment to making timely responses to competitive pressures. Many managers recognized that their firms would have to adapt to technological changes in the future, including learning how to accept innovations pioneered by ventures as if they were in-house products.

Jealousies between partners—as well as between owner and venture—based on the not-invented-here syndrome result in the performance of suboptimal activities. For example, one joint venture had to develop its own sales force and cultivate its own customer contacts because it could not get its products to commercialization through *either* of its owner's laboratories. In both cases, the venture's products created conflict of interest problems because they competed with owners' wholly owned products.

Irreconcilable Difficulties. Foreign partners often find ventures with U.S. firms frustrating because their products are orphaned by the venture's technical personnel. Their products do not receive proper attention from the venture's engineering staff or are dismissed as being too difficult to adapt to U.S. customer tastes. U.S. firms report similar complaints when working with European partners overseas, especially if the U.S. firm holds many patents in an area but has not been able to commercialize its products successfully. (Sometimes the foreign partner's concerns about not-invented-here inertia barriers are unfounded, but in at least one major firm, top management declines to be involved in any more ventures that commit its firm to bringing another company's products into its internal portfolio of products.)

Duplication of Activities. The principal alternative to rewarding engineers and scientists for accepting technology across business units—or across owner–venture boundaries—is to build duplicate facilities to permit each group to create its own products. Few managers viewed such alternative to the not-invented-here problem as being an attractive solution. In many cases, firms cannot afford to duplicate research facilities in several sites. Even when they erect small pilot plants, they encounter difficulties in persuading their in-house research groups to accept the pilot plant's results if these scientists and engineers have not performed the tests themselves or blessed them beforehand. For example, by the 1980s, many local governments required multinational firms that develop products overseas to form ventures to establish local research facilities (because the highest value-added margins are frequently given to R&D activities that yield patentable products). Such investments duplicate existing facilities, and their scope must be small since they are rarely cost-justified. Moreover, managers with experience in these types of duplicate facilities report that fragmented research units are not as productive as a large, centralized research laboratory and that their products are not as well-accepted as those developed by in-house units at the central research facility.

Managers combat the not-invented-here problem by giving business units (including their ventures) missions to develop products for a particular specification or application while *prohibiting* other business units within the firm from duplicating that research mission. In this way, products are shared across the firm, and business units are required to accept each other's components under the umbrella of strategic missions even if the components come from a jointly owned venture.

Other firms require partners to maintain duplicate facilities to replicate research findings and verify their venture's information; alternatively, some firms solve the not-invented-here problem by transferring *all* of their research facilities to the venture and by requiring their business units to use the joint venture as their research arm. Incentive programs are created in some firms to reward *both* (1) the technical personnel that caused information, patents, and products to flow from one division (or venture) to another; and (2) the division (or venture) receiving and using the information.

To combat the not-invented-here syndrome, technical personnel that once could disapprove proposals for cooperative arrangements are being disabused through a variety of incentive plans of their long-held opinions that only their laboratories (and internally developed technology) are always the best. Top management in such firms intervenes in the innovation process to review rejected proposals for joint ventures. They may ask a second team to study the most promising partnerships again to ensure that not-invented-here jealousies do not quash innovative proposals. By elevating such questions to the corporate level within firms where top executives also possess technical skills—and by giving these issues corporate attention—managers attempt to overcome organizational tendencies to reject outsiders' ideas without careful study.

Knowledge Repatriation and Management Systems

Highly diversified firms try to ensure that knowledge gained through exposure to partners within ventures is diffused back to owners' laboratories through meticulous programs of repatriation. At the group level, for example, firms hold annual technical meetings where engineering managers and leading R&D scientists gather divisional engineering and R&D personnel for an interchange of information and ideas. Projects are coordinated through divisional reports concerning who is doing what in technology with which partner.

At the corporate level, highly diversified firms appoint officers such as vice presidents in charge of technology to track major technological changes beyond the corporate sphere of activity and track which potential partners are working in those areas of science. Top technical officers also coordinate transfers of technology that are created within the company where knowledge-sharing might be useful in joint ventures among other divisions or with outsiders. They also coordinate the use of technology that is received from others—through licenses or ventures—that might be useful in some other part of the company.

Tracking Down Innovators. Managers confessed that their attempts to control and coordinate flows of technical information within highly diversified firms are, as yet, imperfect because top technical officers sometimes discover that in-house technical efforts—or technological ventures—that other divisions could have benefitted from have existed inside the firm for years without their knowledge. Corporate technical offices are frequently unaware of bootstrapped technical projects, especially where divisions possess the authority to enter ventures and other cooperative agreements without involving their corporate legal staff.

Integrating Diverse Innovations. Managers repatriate knowledge from their ventures to the sponsoring firm and between business units of the same corporation, using matrix organizations, an integrated sales force, and internal cross-usage agreements. An integrated sales force and marketing organization may sell products from *all* divisions, for example, regardless of the ownership of their originator, to a particular customer. Thus, all products intended for consumption by the paper industry are sold through a sales force with experience in serving paper mills, and the cost of selling is shared by client business units (including joint ventures) that use this service. (Parallel sales forces are prohibited under such arrangements.) Internal cross-use agreements permit firms to apply knowledge developed for one application to all other markets where it possesses strengths.

Managers confessed that it is difficult but necessary to repatriate technical personnel if the joint venture fails to retain the knowledge that it has created. This process is more painful for the engineers than sponsoring firms because the venture's personnel have become accustomed to making their own decisions, running interesting projects, and enjoying more autonomy than owner firms can tolerate from a well-integrated business unit. This problem is developed further in chapter 8.

Personnel Rotation and Collegiality

Information is shared by creating fellowship among technical personnel. Firms try to transfer knowledge by rotating personnel between their ventures and wholly owned laboratories. Returning scientists and engineers present seminars to their colleagues within owner firms to share research findings or to explain the new approaches taken by the research team in the venture's laboratories.

When firms purchase technology, they send a platoon of engineers and scientists through existing plants that are using the patents, machinery, and other assets they are buying to learn how to use it. Personnel rotations in joint ventures are increasingly commonplace as, for example, technical personnel work at the venture's facility for a month, then return to owners' plants for a month, then return to the venture's plants for another month and so on. Because there are many ways that technical personnel can transfer information, partners' employees are encouraged to develop relationships of collegiality, and joint-venture team members are chosen for their abilities to work together. But sponsoring firms must be indefatigable in their quest to understand everything possible about a partner's technological approach—

both to make it work and to pass it on within their own firm. (For this latter objective, technical personnel with communication skills must be chosen for joint-venture team membership.)

Nurturing Creativity. Creativity is encouraged by the intellectual curiosity of the collegial process. It is healthy for sponsoring firms to provoke discussions concerning how product designs, management procedures, and plant set-ups could be changed in ventures, even if doing so irritates partners for a time, because managers find that they reconsider their points after the argument and gain new insights about their problems. In academia, collegial (and un-inhibited) professors sometimes argue ideas for hours and cover blackboards (and themselves) with chalk before they have pushed through a problem to their satisfaction. If the venture's research team can achieve that level of comfort and collegiality in working together, a productive research joint venture is feasible. In many cases, however, R&D ventures are not successful ways to develop knowledge, especially not on a long-term basis, because firms prefer to control the research activity in-house.

In one R&D collaboration, partners exchanged engineers for a short, on-site development effort that was followed by extensive consultation by telephone and computer links. One firm possessed design strengths; that partner supplied creative genius—the type of "mad artists" that invent ideal ways to solve technological problems. The other partner supplied pragmatic engineers who sorted through the pros and cons of the artists' dreams to select projects that would be appropriate for commercialization. The engineering team modified and finished the artists' designs, made plans for automated factory assembly, and installed the manufacturing systems in both partners' plants. Their collaboration was most satisfactory until the artistic partner's viability was threatened by substantial losses in its main line of business and it could no longer afford to fund its joint venture.

Altruistic Innovation. Some managers are more interested in advancing knowledge than in obtaining a quid pro quo when they show their technological files to partners. They tend to be very open in sharing information to encourage a similar openness among partners. In this manner, they hope to enhance their venture's creativity and success rate. Joint-venture partners candidly admit that they use personnel rotation as a means of transferring technology to partner organizations. Moreover, they assert that they pick the brains of the partners' personnel as they are rotated through the venture and expect that their partners are being as meticulous in exploiting the knowledge of their respective technical personnel. These managers sent their firms' very best technical personnel to the joint venture on the theory that to make it work, they should hold back nothing.

The Honor of a Joint Venture. This ease in sharing personnel stood in marked contrast with the policies of other partners. Japanese managers and engineers, for example, allegedly have an inferiority complex about working for a joint-venture organization. Although U.S. managers assert that money cures that malady, many U.S. firms do treat their ventures like stepchildren, and they pull their best technical personnel out of the venture when it is time to spin it off or sell their interest in it to partners. In fact, many partner firms merely "loan" their best technological personnel to ventures. Although their salaries are paid by the venture during their tenure there, the revolving door back to the owner firm is open, and personnel retain their benefits in sponsoring firms' personnel programs. Despite findings that suggested it is necessary at last to close the revolving door and make the management team (as well as the research team) employees of the venture with an interest in improving the venture's well-being, many firms used personnel rotation as a way to transmit knowledge back to partner research facilities. (This point is developed further in chapter 8.)

Choosing Competent Personnel. In 1983, 15 major companies formed a joint research venture, Microelectronics & Computer Technology Corp. (MCC), to speed up gains in technology. Its goal was to share the expense of developing advanced semiconductor, computer, and software technology that the partners could use in their products. Its membership included 20 firms in 1984, including Advanced Micro Devices Inc., Allied Corporation, BMC Industries Inc., Boeing Co., Control Data Corp., Digital Equipment Corp., Eastman Kodak, Gould Inc., Harris Corp., Honeywell Inc., Lockheed Missiles and Space Co., Martin-Marietta Corp., 3M Co., Mostek Corp., Motorola, NCR, National Semiconductor, RCA Corp., Rockwell International Corp., and Sperry Corp., among others. (A research consortium owned by the Bell operating companies had also applied for membership.) The venture was fashioned after the Japanese practice of pooling corporate R&D money and disseminating results.

The MCC experiment illustrates problems that are commonplace to partners' relationships with each other and with their venture. Initially, partners balked at surrendering their very best personnel and proprietary ideas to a consortium that would help domestic competitors. But the venture's manager had negotiated the right to reject any personnel that were contributed by owners if these engineers did not meet the venture's high standards. After rejecting 90 percent of the applicants owners submitted in the first round of staffing, MCC was finally staffed with outsiders when owners would not send top-notch in-house talent. (Six of the seven key project directors were outsiders, for example.) When owners protested that they would have no way to repatriate knowledge back to their laboratories from MCC if its employees were outsiders that were loyal to the venture, they were advised to submit better in-house candidates or forever lose that chance. The caliber of owner-sponsored applicants improved abruptly. Several owner firms developed organizational mechanisms to move MCC technology into their laboratories soon thereafter.

Spider's Webs versus Exclusive Partnership Relationships

Some firms require exclusivity when they enter ventures in areas that are of high strategic importance to them. Other firms prefer exclusivity because they want to keep the management of their joint activities simple, preferring one joint venture per product or concept basis. (Such firms did not rule out the possibility that they would create second-generation ventures with the *same partners* for new projects that had not been perceived when the first joint venture was formed.)

Spider's Webs. Firms create a spider's web of agreements with themselves at the hub when they examine several technological approaches simultaneously with different partners. Spider's webs of agreements are becoming increasingly necessary, and firms create cooperative strategies with many different firms (which are sometimes partners of each other in other ventures) to exploit diverse therapeutic areas of product applications, different markets, or even various geographic territories.

In genetic engineering, for example, established firms create a spider's web of joint arrangements with small research firms, by therapeutic area to gain a "first look" at technology or by right-of-first-refusal to use their partners' research findings. The small genetic engineering firms, in turn, each form a spider's web of alliances to gain financing and potential customers for their particular technology. (Small genetic engineering firms also want to form a spider's web of ventures with established pharmaceutical houses and chemical firms to impress the capital markets and venture capitalists. Listing major multinational firms with strong in-house research facillities as their partners makes smaller firms' financial reports look stronger.)

Strategic Inflexibility. Although there were relatively few joint ventures to make computers, firms used minority investments, OEM vendor arrangements.and many other types of cooperative agreements in this industry. Making computers was so important to major players that they would not cooperate with outsiders or tolerate the extra layers of negotiation needed to manage a joint venture.

There were many joint ventures, as well as many other types of cooperative arrangements, however, in the computer peripherals business. The high

scale economy advantages available from manufacturing computer peripherals in large volumes made close coordination between owner and venture
necessary unless partners pooled their assets in the venture and permitted it
to be totally responsible for their in-house peripheral development, as in the
example of Magnetic Peripherals Inc. In such arrangements, owners could
choose alternative sources for their peripherals if their venture did not perform adequately, and the venture's failure to satisfy owners' needs signaled
its demise since it had no marketing assets of its own.

Minority investments were popular among U.S. computer and computer
peripherals firms because they maintained the illusion that owners could control their venture's activities and gain advance knowledge of its product decisions. Only Fujitsu (in its relationship with Amdahl) provided tangible evidence that it was acting as a marionette master in the examples I examined.

As increasing numbers of information processing and electronics companies joined forces to cooperate, two patterns emerged: horizontal cooperation did *not* create a separate, jointly owned venture. Instead, partners
learned how to cooperate in developing common standards because no firm
had enough research money to risk and enough good results in-house to offer
every product needed to compete effectively. The "not-invented-here" syndrome that had plagued efforts to transfer knowledge from division to division within a single firm (not to mention between autonomous firms) had to
be surmounted. When it became clear that coalitions *would* be important in
hurdling the chasm between computer technology and that of telecommunications, firms scurried to form alliances. But, because there were no competitors that possessed the necessary resources and knowledge to bring this product gap in a timely fashion alone, separate jointly owned entities were formed
more frequently to bridge this gap because partners were not head-to-head
competitors and because a single repository was needed to pool the knowledge that was germane to the task.

The Ease of Changing Partners. The electronic components, computer, computer peripherals, office equipment, and communications industries illustrate
environments where technology changes rapidly and cooperative strategies
are commonplace. OEM arrangements within them are very transient. Firms
obtain products from outside vendors that fit their needs for features or low
costs until another OEM vendor offers better features, prices or the old products' technology is superseded. The old OEM arrangement ends and firms
switch to a new vendor. Thus, unless joint ventures are between firms that
both contributed technology and personnel to keep up with the industry, such
ventures are less flexible than OEM arrangements, cross-licensing relationships, or other alliances that do not create a separate entity. Unless partners
are prepared to permit their joint venture to develop into a stand-alone entity,

few joint ventures are formed (or if formed are not permitted to endure beyond one technological generation).

Patterns regarding autonomy vary substantially when joint ventures are formed. The venture's products fill out owners' product lines, and owners ultimately share in the knowledge their venture creates. But relationships are not always amicable between owner and venture in high technology industries.

The best use of joint ventures in these environments is when scale economies are substantial and partners let their venture produce all of the needed quantity of a particular product for them. In cases where scale economies are not significant (because few firms produce the product in question in significant quantities or it becomes obsolete before they progress far down the experience curve), the creation of joint ventures makes less sense. Moreover, owners seem to enjoy the spider's web nature of their informal alliances, which are buttressed by legal exchanges of patents, knowledge, and computer tapes because they appear to offer greater flexibility.

Effective management of minority investments and joint ventures is an enigma that engineering-based managers do not wish to ponder. One often-expressed sentiment is that because high technology industries change so quickly, it does not make sense to let the venture continue beyond the time when it has completed its purpose. Managers did not want to consider how to dissolve a "dodo-bird" organization.

Defining the scope of joint ventures (as lawyers do) inhibits the flexibility of partners in their innovative activities, but giving the venture an open lifespan (to develop its own line of products) is not regarded as an adequate solution by managers either. Decision making is regarded as cumbersome within a joint venture because it requires a different mentality to make it work than if a business unit is fully owned. Managers become frustrated when they find it difficult to tell the venture's management that something must be done quickly.

Coordination within Rapidly Changing Technological Environments. The venture needs to coordinate its activities closely with owners when it shares facilities, personnel, or resources with them, when it is "captive" in its owners' vertical chains of processing, or when competitive needs for owners' advice, services, and resources are great. The venture's need to coordinate with its owners is greatest when technology changes rapidly and prices change erratically, requiring owners' help in modifying the venture's products or technologies.

The competitive needs of industries where knowledge rapidly becomes obsolete require that the venture control its key facilities. Having such control gives the venture more autonomy than some owners are willing to accept. It is difficult for owners to accept that the venture's employees must be loyal to the joint venture (not its owners) to seek its success. However, it is only when the venture does have employee loyalty that owners thrive from joint activity as suppliers, distributors, or owners.

The Microelectronics & Computer Technology (MCC) consortium offers an interesting counterpoint to the adversity of owners to the suggestion that their venture be allowed to develop into an entity in its own right. Funded by membership fees collected from its owners, MCC has no manufacturing facilities, distribution channels, or marketing organization of its own. It controls patent rights on the technology it develops. Its owners are free to use that technology. After a period of exclusivity, licenses are available to outsiders. Owners are free to develop mechanisms for coordinating their activities with MCC's. They can send personnel to work at MCC. But the large number of nonaffiliated engineers within the venture makes it likely that MCC will develop into a "boisterous" venture, one in which managers want to move faster and more aggressively than its owners are prepared to sanction.

Designing effective ways to repatriate and communicate technology to owner organizations is of greater concern than worries about bleedthrough in high technology industries. In settings where technologies rapidly become obsolete, advantages must be exploited quickly to recover their development costs before they become obsolete. Thus many licenses, joint development projects, and joint ventures are found where the pace of technological change is rapid; crucial knowledge is shared more quickly with the venture under such circumstances. Because knowledge is so highly appropriable as well as perishable, owners must rethink their attitudes regarding the control of technology in their use of cooperative strategies.

If the gestation period needed to move a product from the workbench through development and pilot plant testing to the marketplace is a long time, longer duration relationships are more acceptable than where a technology's half-life rarely exceeds eighteen months. Where technology changes rapidly, firms move on from partner to partner, and sometimes form a spider's web of parallel arrangements to test several technological alternative approaches simultaneously.

Transitory Competitive Advantage. Some market opportunities are so transitory that firms quickly form many ventures (with many partners) in order to snatch a portion of the market. In cable television, for example, spider's webs of ventures proliferate because they are one means for competitors to enter more regional markets and share the high capital costs of doing so. The technological risks of entering the communication service industry are tremendous, which might explain why spider's webs of ventures are used by so many players to enter that market. The window of opportunity in commu-

nications equipment—especially private branch exchange (PBX) systems—
did not open until firms had created technological standards to reassure their
customers against obsolescence. Spider's webs of technical standards agreements are necessary in the PBX market to launch firms' products.

Other market opportunities are transitory because they involve projects
with predefined sunsets, such as military defense contracts, for example. For
such markets, firms form teams until a project is completed. Then relationships are dissolved frictionlessly. Because subcontracting is commonplace in
defense contracts, other members of the industry serve as suppliers to a prime
contractor for a particular project while they compete aggressively on opposing teams for other contracts. Firms form partnerships for one project with
companies that are competitors for another contract.

Exclusivity. As technologies change with increasing speed, one of the difficulties that firms encounter in negotiating rights to use another firm's technologies is their desire for exclusive use of patents. Partners frequently reserve
the right to sell products themselves using their technology in their home
markets. Initially, U.S. firms balk on this point because they want total control and exclusivity. But as this request is made more frequently and as U.S.
firms lose more licensing deals to smaller, more accommodating competitors,
they have become more pragmatic concerning their demands for exclusive
rights. They now tend to develop a cost-benefit argument that evaluates (1)
the likelihood that a licensor will enter the U.S. market later in its own right;
(2) how much market share the firm expects to lose to such late entrants; and
(3) how much benefit is gained by exploiting the license now. To their surprise, some managers conclude that their firm can concede the question of
marketing rights for the patent-holder and later sell consulting services to the
licensor to help it formulate products to suit U.S. tastes without harm to their
own net position. Firms even prosper by letting partners seek new marketing
agents when licensors overestimated their products' market potential. Such
changes are grounds to renegotiate their arrangements on better terms when
partners return sheepishly after their own marketing analyses prove them to
be wrong.

Firms learn with experience that exclusive arguments with sluggish partners will tie their hands from being able to respond to rapidly changing competitive conditions. With hindsight, managers suggested that it is sometimes
wiser to *break* an exclusive agreement and pay the legal costs rather than to
stand by helplessly while competitors capture their market share.

If firms understand what their true competitive advantage is, they can be
in a better position to recognize when granting an exclusive relationship (or
accepting one) is more advantageous for them than associating with several
firms that compete with each other. In one successful partnership, a take-or-
pay contract to buy components was given to a partner that was especially

strong in making certain components in exchange for an exclusive relationship with it to build turnkey equipment. Later, the partner decided that it wanted to build machines on its own and paid the firm to learn how to do so. The partner's renegotiations came at a time when other competitors were entering the machinery market and profit margins were failing. The firm had been building machines originally as a way of selling its components and elements (which used proprietary knowledge and were difficult to make). It was delighted to release its partner in exchange for another take-or-pay contract covering the sale of its elements as well as its components to its partner.

In summary, agreements that create separate entities are not the only forms of cooperative activity firms use to cope with technological problems. Many types of joint activity of varying durations are used to leapfrog technologies, to increase value-added margins, and to keep abreast of state-of-the-art developments in their fields.

Managers recognize that bleedthrough problems are created by pooling information, but they regard this phenomenon as being more helpful to collegiality than harmful for its damage to competitive advantage. Indeed, managers found more problems in *encouraging* bleedthrough than in discouraging it. For them, ventures are a particularly vexing way to adapt to technological changes where in-house personnel harbored not-invented-here biases against the venture's innovations. Where not-invented-here is a problem, firms find it easier to transfer knowledge by using in-house facilities in loosely formed joint research efforts, rather than by forming a venture that might be horizontally related to the sponsoring firm's organization.

8
Guidelines for Forming and Managing Joint Ventures

C ompetitive stakes are increasing in the 1980s as U.S. firms try to assimilate information-processing, telecommunications, and other competitive skills. No diversified firm can hope to develop in-house the many technologies they need; they cannot afford to fund all of the projects they need to remain competitive on several fronts. So they are forming joint ventures.

Well-structured joint ventures offer firms a way to supplement the short-falls that even large companies face in coping with such challenges. Accordingly, findings concerning how firms manage their cooperative strategies should be of interest to managers for the insights they offer concerning how to enhance joint-venture success.

This chapter reflects managers' observations (gathered from field interviews) concerning their experiences in structuring and operating ventures. It draws heavily on examples obtained from oil-exploration ventures because firms in that industry have accumulated a vast inventory of experience concerning how to make joint ventures work.

Based on managers' comments within the other 25 industries studied, there does seem to be a cross-industry experience curve in using cooperative strategies in the sense that *the more that managers understand about what works in their joint ventures,* the more they want to replicate their successes. Some managers—representing both owner and venture viewpoints—are unabashedly pleased with their cooperative strategy arrangements. Moreover, owners and their ventures often concur, when interviewed separately, in identifying how managers might alleviate the stumbling blocks that accompany their firms' cooperative strategies.

Finally, this chapter reflects managers' suggestions concerning what not to do when forming and operating joint ventures. It reflects their experiences in suggesting how cooperative ventures can go awry.

Finding Partners

Successful firms will always be inundated with proposals to form joint ventures. However, managers often prefer to find their own projects—to dance with partners of their own choosing. Occasionally, managers are successful in getting their first-choice partners, but they rarely get agreements with all of the allies they desire. Instead, they learn to compromise.

Managers' expectations and attitudes concerning cooperation carry over to their assessments of potential partners, and these prejudices determine whether managers believe they have entered a shotgun wedding or are allied with a prince. If managers want their venture to succeed badly enough, they find a way to agree with their counterparts on their venture's activities. Managers within the sponsoring firms and their venture make the alliance work.

Successful and experienced managers prefer to work with equally experienced partners. For them, the ideal objective in choosing a joint-venture partner is to find one that offsets their firm's strengths without creating conflicts of interest between partners. Attractive partners are those that offer market access, experience, or technology in addition to cash. Adverse reputations also influence partner selections. Desirable partners have established track records concerning their abilities to work together in joint ventures. Undesirable partners cannot work with outsiders.

Although it is often easier to find "silent" partners that put up only cash, experienced managers tend to welcome the stimulation of partners' insights concerning decision making in risky ventures because no firm can hope to possess all of the knowledge needed to thrive in highly competitive settings. That is why cooperative strategies are increasingly attractive to them. (Exceptions are found where managers in one firm clearly want to operate the venture and are looking for a passive "sugar daddy" as partner. These ventures are usually of limited duration because they ultimately become a drag on the manager's creativity. The passive partner becomes little more than a "banker.")

Partners in Oil Ventures. Terms of joint-venture agreements in oil exploration are strongly influenced by (1) decades of experience in using joint ventures; and (2) homogeneity of interests among partners. Because firms have often been both "operators" and "nonoperators" in the past, they see each other's perspectives more easily. Provisions of their agreements strive for equitable treatment of partners' interests and, since their industry is close-knit, their conduct becomes widely known. Firms quickly learn not to "spit in the community well."

One partner in an oil exploration joint venture is designated as the "operator." A management team from this partner's firm takes charge of the physical work of exploration and makes presentations to a "planning committee" (composed of other partners' personnel) concerning *where and how it will drill*. (Drilling is the single most important decision in oil exploration and all owners devote significant time and energies to this decision.) The operator has budget authority to cover most day-to-day expenses and owners differ substantially concerning how involved they are in activities beyond the drilling decision. There appears to be an inverse relationship between owners' experience in oil-exploration joint ventures and their demands to be consulted by partners on minor expenditures.

Partners in oil exploration ventures frequently use "offsets" to maintain equality between them by forming a series of joint ventures. Each firm serves as the "operator" in one venture, and as nonoperator in the others. Thus, partners may have equal ownership shares but different management responsibilities per venture. Offsets enable partners to see each other's concerns in operating joint ventures. (Note that a pattern of offsetting joint ventures between partners is quite different from the "offset" purchases required by local governments as a condition for purchasing the products of a foreign vendor.)

Find a Way to Agree

If a joint venture is a good idea, it would seem that potential partners should not have to be coaxed into an alliance. But managers' experiences suggest that selling *is* necessary to overcome partners' fears, hesitations, and ignorance concerning this strategy option. It is often easier to say "no" than to find a way to say "yes." For example, a successful joint venture that lasted over ten years almost did not happen. The firm that the management team believed made the best partner had already rejected the proposal, but the initiating partner's chairman called his counterpart and suggested that there must be a way to make such a great alliance work. Even after staff had rejected the idea of a joint venture a second time, top executives from each firm sat down to explore what could be done to make the venture work. Adopting the attitude that the market opportunity the venture would serve sounded too good to reject, they persuaded their operating managers that no problems raised by negotiations were too great to overcome, but that each partner had to compromise in order to reach an agreement. The final agreement to form their joint venture was very different from the original plan by the time it had been worked through the two organizations. The amended venture was eventually done with great enthusiasm on both sides and was quite satisfactory to its owners.

Unequal Commitment. Asymmetries among partners create both an opportunity and a problem. Resource differences give partnerships greater strengths when they combine. But differences in management styles, outlooks, and control systems are disruptive.

The structure of partnership agreements, distribution of ownership shares, and board member composition are less likely to trip up the success of a venture than are individuals who do not disclose their lack of commitment to the success of the venture (or other hidden axes they wish to grind). Individuals with hidden agendas were cited by several managers as being the single most important factor that made ventures fail. Joint ventures are, after all, a marriage where compatible partners are needed; running ventures where owners do not value the venture with equal enthusiasm is difficult for the venture's managers.

Unequal Experience. Having experience with previous ventures makes firms more formidable as potential partners when negotiating deals with naive firms because experienced managers better understand what joint ventures can (and cannot) do. Joint-venture experience makes owners more relaxed in supervising and in evaluating joint venture performance also. The more relaxed partners become about the idea of doing ventures, the more willing they are for a little give and take to occur between them and potential partners in their efforts to hammer out a satisfactory joint-venture compromise.

Shotgun Wedding

The enthusiasm of top managers causes joint ventures to be formed, but the enthusiasm of operating managers makes ventures work. Some managers are not universally enthusiastic about using cooperative strategies and even experienced managers remain uncomfortable about joint ventures after running several of them if they are mismatched.

Characterizing ventures as "shotgun marriages" that they enter without enthusiasm, these disenchanted managers view ventures as unholy alliances with partners that would *never* be their first choices for business associates under other circumstances. Such managers use ventures *only* where they see no other way to attain their objectives.

In retrospect, lukewarm managers suggest that their firm's agreements had been made poorly because their negotiating teams devoted too much attention to questions of who would control technology produced by their venture and what the financial arrangements would be. They suggested that too little attention was devoted to the more important questions of *how their relationships with potential partners and with their venture would be managed*. Consequently, because their authority to act for their owners had been poorly defined, the venture's managers could not roll up their sleeves and find a way to get the job of running the joint venture done. Too often, managers are thrown together by owners without thinking through the details of day-to-day operations, they suggested.

This insight is not offered to suggest that attention should not be directed to details concerning financial arrangements, technology transfer, or other issues concerning assets. Rather it suggests that short-sighted firms make poor partners for cooperative strategies because they do not think through the operating details of the ventures they propose. Such ventures are troublesome to manage because owners fail to give the venture's managers the strong authority and incentives needed to make them succeed.

When managers are just thrown together in joint ventures without the advance opportunity to work out details concerning how their sponsoring firms' respective cultures will mesh, they are especially likely to feel that their hands have been tied. Frequently owners become frustrated by what they perceive as a lack of aggressiveness in their ventures' managers (the "sheltered venture"). Moreover, since corporate memories are often short and sponsoring firms' managers move on to other assignments after the venture they championed has been created, owners sometimes lose sight of their original objectives in forming their joint venture, particularly where the venture's activities require years of subsidization before it can stand on its own. (Poor performance always exacerbates tensions between owners and increases managers' frustrations with their counterparts unless communications flow freely between owners and their venture.)

When firms grow upset with each other, they rarely confront their differing expectations by discussing problems with their partners' managers. Instead, they criticize *the venture's managers*. Alternatively, disenchanted managers balk in making additional investments in the joint venture or quibble about how the venture's managers should make a decision. A variety of "foot-dragging" activities ensue. Sometimes owners take over the reins of management in their ventures. In brief, managers in charge of ventures suffer because managers from sponsoring firms draw the venture closer when they are upset, thereby robbing the venture's managers of the autonomy and flexibility needed to compete effectively and the ability to fairly represent the viewpoints of the venture's other owners.

Someday a Prince Will Come

Expectations concerning potential partners are sometimes unrealistic. Some firms want a prince for a partner and will not settle for those that look like frogs. Rather than discuss the feasibility of a joint venture with available (and eager) partners, some firms' managers hold out for the ideal mate. Managers often do not recognize that leading firms need joint ventures less than followers do. Hence, the prince they desire is *less* likely to approach them with a proposal for cooperation than less attractive firms are.

One successful firm with several ventures to its credit takes a very deliberate approach toward the formation of its ventures. Its managers identify the need for a partnership in a particular business activity. The managers develop a list of potential partners for cooperation and screen them carefully. Then the firm's managers approach *several* potential partners simultaneously to discuss the feasibility of a joint venture and to decide which of several potential firms would be the best partner for the venture in question.

If the managers within both firms agree that cooperation is desirable, they begin their alliance with a long engagement period during which time managers on both sides move slowly to a consensus concerning how to operate their venture; cooperation progresses incrementally. When the marriage is finally consummated, the venture receives all of the assets needed to operate as a stand-alone entity. Subsequent intervention by owners' managers in their venture's operating decisions is minimal because the resulting management team closely reflects the values of its owners. (Note that this approach to cooperative strategies will not work as well in a highly changeable environment or in situations where competitive advantages must be exploited *quickly*.)

Even in ventures that must share facilities with one owner, the search pattern among successful venturers is a careful one. For example, managers often proceed methodically to search the globe for the best possible partners after they are convinced that cooperation is necessary. First, they interview the customers they hope their joint venture will serve. Then they interview research institutes and any other experts with knowledge concerning where the technologies they seek might best be observed or obtained. Finally, when managers have found the technology they desire and chosen the best candidates for cooperation, their negotiating teams learn enough of the potential partners' language to converse with top executives (if their potential partners do not speak English). They court desired partners by offering them access to resources that the candidates lack (such as access to the U.S. market). Briefly, the best joint ventures result from a devotion of time and careful attention to the *complementarity* between potential partners during the search process.

If managers are uncomfortable during their negotiations with potential partners managers, they do not consummate any cooperative agreements, often because they believe that intuition should dictate whether a venture is forged. Managers justify this policy by noting that because so much must be done within a joint venture on the basis of faith and good feelings, owners should give priority to the abilities of their venture's managers to cooperate and learn how to trust the good feelings these managers sense concerning potential partners during negotiations. After all, one venture's manager counseled, "Staff is not running this jointly owned business; I am."

The Changeling. If managers devote themselves to making the alliance work, some frogs later turn into princes, especially when managers from each owner's organization are put into the venture and allowed enough time to learn how to work together. But inattentive owners find that the managers of "boisterous ventures" sometimes have minds of their own. One very successful joint-venture management team exploited the pressures they felt from their respective owners and formed an atmosphere of great camaraderie *within the venture*. When such ventures mature, this camaraderie can create some difficulties at its owners' headquarters (because the venture's management team has become so successful in working together that they will outperform the jealous wholly owned units of the sponsoring firms). Not until the venture's success has buoyed its owners through hard times in their respective industries, will the venture's management team finally win respect and recognition from its owners' managers as being the prince it really is.

Managers within sponsoring firms suggested that the best way to make a successful joint venture is to choose skilled managers, trust their operating decisions, and focus on the common interest that brings partners together in judging the venture's performance. Partners must learn to make the best of their alliances, some managers suggested. Advance the common interest of the partnership, and stop worrying about what might have been if other firms were in the partnership. If questions arise later about whether one's partners bring more to the party than the firm does, develop a means for readjusting partners' interests as conditions change, experienced managers advised.

The Alaska Pipeline joint venture provides an example of how partners adjust to unforeseen events in their cooperative ventures. The agreement, which was written in 1977, provides maximum flexibility in terms of the shares of crude oil each partner ships through the pipeline. It provides for the contingency of additional Prudhoe Bay oil discoveries and for other events that could occur when resources are commingled. The original capacity of the pipeline was determined by *estimated* reservoir capacity and each partner's ownership share parallels the proportion of capacity it will use in shipping crude oil. If partners' relative shipping volumes change, the contract provides for them to adjust their ownership shares, as well. (This adjustment is done to ensure that no partner is predominantly a shipper or predominantly a customer. Conflicts of interest are avoided by making all partners' interests in the buyer-seller relatively equal.) If another large oil basin were discovered in acreage in the Prudhoe Bay adjacent to that originally covered by the Alaska Pipeline agreement, the contract provides a right-of-first-refusal to original partners if the pipeline must be expanded.

Silent and Unitiated Partners

The majority of managers who represented the owner firm's viewpoint suggested that the best partners are horizontally related to each other and understand well the business activities of their venture. Partners that contribute only cash and cannot act as "operators" often become a source of irritation as ventures proceed. Schisms occur between partners because if a passive (and inexperienced) partner's managers do not understand the business activity of the venture, they cannot contribute meaningfully to the venture's governance. Doubt exists in the minds of managers from passive firms concerning whether they have been told the truth by their partners' managers, especially when they do not like the results of those facts.

If a joint venture is in trouble, managers from passive partners are more likely to think that the true condition of the business cannot possibly be as bad as it has been represented to be by the venture's managers because they cannot judge the situation on their own. But if a venture between a knowledgeable firm and a passive (or unschooled) partner thrives, the venture's managers begin to look on the demands for information from a passive or unknowledgeable owner as a drag on their efforts. Their resentment develops because, although passive owners may have been "silent" with respect to their more knowledgeable partners, they often ask detailed questions of their venture.

If relationships between partners deteriorate to the worst case, the active owner and the venture (which is often managed by the active owner's personnel) come to resent sharing the fruits of their successful labors with untutored partners that have acted as little more than bankers or venture capitalists. Even if the passive owner insists on being actively involved in the venture's decision making, venture managers from the active owner's ranks often do not consult or brief managers from the passive owner regularly. Managers from active partners may even begin to think that they need not bother explaining facts to managers from unversed partners who do not know what they are talking about (or who challenge everything their knowledgeable partner says). Eventually a schism develops between the knowledgeable "insiders" and the inexperienced "outsiders" unless the outside partners' managers can find a way to become insiders themselves without becoming a drag on their partners or their venture. A program of educating the silent (or uninitiated) partner's managers (and of supplementing the partner's knowledge of the venture's industry) is needed to make partners' outlooks more homogeneous if partnerships are to endure.

One Step at a Time

Cautious managers suggested that a step-by-step relationship is prudent when forming a joint venture with potential partners that they do not know well. They suggested an incremental approach, such as giving potential partners a proposal to study and some issues to discuss. If the potential partner returns to discussions with suggestions and is comfortable in negotiating on the critical points of the proposed venture, a small project between partners may be warranted. If the first cooperative venture works out, another joint venture can be formed.

Some managers believe in long engagement periods or trial marriages as a precursor to larger ventures. These firms form study teams composed of managers from each potential partner. The managers on the "prenuptial" teams suggest how the proposed venture—representing the combined assets of its partners—should change its sourcing arrangements, its resource deployments, and the mix of products made at each plant, among other details. The prenuptial management team also suggests whether particular plants should be closed (regardless of which partner owns them) as they work through the most economical way to run the proposed venture. (The prenuptial team's objective is to significantly lower the cost of joint operations. Valuation questions associated with contributed assets are left to other negotiators.) No joint venture is formed (1) if the prenuptial management team cannot develop a useful set of suggestions concerning how to rationalize the operations and productive capacities of assets contributed by potential partners; or (2) if the management team (which is, in fact, understudying for the role of managing the venture) cannot work together.

Managers that take a cautious approach—a small project, then another one if the first experience with a potential partner is a good one—seem to be more satisfied with the use of cooperative strategies than those who move too fast or who were not careful enough in forming alliances. This incremental approach to forming partnerships enables managers to add to the complexity (or breadth) of things that they trust a joint venture to do on the basis of their previous experience with a particular partner. This approach keeps managers' expectations for a particular partner lower and enables them to be more analytical in assessing why a particular venture does not work out. Hence, a firm does not have to give up hope of working with a particular partner if one venture flounders due to uncontrollable factors that make it more costly than expected—such as product obsolescence, rabid competitors, or economic recession.

Finally, managers suggested that it is important to be ready for a successful venture. Despite their advocacy of an incremental approach, managers advocated that adequate funding be provided to exploit the exciting opportunities that develop for ventures. If partners cannot provide the needed cash for new opportunities, they must be prepared to let their venture approach the capital markets in its own right to obtain funding or to let the distribution of ownership shares pass to the partner who is willing to fund the venture.

For example, because the daily operating expenses in oil exploration are so very high, delays due to decision-making stalemates among partners can be costly. Instead, "side-payments" are made to disgruntled partners (as covered in partnership contracts) if they disagree on an action taken by their venture so that exploration may proceed. Exploratory drilling activities can be undertaken by a firm under a "sole-risk" provision if one partner wishes to stop a venture from going forward. The entire costs of drilling are borne by subscribing partners in this case. But if the venture strikes oil and some partners have not paid their share of drilling costs, subscribing partners are indemnified for their costs (plus a bonus which is often 200 percent to 300 percent of their costs) before nonsubscribing partners share equally in the venture's findings. Such stiff penalties for not participating reduce deadlocks once joint ventures are formed in oil and gas exploration.

"Farm in" (or "farm out") agreements in the oil industry enable firms possessing yet-unexplored mineral rights to take on partners who typically offer cash and exploration technology. The entering partners may pay for exploration costs to obtain a 50 percent interest in the oil field, for example. Alternatively, the partner possessing the mineral rights may have drilled with discouraging results and may lack the funds to drill further. At this point partners may be "farmed in" who make contributions up to some portion of sunk costs (sometimes plus a premium) to obtain a position of parity in the acreage under exploration.

Many Dancing Partners

Success in some industries requires that firms be promiscuous. It is advantageous for firms to take several partners in a spider's web of cooperative strategies in certain industry settings, such as those where technology changes rapidly or the infrastructure is still embryonic. For example, liaisons among military contractors and subcontractors are necessary for political expediency. Partners take a pragmatic attitude concerning alliances for military contracts. One day firms may compete neck and neck on one project; the next day they are on the same team for a different project.

Whirlwind Romance. When a firm must move quickly to exploit a transitory competitive advantage, it selects partners according to their ability to solve the problems of particular customers that the firm wishes to serve. The short-term nature of a firm's competitive advantage makes it take on *several* dancing partners in order to reach many new customers quickly. Few stand-alone ventures result from these whirlwind romances because partners work together for as long as necessary, but their alliances are hardly marriages. Like the musical-chairs pairings of the electronic components industry, no firm is expected to solve all of its problems alone and no firm limits itself to one partner for every turn around the floor.

A willingness to dance for a short time with several partners allows a firm to move faster in responding to changes in market demands than an exclusive arrangement of longer duration would. Part of the flexibility in using a spider's web of agreements arises from the informality of such alliances. (Firms accustomed to forming coalitions in this manner are frequently adept at internal venturing arrangements.) However, dissimilarities in the ease with which a firm makes (and breaks) ventures and reaches decisions when operating within joint ventures sometimes creates irritations in managing partnership relationships. It is unwise, for example, to use loose arrangements where intellectual property rights are poorly protected or where the venture's activity must be closely meshed with the assets of one of its owners if the partners' management styles are mismatched.

Ventures with Dissimilar Partners. Loose alliances—personal-service contracts, OEM-vendor agreements, or other arm's length arrangements—are preferred by managers when dealing with highly dissimilar partners, entrepreneurs, and in other situations where managers feel uncomfortable about forming long-term, shared-equity ventures. Limited-term alliances with low exit barriers are preferred by many creative people who want an equity participation in their creations but do not want a salary from (or to be otherwise closely affiliated with) a corporate monolith. Astute managers suggested that large firms should help such entrepreneurs to incorporate and deal with them on a contractual basis. Some managers go so far as to suggest that joint ventures (or other enduring forms of alliance) are a bad idea when the partners are trying to achieve incompatible objectives. Their comments reflect the difficulties they envision (or have experienced) in overcoming the exit barriers associated with joint-venture agreements.

Reducing Hostilities. Joint ventures were endorsed for selling jointly developed products to competitors. Expressing motivations such as those that caused Exxon and General Motors to form Ethyl Corp. in the 1920s, several managers suggested that vertically integrated customers are reluctant to purchase products that are too closely associated with their rivals. (This fear is analogous to the problem faced in oil-well drilling when a firm will not buy drilling services from an oil-exploration firm too closely allied to the firm's competitors in order to avoid revealing the location of good oil prospects to rivals.)

Whose Turn Is It to Lead?

Successful ventures enable partners to see each other's viewpoints. Sometimes offsetting ventures are formed in which partners take turns being the operator, as in the Alaska Pipeline agreement, so that partners balance the perspectives of buyer and seller in making decisions.

In 1975, Control Data Corp. (CDC) and Honeywell formed a 70%–30% joint venture, Magnetic Peripherals Inc. (MPI), to design, develop, and manufacture rotating mass memory products for the computer industry. Honeywell and CDC contributed their respective computer peripheral assets to create a venture that could compete with IBM. MPI had lower costs than either parent because it eliminated duplicate activities and exploited economies of scale. CII-Honeywell Bull later purchased a 3 percent interest in MPI from Honeywell. Sperry became a partner in 1983 with a 13 percent interest, reducing CDC's interest to 67 percent and Honeywell's interest to 17 percent.

MPI was a captive supplier for its owners, selling on an OEM basis only to them. CDC and Honeywell did not purchase their magnetic memory devices from in-house business units because neither company maintained parallel facilities that competed against MPI. As long as MPI's products were updated and competitive with those of outside suppliers MPI was their only vendor.

MPI was used as a vehicle to enter other joint ventures on behalf of its owners. For example, in 1982 MPI and Memorex formed a set of 60%–40% joint ventures to develop a magnetic plating for MPI's memory devices. MPI and Memorex took turns being operators. The joint ventures invested in generations of technology to develop thin-film heads and applications for thin-film heads in semiconductor technologies. These joint ventures were also captives that sold only to their owners, using their owners' respective market access to sell their outputs. As the MPI–Memorex ventures became increasingly successful, their owners relied on them to be major suppliers, especially when other firms failed to commercialize similar products.

In 1982, MPI also formed a set of joint ventures with Philips NV to develop laser-optical memory devices. Philips was a majority owner (52 percent) in the partnership to develop the substrate for the memory device, whereas MPI was the majority owner (52 percent) in the partnership to develop the drive, its rotation mechanism, and read/write head. Although CDC was strong in magnetic memory devices, it wanted to have access to knowledge concerning alternative technologies that could supplant its ongoing products. The joint ventures were structured to provide complementary bargaining power while putting one owner in charge of each venture's activity. When their development phases were completed, the two ventures were melded into one 51 percent–49 percent joint venture, Optical Storage International (OSI), with Philips NV as majority owner and CDC as its partner. (CDC had obtained the rights to the OSI technology from MPI, the original venture partner.) OSI was permitted to have its own manufacturing and marketing facilities, but it was expected initially to contract for marketing and distribution services from CDC.

Don't Shortchange Your Partner. Many managers cautioned that their joint ventures died when other managers began to think about how they could shortchange their partners. (Many announced ventures fell through because the managers in potential partner firms could not see each other's needs as negotiations proceeded. Their greed killed the cooperative spirit of their ventures.) The name of the game should be cooperation, one manager suggested, not rape.

Ventures with Small Firms and Entrepreneurs

Joint ventures between a large firm and a small one (an entrepreneur) pose difficulties because of the dramatic differences in vision each firm has for the venture and in how they evaluate each other's contribution. Joint ventures often are necessary to cooperate with an entrepreneurial manager/inventor because when firms try to acquire the rights to or interests in a small firm's products or devices, they discover that the inventor wants an outrageous sum of money—far more than potential investors will pay.

Inventors often want compensation for their discoveries based on the enormous market potential they are certain exists for their products. They are, more often than not, overly optimistic about their product's success and do not see the risks and expenses of launching their discovery. Corporate rate partners might have to bear additional expenses that could include more engineering and substantially more testing. A joint venture forces the entrepreneur/inventory to share in the risks that the cautious corporate partner envisions in order to realize the higher rewards that the entrepreneur envisions for the venture's products.

Since the entrepreneur/inventor is more informal in transacting business than a corporate partner would be, the incremental approach to joint-venture formation works especially well with them. A joint venture with an entrepreneur/inventor initially can proceed on the basis of a handshake. The venture actually is more like a venture-capital project than an operating partnership until the product reaches the commercialization stage. If demonstration projects are successful, a formal agreement to fund test-marketing can follow.

Writing Contracts

Prudent managers realize that there are limitations to what can be written into a contract to ensure joint-venture success. *Alliances fail because operating managers do not make them work, not because contracts are poorly written.* An unsatisfactory contract reflects a fundamental misunderstanding among partners concerning the venture's mission. When partners reach a meeting of minds, it is time to negotiate a contract, but many firms cannot translate their agreement to cooperate into a legal document.

The most frequent answer offered by interviewed managers as to why announced ventures never went beyond the discussion stage was that ventures were sunk by lawyers. From this response, one might conclude that managers from partner firms were homogeneous in their outlooks; their firms' lawyers were too adversarial. A more likely explanation for joint-venture deaths at the contract-writing stage is that partners do not adequately think through their arrangements before they reach the altar. The lawyers' probing questions in anticipation of drafting the formal agreement expose these shortfalls in the partners' understandings and the venture falls apart.

Part of the cause of partners' being abandoned at the altar is their lawyers' job descriptions of products. Lawyers are very good at spelling out the legal scope of ventures, but in doing so they often limit the life of the joint venture to a particular undertaking. Although they are merely doing their jobs in renegotiating joint-venture agreements at the horizon point of a project, lawyers often seem to accentuate the fact that partners have grievances with each other. When lawyers convene to modify ventures, their renegotiations reveal areas of discontent with partners that their firms' managers have borne without comment during the venture's operations. Frequently, the new terms lawyers request to rectify areas of dissatisfaction come as a surprise to the other firms' managers. By calling attention to inequities, lawyers make it more difficult for partners to agree to work together thereafter.

Lawyers prefer to write explicit agreements that specify performances for every contingency. In particular, they suggest that a divorce settlement be negotiated before the marriage is consummated. Many managers, by contrast, find the act of writing contracts unpleasant. Furthermore, managers are often not actively involved in contract negotiations to form their own ventures; the only time some firms' managers consult their contracts is when their ventures fail, managers confided. (Then they hope that their lawyers have written a good divorce settlement for them.)

Prenuptial Agreements

Prenuptial agreements are necessary to record the intentions of the parties when the joint venture is formed. The major reason to write contracts as carefully as possible (and within legally accepted guidelines) is to capture the understandings that are so firmly in everyone's minds and so beautifully understood by everybody at the original negotiations because the managers that build ventures do not necessarily continue to operate (or monitor) them as their careers progress.

In order for a joint venture to succeed, partners must agree on (1) their venture's mission; (2) the markets it will serve; (3) the products it can offer; (4) the obligations of each partner in assisting their venture; and (5) the process by which the venture will be dissolved when it has outlived its usefulness. It is more difficult to write out operating details concerning how managers from diverse cultures will blend their partners' management styles to work together within the venture. Some managers also found it difficult to write contracts for supplies and purchasing relationships, horizon points for reviewing their venture's progress, renegotiation thresholds, and other terms that recorded the original meeting of partners' minds.

Some managers create joint ventures without writing formal agreements. Sometimes partners race ahead in a joint venture with great euphoria. In their interest to get the project done, they form a ragged agreement that they may intend to amend and refine later. If they miss a key point in their agreements, managers confided, such haste often comes back to haunt them later.

Anticipate Impasses. Despite the temptation to forge ahead in a joint venture, great care should be taken to anticipate every possible change in partners' business relationships and to develop a means of handling any events not foreseen by negotiating teams. As negotiating teams work through this process (which can take from five months to three years, or more), managers learn about their counterparts (assuming the managers who will oversee or manage the venture are a part of the negotiating team). With several good experiences together, partners come to rely on each other's word in solving unforeseen problems, and satisfaction with a partner's word becomes the bond that contributes to a venture's stability.

Reputation as a Firm's Key Asset. It is important to have experienced managers as well as talented lawyers engaged in joint-venture negotiations. Because the integrity of each partner's managers is important for the venture's stability and because firms will undoubtedly have to "go to the well" several times in the future as competitive conditions make cooperation an increasingly attractive option, the selfish, dishonest, or devious manager is recognized over time as being one who "spits in the community well." Venture managers that did not bargain for equitable treatment for all of the venture's owners had less joint-venture success than managers that remembered to include all owners' viewpoints in the decision-making process.

Protecting Property Rights

As chapter 7 notes, knowledge that is shared with a jointly owned venture is difficult to protect. Proprietary nondisclosure agreements are sometimes difficult to enforce. Some firms protect their intellectual property rights by pooling them in the joint venture. (Making the venture the owner of valued knowledge increases its self-esteem. Indeed, managers suggested that their ventures are even more aggressive in protecting against violations of their patents—even against unauthorized infringements by owners—than owners themselves might have been.)

However, where technological bleedthrough is a recurring problem, managers had few practical suggestions. Lawyers suggested that owners could license their venture to use their knowledge or withhold the information altogether. The latter suggestion defeats the purpose of cooperative strategies, however.

Keeping Key Personnel. As is the case in any highly competitive industry, firms must understand the nature of their competitive advantage when writing joint-venture contracts if they hope to protect those advantages. Astute lawyers inserted a clause into one joint venture agreement that made key personnel of the venture employees of the surviving partner in the event of venture termination. Owners had not consciously set out to structure their agreement in that manner (although such a provision is surely a sensible way to protect the value of the venture's business interests in an activity where personnel are the venture's principal assets). However, in this case, owner *A*, who wanted to sell its interest to partner *B*, had contributed the services of its top personnel without realizing that they stayed with the venture when partner *B* acquired its interest. Thus, having a savvy lawyer negotiate the contract paid off for firm *B* who had delegated the task in this example, much to the chagrin of firm *A* (who had also delegated the task to its lawyers).

Demanding Fidelity

Managers agreed that, although it is often necessary to circumscribe partners from creating facilities that will compete with their venture's activities, it is unwise to restrict partners' activities in another field. (Lawyers advised that it is illegal to try to do so.) That means, for example, that partners to a pharmaceutical joint venture that makes products for the care of gastrointestinal problems would not want to restrict their partner from doing research in psychotherapeutics. Owners can better help their venture in unforeseen situations if they are unconstrained to develop expertise in related fields, because the venture benefits from its owners' ideas concerning analogous approaches that could be applied to its own sphere of responsibility.

With experience comes a more relaxed attitude from managers on questions of exclusivity in their ventures with particular partners. One manager suggested that all the firm wanted from its venture partners was a telephone call to advise them when the relationship ceased to be an exclusive one because recriminations were fruitless in that industry; technologies change too rapidly, penalties are too difficult to extract from unfaithful partners, and patents are virtually worthless in such industries.

Divorce Settlements

Termination clauses are treated as being very important by lawyers. In a typical joint-venture document, approximately 80 percent of the content is devoted to details concerning who will buy out whom, at what price, who will act as source to whom after the venture terminates, and other arrangements created to replace the venture. The divorce settlement clauses also determine which partner gets what assets when the venture folds and what happens to the personnel, to the trade secrets generated, to the patents generated, and to everything else associated with the venture's activities when partners no longer wish to cooperate.

Most ventures contain divorce settlements because lawyers are worried about partner firms' obligations on exit during the negotiation phase. Creditors (especially banks) also demand divorce-settlement clauses in joint-venture agreements in order to know what their rights will be if the venture goes bad.

The venture's managers, by contrast, rarely believed that divorce settlements were needed because nobody can foresee accurately what events may arise. They preferred to sail along, operating the joint venture and negotiating problems on a day-to-day basis with owners until the alliance between their firm's owners broke down. (Successful ventures never reached deadlocks, apparently, because the managers within each sponsoring firm always found a way to resolve conflicts among partners until firms mutually agreed that the formal agreement had to be renegotiated.)

Why Ventures Fail. Some ventures failed because (1) partners could not get along; (2) their markets disappeared; (3) managers from disparate partners within the venture could not work together; (4) managers within the venture could not work with owners' managers; (5) what was thought to be good technology from one partner (or whatever the contribution was to be) did not prove to be as good as was expected; (6) owners that were to contribute information or resources could not get their personnel down the line to deliver what had been promised; (7) partners simply reneged on their promises to deliver on their part of the agreement, or (8) other reasons destroyed partners' cooperative spirits. Even good ventures endure for short periods, at best, because the necessity that spurs their creation does not endure forever in evolving, competitive market-places. Moreover, when managers within sponsoring firms rotate to other responsibilities, relationships between partners may change dramatically if the new personnel can no longer recall the logic that once stimulated the joint venture's creation. For the new managers (who were not involved in the venture's birth), maintaining their firm's relationship with its partners becomes a nuisance if they do not share the same vision as the venture's founders. Without the attentions of the managers who gave birth to the joint ventures, interest in their well-being wanes. If the venture becomes ill after its sponsoring manager moves on, the new manager left in charge is more likely to terminate the venture than to nurture it.

Paradoxically, ventures between firms of unequal size are unstable and difficult to maintain even if the venture *is* successful because satisfying the venture's working capital requirements (not to mention its capital require-ments) will stretch the small partner beyond its debt capacity. If the smaller sponsoring firm has neither the cash nor the credit to supply its fair share of funding, ownership shares must be reallocated or the venture must end. Sur-rendering equity (and ending the venture) is a painful process for entrepre-neurial, high technology firms that feel as though they are selling their birth-rights when they cannot afford the capital demands placed on them by their ventures. Yet these same firms cannot afford to buy out the ownership inter-ests of their larger partners (because they were undercapitalized at the onset). Frequently, small firms are operating on slim margins in their primary busi-ness activities even before the joint venture is formed. (Some large firms enter such ventures with the knowledge that they may later have to buy out smaller partners.)

Ending It. Some firms use the Russian roulette system to value partners' in-terests when ventures are terminated. (In this system equitable treatment for all partners is ensured by letting one partner split a property while the other partner distributes the pieces between them, as chapter 4 notes.) Other firms do not let partners back out of ventures without some difficulty. One firm with many successful ventures to its credit does not believe that ventures should necessarily terminate after a certain number of years. Arguing that the managers who create the venture have no idea how well that venture will fare when the first horizon date is reached, managers from this firm sought ways to ensure stability during the first phase of their joint-venture arrangements. To do so, this firm insists that no partner can sell its interest in their joint venture for a predetermined number of years. Partners are locked into the first round of funding obligations to give the venture a chance to develop. For the second phase of its joint-venture agreements, this firm stipulates that a disgruntled partner can sell its interests—but only after offering its shares to other partners first and only by *selling the stock in a block*. (In this ar-rangement, a departing partner cannot bring in more than one new partner.) For the third phase of its joint-venture agreements, this firm insists that the venture be transformed into a corporation with the opportunity to sell shares to the public if it survives the first two phases of development. (Making the venture a public company terminates the previous partnership but not the venture's business activity or any vertical relationships that may have existed. Phase three of this arrangement is a way for partners to liquidate their in-vestments in the venture).

Other managers eschew such arrangements because they do not believe that the venture should be allowed to have a life of its own. (In many cases, letting the venture issue its own securities creates a horizontally related com-petitor, managers noted.)

Ownership versus Control

Most managers prefer that their firms hold majority equity control in their ventures. Several managers distinguished equity ownership from operating control. The distribution of equity shares is important for accounting, consolidation of interests, and qualification for tax benefits. Operating control is important for running a joint venture frictionlessly. Some managers are comfortable with asymmetric profit splits (distribution of profits that does not match distribution of equity ownership). They also accept management control splits that do not mirror the distribution of ownership interests, as long as *their firm* is the venture's operator.

Although there is no rule in such matters, if a partner wants to take less than 25 percent ownership in a joint venture, it is considered a financial investor by many firms and is not entitled to much of a voice in managing the venture's activities. Although majority owners may consult such partners if the size of their joint-venture investment is to be increased substantially or if another major change is contemplated, such minority partners usually are expected to be passive. There are exceptions to this pattern. In one situation a partner with a 24-percent interest in a joint venture was asked to supply the managers for and to operate the venture on behalf of the majority owner. Sometimes a comparison of each partner's skills determines which firm will be the joint venture's operator.

Division of Ownership Shares—Owners' Perspectives

Managers from sponsoring firms who favored an unequal distribution of ownership shares believed that it is desirable to have one partner who is clearly in charge of the venture and that the split of ownership shares should reflect this power structure. Too many failed ventures, these managers argued, have 50%–50% ownership splits and the partners cannot agree on the venture's direction. All that 50%–50% ownership really guarantees partners is the right to fight, one manager noted.

Even managers who represented owners' viewpoints within excellent 50%–50% ventures said that they distrust the idea of equal ownership splits in general because when the venture is established as a 50%–50% joint venture, it is presumed that partners will be able to work out every problem along the way. Managers find that such presumptions are not realistic. They insist that one of the venture's owners should be identified as having primary responsibility for overseeing and running the venture. The other owners of the venture, they suggested, should hold the operator accountable for the venture's performance.

Some managers suggested that three owners are more desirable than two when a means of governing and resolving conflict within ventures is sought because it is less likely that owners will fall into a deadlock. The experiences of ventures with three owners suggest, however, that running a three-party joint venture is extremely difficult, especially with respect to its direction and control.

Division of Ownership Shares—Venture's Perspective

Managers who represented the venture's perspective and were charged with running the jointly owned firm expressed dramatically different attitudes concerning ownership splits and the relative influence exerted by the venture's owners. *Many joint venture managers expressed a preference for two (not more) owners and for 50%–50% joint ventures rather than uneven equity splits.*

Venture managers who favor equal ownership shares believe that they ensure that each owner's interests and opinions will not be quashed. These managers fear that a minority owner's interests will be shortchanged in asymmetric ownership structures (such as 51%–49% or 75%–25%). Venture managers often are placed in the uncomfortable position of implementing the orders of their owners. These managers were most sensitive to the need for a consensus because a joint venture cannot be managed for long against any owner's wishes. They felt that equal ownership shares are the outward symbol of the owners' equality in the joint venture.

Although 50%–50% ventures are widely acclaimed as being difficult to manage, such arrangements best capture the spirit of a partnership. They are desirable in high technology ventures (especially with entrepreneurial firms) to ensure that owners remain interested in and involved with the venture's technological development activities. Equally distributed ownership is the only way, some managers argue, that top management stays interested enough in a venture's activities to avert problems before it is too late. The long-publicized dislike by managers of equally owned joint ventures may have originated in interviews with managers from sponsoring firms, not with the managers of the jointly owned ventures. The venture's managers tend to be more interested in sustaining harmony among owners by ensuring that no owner shortchanged the others than their counterparts in owner organizations were.

At the basis of a successful 50%–50% joint venture, most venture managers conceded, is personal trust, usually between the managers from the sponsoring firms who originally formed the joint venture. Venture managers emphasized that the spirit of the founding relationship must be kept healthy and vibrant in order for a joint venture to run successfully. Although examples from the oil industry suggest that ownership shares should be renegotiated when owners' interests change, some managers disagreed with this practice, suggesting that if owners had to *renegotiate* ownership terms, they probably had made a poor deal in the first place and should back out. If a joint venture is not right on a 50%–50% basis, it is not likely to be right on a 90%–10% basis (or any other split either, they suggested).

Managerial Control

Ownership share distribution matters less than how operating control and participation in decision making), are actually apportioned. It is often necessary to spell out each owner's responsibilities carefully and to keep the lines of authority clear (between the owners' managers and the venture's managers) in order for a joint venture to succeed. Otherwise, squabbles ensue. Firms are pragmatic concerning control over ventures where project leadership can be determined by owners' skills and experiences, as in the example of letting an owner with navy experience lead a navy contract team. Sponsoring firms find it easier to work together where each partner respects the other's knowledge and personnel well enough to send in their engineers, go through the facts, and reach agreements concerning what should be done. When firms cannot evaluate information from their venture or their partners, they become uneasy with their partnerships.

Shared Decision Making in Volatile Settings. Confusion about who is operating a joint venture cannot be tolerated in highly competitive settings where conditions change so rapidly that ventures need great flexibility in order to respond fast enough. For example, clear leadership authority is needed in volatile businesses like the financial services industry where communications are important. It is very difficult to operate a successful financial services company using a bureaucratic decision-making process, for example, because it is necessary to be able to move fast when prices swing erratically. In such settings, there cannot be any management by committee, unless the decision-making committee can be convened immediately and possesses the power to bind the corporation in making difficult decisions. Although partners can use their veto power and the joint venture's voting structure to protect their ownership interests when they review the venture's performance, somebody must be able to obligate the venture contractually until owners can make their review.

Using Managers Effectively

Managers sometimes erroneously believe that they can set up ventures and let them run themselves. Most ventures require much more management time than many owners expect. Choices concerning who to appoint to the venture's management board and which managers to place in charge of the venture's operations are crucial to its success. A joint venture runs the risk of failing if it does not receive a tremendous amount of attention from its owners' executives as well as from the managers who run it.

Joint ventures take twice as much time to manage as wholly owned business units if owners are unwilling to delegate decision making to the venture managers. Somebody must be responsible for coping with the many possible conflicts that arise concerning owners' egos, venture manager motivation, and other operating problems. These responsibilities absorb significant amounts of time and require negotiation skills, people skills, and selling skills. It is unclear whether the executive who shoulders these responsibilities must be in the venture's organization or in the owners' organizations, but a central coordinator is needed to bring owners to rational agreements and avert dissention.

Joint-Venture Management Style

Several managers blamed joint-venture failure on the choice of the wrong manager to lead it. The managers best suited to run a joint venture must be trained in diplomacy, one executive noted, because they have to approach the chief executives of *all* sponsoring firms to explain the venture's activities. Working only through the board members who oversee the venture's activities is not sufficient to gain the trust and sponsorship of owner firms. Unless the venture's manager can capture the support of its owners, the venture is treated like an unwelcome stepchild.

The best joint-venture managers are those who do well within a matrix organization because they can deal with the political differences of owners in a diplomatic fashion while satisfying their diverse needs. In managing points of obvious controversy between owners, it is important for the venture's manager to gather the opinions of the "experts" within sponsoring firms. (These are the managers within owner firms whose opinions on a particular topic are most likely to be asked when a venture's proposal is evaluated *whether* the owner knows the venture's business or not.) These opinions should be solicited and the proposal should be modified to reflect them before making a recommendation to the joint venture's management board. If the venture's manager incorporates each owner's viewpoints into the proposal, these recommendations become the plan that owners' own experts have recommended and are more likely to be accepted.

One sure way for a joint venture to fail is for its managers not to consult all of the venture's owners on decision alternatives, planned expenditures, and other proposals. Although giving joint-venture managers more of a free rein in decision making may improve the joint venture's return to its owners, venture managers should remember that owners' managers want to share in the venture's success, especially if founding managers' egos are closely tied to that success. (As one successful venture manager noted, not bringing owners along on a joint venture's decisions is like excluding biological parents from their child's wedding.)

A Human Dumping Ground

Owners miss an opportunity to tap their venture managers' entrepreneurial tendencies when they let the ventures be used as personnel dumping grounds. If owners place their burnt-out, low-potential, or politically embarrassing managers in their ventures (and treat them accordingly), their failures are self-fulfilling prophesies. Failure is also likely if owners remove high performers from the joint-venture assignment soon after the first honeymoon is over and deny the subsequent venture management team the high-level attentions reserved for managers of wholly owned business units. When they receive poor treatment, managers assigned to the venture become jaundiced because they know that running the joint venture is not considered to be a great honor within the owners' organizations. Rather than making the joint venture a convenient parking place for senior executives awaiting retirement, firms should make venture management a *reward* for enterprising managers and encourage them to engage in innovative behavior.

It is not surprising that the strategies of owners will become different from the venture's strategy or that partners will have different corporate cultures that their respective managers carry with them into the venture. Problems arise, however, when the joint venture is treated as an inferior child or is not given the means to succeed. Sometimes owners undercut their venture's chances for success through their personnel policies, for example. Because they are thinking of the revolving door that will bring them back to their old jobs in their respective owner firms, venture managers identify with their owner's interests rather than with the venture's success needs. If venture managers cannot think of themselves as employees of the venture, their decisions will reflect this schism (as will the joint venture's ultimate failure).

No Revolving Door. The venture's general manager must be detached from loyalties to either partner in decision making, even if that means that managers must be recruited from the outside. (The general manager can come from either one of the venture's owners if the manager can maintain a neutral attitude and can win the confidence of all owners. However, since it is often difficult to persuade the other owners to trust a manager that comes from one partner, a more radical solution is often needed.) To combat the problems of split loyalties, some firms close the revolving door (thereby focusing a venture manager's attention on the venture's problems). Some firms hire talented outsiders—with loyalties to neither owner—to lead the venture and hold its critical jobs if they cannot close the revolving door.

With time and success, ventures develop their own management teams and assert their independence. Employees from each owner are still needed if the venture's activities are to be coordinated with those of its owners' because it is helpful for the venture to have someone on hand who knows the corporate people and where to go to get things done. It is helpful to have employees on hand who can call in old favors—as when the venture needs something pushed through its owner's organization—to make day-to-day operations of the venture run smoothly. But the message-carrier does not have to be the president of the venture.

A Serpent in Our Bosom

When the venture managers become more loyal to the venture than to the owners, conflicts with the owner's personnel are inevitable, especially when owners have encouraged the development of a guerilla mentality on the venture managers' part because of their own past treatment of them. In many cases, the venture has been an underdog. Its management team started as groups of rag-tag people sent from the owners to make the venture succeed. With time, this management team develops a closeness because they are the black sheep of their respective owner firms and receive little respect from them as the venture's managers. For example, the venture may have operated for a decade but the owners' managers still misspell and mispronounce the venture's name. Perhaps the venture's organization has been kept lean (or understaffed) while important decisions are made at owners' headquarters.

Despite these deterrents, the venture's management team may thrive (sometimes to the chagrin of the venture's sponsors). When managers within owner organizations finally realize that their venture has grown into an independently minded entity with its own markets and its own priorities, their feelings of alienation are scarcely surprising. After all, the venture may have occupied a corner on one floor of its owner's sixty-story office complex for years, for example, and its revenues may have been a pittance when compared with those of its owners. Suddenly the venture is stealing top management talent from its owner and competing for resources. Moreover, going back to an owner firm that resembles a paramilitary organization after a decade of autonomy rarely appeals to the venture's "black sheep" managers.

A Family of Ventures. As a venture matures, its managers often want freedoms, such as the freedom to enter into new ventures in its own right. (If the venture is allowed to forge its own joint ventures, its experienced venture managers make excellent overseers of the subsequent joint ventures because they know what works and which policies owners impose that make a venture's manager impotent.) Whether owners permit their ventures' managers to go to the stock market in the ventures' own right, develop competing facilities, or form their own ventures depends very much on what owners want from their alliance. Some firms' managers asserted that a joint venture should be terminated as soon as its goal is attained (project-by-project basis). Other managers favor cascades of ventures (if appropriate) and will let their ventures develop into autonomous entities.

Overcoming Impasses

Managers of owners' firms noted that many mistakes common to starting any new business are made with joint ventures. These include underfinancing the venture, choosing the wrong management team, defective technology, and other mistakes that affect any new business unit adversely. But joint ventures create a unique problem due to their shared ownership; disagreements among the owners halt the venture's progress. Conflicts between owners are a natural part of daily life because the interests of owners in joint ventures are rarely identical, yet somehow they must be managed.

Joint ventures that rely on the personal friendship of top executives to resolve owners' disputes are in a highly unstable position. When the joint venture owners reach a crossroads where decisions cannot be made unanimously, it often is time to unearth the legal documents to see what the lawyers agreed on when they created the venture.

Decision making is cumbersome in a joint venture. It requires a different mentality on the part of *owners* to make a venture work. Owners' managers reported that they became frustrated when they found it more and more difficult to get something done quickly. They could not simply call down to the venture to tell its managers that another 10 percent of a certain output was needed, for example, or to do this or to do that if the venture was jointly-owned. An arm's length relationship with a jointly owned venture means that negotiations with the other decision makers are needed, especially if both owners draw outputs from the venture.

Such restraints on an owner's autonomy are especially difficult for managers within firms that instinctively overmanage their subsidiaries and for managers that are unaccustomed to techniques for managing cooperation. A regular flow of requests from owners' managers to the venture's managers for figures, status reports, and other information fairly overwhelms the venture managers, especially if the joint venture is small and the inquiring owner is large. When frustrated managers in sponsoring firms slam against the constraints of the matrix organization they created for monitoring their venture, they do not change their control mechanisms. Instead, they layer in more and more people and procedures to solve their personality conflicts with the ventures' managers or with their partners by *buffering them* from direct contact with them. As the situation grows more hidebound, owners lose track of the original benefits that motivated the venture's formation.

How do managers within sponsoring firms break out of this quagmire? Some firms prefer to negotiate as they transact business together on new subjects. Since they cannot foresee everything the venture will face and the success requirements of the venture's industry change so rapidly as to make the venture's products obsolete before owners' lawyers can write a contract to cover all contingencies, partners simply trust each other when they reach an impasse. Or owners give the venture's managers more authority and autonomy. But other managers from sponsoring firms pull their venture even closer to their firm's ongoing activities and run the venture as a part of their regular management responsibilities. Some owners' managers relied on the close personal friendships of their respective chief executive officers to resolve disputes. Other managers simply trash the joint venture when managing it becomes too difficult.

Clinging Owners. Managers that draw their ventures closer often believe that firms cannot expect to set up ventures, delegate their management to a venture team, walk away from them, and expect everything to run without a hitch. Some managers believe that their joint venture needs constant supervision and intervention from them in order to ensure that joint-venture managers know what their owners want. Some managers are very involved in their venture's activities to ensure that the technology partner, for example, is spending enough time, money, and effort to find the best technology for the venture or that the marketing partner is doing a good job of distributing the venture's outputs. When managers within owner firms insinuate themselves so deeply in their venture's day-to-day activities, the role remaining for the venture managers is primarily that of a caretaker.

"Hands-Off" Owners. Managers from sponsoring firms that give their ventures more authority and autonomy often believe that the fatal flaw in many joint ventures is that owners are not prepared to let the venture live its own life. "Hands-off" managers tend to believe that if the venture is run on a day-to-day basis by its owners' managers, it is doomed to failure. Moreover, they argue that the venture's managers must have control of the venture's whole business activities and all of the assets needed to do its job. Successful ventures should stand on their own, they argue, and owners that will not transfer salient assets to the venture are creating their own nightmare of interface problems with the joint venture's managers.

Letting Go. If managers in sponsoring firms can acknowledge that the venture must eventually evolve into a stand-alone, independent entity with a life of its own, they can manage this transition with greater ease. Maturation and self-sufficiency are not grounds for its owners to abandon the venture or deprive it of the sustenance that any fledgling needs. In order for a joint venture to survive (even if that means it will eventually become a competitor of its owners), high-level attention is needed from the chief executive officers of its owners, from its board members, from owners' financial officers, and from other functional heads in the owner firms. Unless this attention is given with statesmanlike, nonparochial skills, another source of conflict will erupt.

Managers from sponsoring firms who were on both sides of the question of venture autonomy recognize that owners' interests and desires regarding their joint venture will diverge with time, particularly if industry conditions (and thus profitability) deteriorate. Some firms negotiate management control buy-out arrangements, whereby one owner maintains operating control until the products of their joint venture generate enough income (using a prespecified formula) to purchase the other firm's equity position. When the minority owner's equity position reaches 80 percent (or a similarly high plateau) for example, it takes operating control from the other owners. Such arrangements help to ease the transition problems associated with joint-venture termination because they ensure that the surviving operator is committed to the joint venture's success. The high threshold before letting go ensures that the venture is healthy.

Boards of Directors

It is important to select the right people to serve on the venture's board of directors to oversee its activities. In addition to possessing competent management and diplomatic skills, directors need time to follow up on the activities of the venture. Although a few ventures were examined that attribute their success to their owners' willingness to leave them alone, these ventures are exceptions. Most ventures need more than just cash to succeed, and the closer their activities are to those of their owners, the more they need day-to-day contact with their owners' representatives.

Excessive coordination could unduly shelter ventures, making them unfit to solve problems on their own. (During one interview, for example, a management director responded to five telephone questions from the president of his firm's joint venture. The venture's managers had little or no autonomy concerning operating decisions and at least one of the venture's owners expected its life span to be short.)

As chapter 6 notes, managers within owner firms can become jealous of ventures that they regard as being their firm's horizontal competitors. Owners of successfully coordinated, horizontally related joint ventures identify pressure points in product development activities that will require close coordination between owner and venture well in advance of the competitive conditions that make them necessary. Then they choose the venture's board of directors carefully to avert areas of potential conflicts. Most joint-venture board members are in positions that are functionally related to the venture's activities, ensuring that they have the knowledge to coordinate owner and venture. Managers suggested that these board members should not be too highly placed within the owners' firms if the venture is still young. Executives in foreign firms with ventures in the United States suggest that contacts with the venture in addition to the management board are needed. For example, small offices should be established near the venture because the venture's managers will pay more attention to the viewpoints that they encounter most frequently and understand most clearly when making policy decisions.

Evaluating Joint-Venture Performance

Managers in sponsoring firms and ventures alike recognize that ventures are very complex to manage, that the probability of joint-venture stability is pretty low, and that the U.S. track record of domestically based joint ventures is not good. Moreover, they recognize that every joint venture is unique because of the many possible ways in which firms might combine as well as the diversity of the owners themselves. Thus, attempts to make any two joint ventures work under identical constraints in time, size, profitability, and so on will probably yield very different results. Nevertheless, many managers realize that ventures are becoming increasingly important as a strategy option for their firms. Accordingly, they are learning how to make them work.

When ventures become of increasing strategic importance to their owners, the venture's information-reporting systems must be separated from those of its owners in order to facilitate better measures of its activity, free and clear of commingling with information about its owners' activities. Without such information, it is impossible to ascertain whether the venture is in good health. Allocations of costs, such as those of shared personnel salaries or other shared assets are frustrating, but these practices must change over time as the venture's relationship with its owners evolves.

Are joint ventures overrated in their usefulness? Managers suggested that any evaluation of joint-venture performance depends on the joint venture's purpose. If firms can do everything themselves equally well without partners and are blessed with infinite cash resources, there is no need for them to form joint ventures. The problems of coordination between owner and venture are formidable, and they rarely outweigh the benefits managers expect to receive through cooperation.

A more realistic vision of joint ventures is needed in order for them to be used effectively by most U.S. firms. Ventures are formed to permit owners to make smaller investments in risky projects than they would otherwise have to tackle on their own. Managers in sponsoring firms hope that the rate of return from cooperation will be the same as if they had invested a larger amount alone. If they are lucky, their returns on investment are higher than going it alone while their ticket to entry is smaller (due to their pooled resources). In addition, their firm is exposed to less risk. The net effect of the risk-return tradeoff makes many joint-venture owners better off than if they ventured alone.

Joint ventures are a transitional form of management—an intermediate step on the way to something else. Since ventures are a means to an end, their owners need to create a system of incentives among their respective managers—both as partners and as owners—to cooperate in ventures. Acquisition is usually a zero-sum game, but joint ventures can be a nonzero-sum game if firms are trying to cooperate, not trying to coopt their partners. The fact that the knowledge, products, or other necessary resources are obtained through a joint venture (rather than through an outright acquisition) matters less in determining whether an activity was successful than whether the relationships among the people who operate the venture were amiable enough to attain its objectives. The U.S. joint-venture success rate has been improving as more firms apply creative solutions to their old ideas concerning how long ventures must last, who must be the operator, and what each player should bring to the party. There is more profit available through joint ventures because of scale economies, because of integration economies from better balances between adjacent stages of production, and because of other cost savings from pooled resources that reduce the total cost of doing business, and U.S. firms must learn to exploit these economies. From a wealth-creating partner's perspective, the joint venture always offers an opportunity to improve on what firms can do alone. When managers have cracked the secret of how to maneuver within them, they are sold on the idea of joint-venture strategies as a means to attain successful performances for their firms.

Appendix:
Cooperative Strategy Alternatives

The strategy alternatives sketched in table 1–1 are discussed here with respect to their benefits and costs. Key issues that managers must distinguish in choosing a cooperative strategy include: (1) owners' abilities to cope with diverse management controls and integrating mechanisms; (2) time required to complete strategic mission; (3) autonomy required for the venture to compete effectively; and (4) whether synergies, technology transfers, exposure to innovative practices or other activities requiring numerous, multilevel owner–venture contacts are intended. In brief, managers should be realistic in assessing their firm's motive for cooperating and in how they intend to manage their firm's relationship with the venture.

Joint ventures are no panacea; if managers cannot stimulate innovative behaviors using the full-equity ownership alternatives (developed below), they will do *no better* in ventures, especially if they also expect to rule them with an iron hand. Distasteful as it may be, some firms would do well to accept a passive managerial role in exchange for their skills, patents, and personnel contributions and let another team run their joint venture.

Alternatives Involving Full-Equity Ownership

Mergers or Acquisitions

This category is included to offer a robust treatment of alternatives. Some firms will *not* cooperate with others in developing new skills, penetrating new markets, or attaining other objectives. They will purchase the resources and knowledge that they desire (or will develop them in-house), assuming they are available. Unfortunately for these firms, some assets and skills are not for sale and some risks are too large to shoulder alone. Even if firms devoted their full energies to achieving some tasks, they would need the assistance of outsiders to succeed. Acquisitions are not a solution to all strategic problems.

Some managers may prefer fully owned ventures because they enjoy being in charge of large and complex projects, or they may consider shared ownership (and authority) to be too cumbersome to be effective. Many managers believe that wholly owned ventures are less likely to fail than partially owned ones, and they expect wholly owned ventures to provide them with maximum returns (as well as the highest degrees of secrecy). If a venture is fully owned, they reason, their firms need not share their unique competitive edge with outsiders. If they cannot buy the skills they seek from outsiders, the managers of such firms are undaunted. Their preferences for full ownership lead them to believe that they can *develop* the needed skills in-house themselves if they cannot buy them.

Internal Venturing

Use of internal venturing also assumes that managers prefer to control expansions, innovations, diversifications, or other strategic investments *alone* for reasons outlined above. But this option recognizes that the dominant cultures of some firms are poor incubators for entrepreneurial ideas. In this strategy option, managers who recognize that their employees' good ideas are not getting to the marketplace create internal venturing units. They hope that by supporting entrepreneurial ideas and keeping these business units out of the firm's mainstream, their personnel will be able to create a regular menu of innovations. Unfortunately, successful entrepreneurial ideas become mainstream issues quickly so they must run faster and faster just to keep up with competitors that may be using joint ventures effectively. Moreover, entrepreneurial employees often want equity in the ideas they develop. Soon managers find they must create equity-sharing programs to prevent such employees from starting their own firms. Before they recognize what has happened, managers find that their firms have entered into joint ventures with their employees in order to keep their innovations in-house.

Internal venturing is like venture-capital activities by outside investors in the sense that capital (sometimes managerial assistance and advice as well) are entrusted to the start-up businesses. Investors could adopt a "hands-off" attitude regarding the start-up venture, or they could foster its development by actively intervening in the start-up firm's decisions.

Whether funding comes from corporate sponsors or from venture capitalists, the outcome is similar. As the venture develops and incurs expenses, somebody must pay the piper if it succeeds. Corporate investors will expect their ventures to generate cash and other internal, competitive, and strategic benefits for the firm. Venture capitalists will expect their payoffs. Impatience from either financing source compounds the internal venture's difficulties in developing a position of long-term competitive advantage. Successfully integrating internal ventures with corporate owners will be as problematic as it will be for other shared-equity arrangements described below. (Recalling that strategic business units (SBUs) develop identities and competitive strategies that make them seek autonomy from corporate systems, provisions will be needed to ease start-up ventures into the corporate family if they are successful in serving their marketplace. Unless corporate management sends strong signals to the contrary, the attitudes of sister SBUs when it is time to integrate the new venture will be adversarial.)

Internal ventures have been used successfully by international firms to mediate between strong-willed managers in sister SBUs. For example, when General Electric sought to integrate electric iron manufacturing on a worldwide basis, it created internal ventures within its international sector to permit SBUs to share the benefits of a new technology as well as its risks and costs. Formal organizational arrangements to mediate between conflicting viewpoints, like the matrix form of organization structure, are other ways to attain the benefits of internal venturing.

Alternatives Involving Partial Ownership

Joint Ventures

Joint ventures offer shared returns with lower risks than if firms pursued their strategic objectives alone. Managers within ventures that include one *passive* owner allow the active owner to lead in decision making; managers must mediate between owners' viewpoints within ventures where owners are *actively* involved in the venture's activities. Indeed, if owners become too involved in formulating strategies for their ventures, cooperation becomes too unwieldy to govern, and will *not* be appropriate strategic responses within all settings.

A robust analysis of joint ventures considers owners' perspectives; and their concerns include: (1) *whether* they should cooperate (or not) and *when*; (2) *what type of partner* they want; (3) *who contributes what resources* and expects *what outputs* or other benefits in exchange; (4) how each owner's *contributions* (and receipts) *are valued;* and (5) how the *balance of power* is evaluated when asymmetries develop. It also considers the venture's perspective, and these concerns reflect the success requirements of the venture's industry. These include: (1) how to obtain or develop the *crucial resources,* skills, or other factors needed to become an effective competitor; and (2) how to gain the *autonomy* needed to compete effectively. Finally, a robust analysis of joint-venture strategies considers the dynamics of relationships between the players—owners and venture—in their protean triangle (or quadrangle).

In theory, the joint venture should create a superior competitor that can draw on the strengths of its two or more owners. Synergies (not to mention eugenics) should arise from such mutually beneficial contacts. In fact, the synergies and other benefits that chapter 2 enumerates must be consciously managed by all players if they are indeed to be realized.

Minority Investments

Minority investments do not create a new entity; investors purchase the equity of an ongoing firm, instead. Investments are made in ongoing firms who may possess skills or resources that investing firms wish to understand better. Minority investments can be a means of fortifying a fledgling supplier or other pioneering firm without acquiring them outright. Minority investments could be a form of venture capital, used where entrepreneurs have little interest in being acquired but need infusions of capital. (If larger firms tried to buy their firms, the founders and key personnel might resign, as in the example of many small, Silicon Valley types of firms.)

A minority investment by a larger firm may be the only way for the investing firms' managers to obtain the knowledge or access desired from smaller firms, as in the example of the genetic engineering firms. Like the internal venturing option (described above), issues concerning what level of *owner intervention* will be appropriate in operating decisions, how to manage *intrafirm relationships,* what *capabilities* (other than cash) investing firms might provide, and other issues must be resolved in order to make minority investment strategies effective.

Alternatives Involving No Ownership Control

Cooperative Agreements

Cooperative agreements refer to *nonequity* forms of cooperative strategies. These are a generic alternative to those activities where owners share equity, create a separate entity, or acquire one another. Cooperative agreements can be a variety of nonequity arrangements between two or more separate firms for the exchange of performances. Such agreements do not provide for jointly owned entities nor do they generally provide for future joint decision making beyond the life of their performances as equity ventures do.

In cooperative agreements, tasks are performed by cooperating firms within their respective facilities, as in the example of agreements to act as second-source vendor for a well-specified product. Partners control the cooperative agreement through contracts that specify product configurations, delivery schedules, price, or other terms. It is unlikely that skills are transferred from one partner to another in cooperative agreements, since the most efficient way to perform tasks may be to do them in the proficient partner's facilities and provide outputs to other partners. If knowledge or skills transfer *is* desired, another arrangement (such as *licensing*) may be more appropriate than cooperative agreements, especially where control of technology is central to a venture's well-being. In such cases, licensing partners must train licensees in the use of their processes and products or transfer skills and know-how in other ways.

Research and Development Partnerships

Research and development partnerships are agreements to fund research. Technological cooperation through research consortia offer firms an opportunity to accelerate their industries' rates of innovation.

In the past, the principal constraints on the widespread use of R&D partnerships in the United States had been those of antitrust policies. In general it had been feared that joint research ventures could harm competitive vigor and prevent independently conceived inventions from ever competing in the marketplace (a concern that could be overcome by running parallel research projects.

U.S. firms traditionally avoided such arrangements before their technological leadership was challenged; but relaxed federal antitrust guidelines concerning R&D partnerships (and concerns about being noncompetitive global players) now encourage greater use of joint licensing consortia. Federal research support—even among horizontal competitors (to form a horizontally related venture)—is no longer unusual. What is novel is the recent willingness among U.S. antitrust agencies to allow the formation of jointly owned entities like Microelectronics & Computer Technology Corp. that presumably will have a life of their own and hold property rights.

Under the terms of many new R&D partnerships, a general partner contracts with the user group (the consortium) to take or pay for a certain volume of the product in question (such as megabyte semiconductor chips), contingent only on meeting predetermined cost and performance specifications. The general partner contracts with appropriate laboratories to do the work that is necessary, using arm's length contractual arrangements. Funding is obtained by syndicating venture capital money from the private sector. (The investment is relatively low in risk, since commercial success is guaranteed in advance and since the best partners' laboratories are doing the research.)

When the product is developed, the general partner either licenses the technology back to the individual companies (the consortium) or manufactures the product for the consortrium to exploit scale economies and surge far down the experience curve. (The general partner also may hire an individual firm to do the manufacturing for the benefit of the group.) The consortium partners can obtain proprietary rights to the new technology without putting in any money because they are bound by take-or-pay contracts. Often the consortium's members' laboratories perform the development work that they wanted to do while being paid to do so by investors. Finally, if the general partner in the R&D partnership is a nonprofit organization, then the cash flow that accrues to it after paying off the limited partners will be available to fund second- and third-generation projects.[1]

Critics of these arrangements have argued that the patents granted to research consortia could constitute bottlenecks that might convey substantial bargaining power to the partners. Thus provisions for access to patents by nonmembers through licensing may become necessary if joint R&D partnerships are to become widespread.[2] But such licensing provisions may instead *retard* the use of R&D partnerships, especially in light of the preferences of many managers for control over their operations and over the technologies that give them competitive advantages.

Cross-licensing and Cross-distribution Agreements

Cross-licensing arrangements cover technology developed independently by separate firms for the same (or similar) products or processes. Firms trade licenses to gain knowledge about processes that other firms may have developed. *Cross-distribution* arrangements permit one firm to market the products of another in a specified geographic region. Firms sometimes trade product lines to offer each respective customer group a wide array of products. Cross-distribution agreements can be a way of forestalling entry into firms' home markets. Their use suggests that local firms possess sufficient bargaining power to control the autonomy of newcomers that seek market penetration (a point developed at length in chapters 3, 4, and 5).

The geographic limitations imposed by these swaps of technology, brand names, and other resources look like divisions of markets to some antitrust authorities. Accordingly, partners that form cross-licensing or cross-distribution agreements must be sensitive to local antitrust policies and accommodate them in their agreements as well as their implementation.

Joint Bidding Activities

A consortium of contractors who bid together for a job may subdivide it later (so that each firm has a separate contract with the customer for a portion of the work) or delegate it to one member to operate for the welfare of all consortium members. Offshore oil-exploration drilling ventures are an example of joint bidding activities that operate through a consortium. Although many joint bidding activities include some sort of binding agreement in the event that the bid is accepted, the duration of the venture could be quite brief. By contrast, other bidding consortiums do not provide for any ongoing commercial relationships after tasks have been subcontracted. (Customary agreements, friendships, and historical precedent sometimes supersede the need for binding agreements, especially in regions where managers are quite homogeneous in their outlooks.)

Joint bidding activities have become a structural characteristic of the offshore oil exploration industry, where joint activities include not only bidding arrangements but also unitization agreements, jointly owned pipelines (or production properties), crude oil exchanges, and processing agreements. The rules underlying such agreements provide for the protection of pioneers' risk-taking investments when new firms join the group. Latecomers cannot obtain access to the fruits of the joint bidding activity without paying some premium to compensate the original venturers.

Oil firms have so many joint activities that the terms of a typical contract are well understood (and accepted) by all players as being a standard that protects their interests fairly. Accordingly, oil firms have learned how to move in and out of ventures with minimum disruptions to their ongoing ativities, and some have learned to maximize the advantages of joint ventures so well that when these firms invested heavily in the petrochemicals industry, they used their knowledge of ventures to gain competitive advantages in that industry as well.

Notes

1. D. Bruce Merrifield, 1983. "Forces of Change Affecting High Technology Industries," *National Journal,* January 29: 253–256; "High Tech Companies Team Up in R&D Race," 1983, *Business Week,* August 15: 94–95; Kenneth E. Krosin, 1971. "Joint Research Ventures under the Antitrust Laws," *George Washington Law Review* 39(5): 1112–1140. The U.S. Department of Justice has challenged only three research coalitions in the last two decades and each involved significant collateral restraints that retarded innovation: (1) an automobile manufacturers' association was accused of deliberately delaying development and installation of emission control devices; (2) the Wisconsin Alumni Research Fund was charged with using grant-back licensing arrangements to acquire exclusive control over patents involving the Wurster process for coating pharmaceutical products; and (3) the Aircraft Association and twenty major aircraft firms were attacked due to their long-standing patent-pooling and cross-licensing agreements. See Ky P. Ewing, Jr., 1981, "Joint Research, Antitrust, and Innovation," *Research Management* 24(2): 25–29.

2. Kenneth E. Krosin, 1971, "Joint Research Ventures under the Antitrust Laws," *George Washington Law Review* 39(5): 1112–1140; Ky P. Ewing, Jr., 1981, "Joint Research, Antitrust, and Innovation," *Research Management* 24(2): 25–29.

Table A–1
Cooperative Strategy Alternatives

Full Ownership Control	Partial Ownership and Contractual Control	Contractual Control Only
Mergers (or acquisitions)	Operating joint ventures	Cooperative agreements
Internal ventures (and spin-offs to full business unit status)	Minority investments	R&D partnerships
		Cross-licensing or cross-distribution arrangements
		Joint activities

Notes

Chapter 1

1. Robert E. Taylor, 1984, "Joint Ventures Likely to Be Encouraged by Friendlier Attitude of U.S. Officials," *Wall Street Journal,* November 5:8; "Joint Ventures: Justice Becomes a Cheerleader," 1984, *Business Week,* November 19:48–49.

2. The industry studies that tested the framework of chapters 3, 4, and 5 are presented in Kathryn Rudie Harrigan, 1985, *Strategies for Joint Ventures* (Lexington, Mass.: Lexington Books).

3. Robert J. Ballon, ed., 1967, *Joint Ventures and Japan* (Tokyo: Sophia University); Paul Beamish and Henry W. Lane, 1982, "Need, Commitment and the Performance of Joint Ventures in Developing Countries," working paper (Toronto: University of Western Ontario); Business International, 1965, *Ownership Policies at Work Abroad* (New York: Business International); Business International; 1971, *European Business Strategies in the United States: Meeting the Challenge of the World's Largest Markets* (Geneva: Business International); Business International; 1972, *Recent Opportunities in Establishing Joint Ventures* (New York: Business International).

4. J. Peter Killing, 1983, *Strategies for Joint Venture Success* (New York: Praeger Publishers).

5. See S. E. Boyle, 1968, "An Estimate of the Number and Size Distribution of Domestic Joint Subsidiaries," *Antitrust Law and Economics Review* (1):81–92; J. L. Pate, 1969, "Joint Venture Activity, 1960–1968," *Economic Review* (Cleveland: Federal Reserve Bank of Cleveland) 16–23; J. Pfeffer and P. Nowak, 1976, "Joint Venture and Interorganizational Interdependence," *Administrative Science Quarterly* 21(3):398–418.; Jerome L. Duncan, 1980. "The Causes and Effects of Domestic Joint Venture Activity," Ph.D. diss., University of Florida; Roger W. Ferguson, 1981, "The Nature of Joint Venture in the American Manufacturing Sector," Ph.D. diss., Harvard University; and Sanford V. Berg, Jerome Duncan, Jr., and Philip Friedman, 1982, *Joint Venture Strategies and Corporate Innovation* (Cambridge, Mass.: Oegleschlager, Gunn & Hain) for patterns of partner linkages to progeny and relationships of partners to each other.

6. Henry W. Nichols, 1950, "Joint Ventures," *Virginia Law Review,* 36:425–459; Frederick M. Eaton, 1952. "Joint Ventures," *Antitrust Law Symposium 1952— Proceedings of the Fourth Annual Meeting, Section on Antitrust Law, New York State*

Bar Association 135–144; Walter H. E. Jaeger, 1960, "Joint Ventures: Membership, Types, and Termination," *American University Law Review* (9)2:111–129.

7. G. E. Hale, 1956, "Joint Ventures: Collaborative Subsidiaries and the Antitrust Laws," *Virginia Law Review,* 42:927–938; Michael Bergman, 1962, "The Corporate Joint Venture under the Antitrust Laws," *New York University Law Review,* 37:712–734; Paul Rand Dixon, 1962, "Joint Ventures: What Is Their Impact on Competition?," *Antitrust Bulletin,* 7(3):397–410.

8. Stanley E. Boyle, 1960, "The Joint Subsidiary: An Economic Appraisal," *Antitrust Bulletin,* 5(3):303–318; "Joint Ventures and Section 7 of the Clayton Act," 1962, *Stanford Law Review,* 14:777–799.

9. Boyle, "An Estimate of the Number and Size Distribution of Domestic Joint Subsidiaries."

10. Charles Baden Fuller and R. Hill, 1984, "Industry Strategies for Alleviating Excess Capacity: The Case of the Lazard Scheme for UK Steel Castings," working paper, London School of Business; Charles Baden Fuller, 1984; "The Economics of Closure and Industry Dynamics," working paper, London School of Business.

11. Kathryn Rudie Harrigan, 1976, "Antitrust Implications of the Data Communications Industry," M.B.A. thesis, University of Texas at Austin; Harrigan, *Strategies for Joint Ventures.*

12. Kathryn Rudie Harrigan, 1983, *Strategies for Vertical Integration,* (Lexington, Mass.: Lexington Books).

13. Michael E. Porter, 1980, *Competitive Strategy: Techniques for Analyzing Industries and Competitors* (New York: Free Press); Thomas Hout, Michael E. Porter, and Eileen Rudden, 1982, "How Global Companies Win Out," *Harvard Business Review* 60(5):98–108.

Chapter 2

1. Yair Aharoni, 1966, *The Foreign Investment Decision Process* (Boston: Division of Research, Graduate School of Business Administration, Harvard University); William A. Dymsza, 1972, *Multinational Business Strategy* (New York: McGraw-Hill); Stefan O. O. Gullander, 1975, "An Exploratory Study of Inter-Firm Cooperation of Swedish Firms," Ph.D. diss., Columbia University; G. Richard Young and Standish Bradford, Jr., 1977, *Joint Ventures: Planning and Action* (New York: Arthur D. Little and the Financial Executives Research Foundation).

2. Jeffrey Pfeffer, 1972, "Merger as a Response to Organizational Interdependence," *Administrative Science Quarterly* 17:382–394; Jeffrey Pfeffer, and P. Nowak, 1976, "Joint Ventures and Interorganizational Interdependence," *Administrative Science Quarterly* 21(3):398–418; Oliver Williamson, 1975, *Markets and Hierarchies: Analysis and Antitrust Implication* (New York: Free Press).

3. Peter Drucker, 1974, *Management: Tasks, Responsibilities, Promises* (New York: Harper & Row); James D. Hlavacek and V. A. Thompson, 1976, "The Joint Venture Approach to Technology Utilization," *ILEE Transactions on Engineering Management* EM-23(1):35–41; Hideki Yoshihara, 1971, "The Japanese Multinational," *Long Range Planning,* pp. 41–45; Sanford V. Berg and P. Friedman, 1980,

"Corporate Courtship and Successful Joint Ventures," *California Management Review* 22(2):85–91.

4. Robert J. Ballon, ed., 1976, *Joint Ventures and Japan* (Tokyo: Sophia University); Lawrence G. Franko, 1971, *Joint Venture Survival in Multinational Corporations* (New York: Praeger); John D. Daniels, 1971, *Recent Foreign Direct Manufacturing Investment in the United States: An Interview Study of the Decision Process* (New York: Praeger).

5. K. R. Harrigan, 1984, "Joint Ventures and Global Strategies," *Columbia Journal of World Business* 19(2):7–16.

6. J. Peter Killing, 1983, *Strategies for Joint Venture Success* (New York: Praeger).

7. Karen Kraus Bivens and Enid Baird Lovell, 1966, *Joint Ventures with Foreign Partners* (New York: National Industsrial Conference Board); I. C. MacMillan, 1980, "How Business Strategies Can Use Guerilla Warfare Tactics," *Journal of Business Strategy* 1(2):63–85; I. C. MacMillan, 1982, "Seizing Competitive Initiative," *Journal of Business Strategy* 2(4):43–57; I. C. MacMillan, 1983, "Preemptive Strategies," *Journal of Business Strategy* 4(2):16–26.

8. C. Kenneth Orski, 1980, "The World Automotive Industry at a Crossroads: Cooperative Alliances," *Vital Speeches* 47(3):89–93.

9. Jules Bachman, 1965, "Joint Ventures in the Light of Recent Antitrust Developments: Joint Ventures in the Chemical Industry," *Antitrust Bulletin* 10:7–23; Joseph F. Brodley, 1979, "Joint Ventures and the Justice Department's Antitrust Guide for International Operations," *Antitrust Bulletin* 24:337–356.

10. Anders Edström, 1975, "Acquisition and Joint Venture Behavior of Swedish Manufacturing Firms," working paper, University of Gothenburg; Jeffrey Pfeffer and Gerald R. Salancik, 1978, *The External Control of Organizations: A Resource Dependence Perspective* (New York: Harper & Row).

11. Estimates of the patterns between partners and between owner and venture business entities have varied substantially in the past. See Stanley E. Boyle, 1968, "An Estimate of the Number and Size Distribution of Domestic Joint Subsidiaries," *Antitrust Law and Economics Review* 1:81–92; J. L. Pate, 1969, "Joint Venture Activity, 1960–1968," *Economic Review* (Cleveland: Federal Reserve Bank of Cleveland), pp. 16–23; Jeffrey Pfeffer and Phillip Nowak, 1976, "Patterns of Joint Venture Activity: Implications for Antitrust Policy," *Antitrust Bulletin* 21(2):315–359; Roger W. Ferguson, Jr., 1981, "The Nature of Joint Ventures in the American Manufacturing Sector," Ph.D. diss., Harvard University. Boyle (1968) found that 44 percent of the joint ventures he studied were horizontal and less than 10 percent were unrelated or conglomerate diversifications. Pate (1969) found that nearly 50 percent of the firms forming joint ventures were already horizontally related; nearly 80 percent of the firms forming joint ventures from 1960 through 1968 were either horizontally or vertically related. Pate also found that more than 50 percent of the relationships between firms and their ventures in the joint ventures formed between 1960 through 1968 were vertical and more than 80 percent of the arrangements resulted in horizontal and/or vertical relationships between one or more partners and the joint venture. Pfeffer and Nowak (1976) found that 56 percent of the joint activity in their sample was undertaken between horizontally related firms.

In Ferguson's (1981) study, of the 145 joint ventures for which full information on SIC codes of owners and venture were available, the principal outputs of only thirteen were in the same three-digit SIC industry as *both* owners; less than 10 percent of the joint ventures represented no diversification on the part of at least one of the owners in Ferguson's study.

12. K. R. Harrigan, 1983, *Strategies for Vertical Integration* (Lexington, Mass.: Lexington Books).

13. W. J. Mead, 1967, "The Competitive Significance of Joint Ventures," *Antitrust Bulletin* 12:819–849; Joel Davidow, 1977, "International Joint Ventures and the U.S. Antitrust Laws," *Akron Law Review* 10:161–173; Frederick M. Rowe, 1980, "Antitrust Aspects of European Acquisitions and Joint Ventures in the United States," *Law and Policy in International Business* 12(2):335–368.

14. "Joint Ventures: Justice Becomes a Cheerleader," 1984, *Business Week,* November 19:48–49; Robert E. Taylor, 1984, "Joint Ventures Likely to Be Encouraged by Friendlier Attitude of U.S. Officials," *Wall Street Journal,* November 5:8; James T. Halverson, 1984, "Transnational Joint Ventures and Mergers under U.S. Antitrust Law," in *Proceedings: Fordham Corporate Law Institute* (New York: Bender).

15. Thomas F. Broden and Alfred L. Scanlon, 1958, "The Legal Status of Joint Ventures Corporations," *Vanderbilt Law Review* 11:689; Paul Tractenberg, 1963, "Joint Ventures on the Domestic Front: A Study in Uncertainty," *Antitrust Bulletin* 8(4):797–841; John C. Berghoff, 1964, "Antitrust Aspects of Joint Ventures," *Antitrust Bulletin* 9(2):231–254; Donald F. Turner, 1980, "An Antitrust Analysis of Joint Ventures," unpublished manuscript, of counsel, Wilmer & Pickering, Washington, D.C.; Joseph F. Brodley, 1982, "Joint Ventures and Antitrust Policy," *Harvard Law Review* 95(7):1523–1590.

16. D. G. Turner, 1965, "Conglomerate Mergers and Section 7 of the Clayton Act," *Harvard Law Review* 78:1790; Gerhard A. Gesell, 1965, "Joint Ventures in Light of Recent Antitrust Developments: Joint Venture and the Prosecutor," *Antitrust Bulletin* 10(1 + 2):31–40; Jules Bachman, 1965, "Joint Ventures and the Antitrust Laws," *New York University Law Review* 40:651–671; Joachim Treeck, 1970, "Joint Research Ventures and Antitrust Law in the United States, Germany and the European Economic Community," *Journal of International Law and Politics* 3(1):18–55; K. P. Ewing, Jr., 1981, "Joint Research, Antitrust, and Innovation," *Research Management* 24(2):25–29.

17. Raymond Vernon, 1971, *Sovereignty at Bay: The Multinational Spread of U.S. Enterprise* (New York: Basic Books); Raymond Vernon, 1977, *Storm Over the Multinationals* (Cambridge, Mass.: Harvard University Press); Richard W. Wright and Colin S. Russel, 1975, "Joint Ventures in Developing Countries: Realities and Responses," *Columbia Journal of World Business* 10(2):74–80; Gene Gregory, 1976, "Japan's New Multinationalism: The Canon Giessen Experience," *Columbia Journal of World Business* 11:122–126; Richard W. Wright, 1977, "Canadian Joint Ventures in Japan," *Business Quarterly,* pp. 42–53.

18. Raymond Vernon and Louis T. Wells, Jr., 1976, *Manager in the International Economy* (Englewood Cliffs, N.J.: Prentice-Hall); G. Richard Young and Standish Bradford, Jr., 1976, "Joint Ventures in Europe—Determinants of Entry," *International Studies of Management and Organizations* 12(6):85–111.

19. L. G. Franko, 1976, *The European Multinationals* (London: Harper & Row).

20. Raymond Vernon, 1966, "International Investment and International Trade in the Product Cycle," *Quarterly Journal of Economics* 53(2):191–207; Peter P. Gabriel, 1967, *The International Transfer of Corporate Skills* (Boston, Mass.: Harvard Business School, Division of Research); Kathryn Rudie Harrigan, 1984, "Innovations by Overseas Subsidiaries," *Journal of Business Strategy* 5:7–16.

21. Howard Davis, 1977, "Technology Transfer through Commercial Transactions," *Journal of Industrial Economics* 26(2):161–175; Edward John Ray, 1977, "Foreign Direct Investment in Manufacturing," *Journal of Political Economy* 85(2):283–297.

22. W. Friedman and G. Kalmanoff, 1961, *Joint International Business Ventures* (New York: Columbia University Press); Anders Edström, 1975, "The Stability of Joint Ventures," working paper, University of Gothenburg; Jacques Picard, 1977, "How European Companies Control Marketing Decisions Abroad," *Columbia Journal of Business* 8(1):113–121.

23. Kenneth E. Krosin, 1971, "Joint Research Ventures under the Antitrust Laws," *George Washington Law Review* 39(5):1112–1140; Jerome L. Duncan, Jr., 1980, "The Causes and Effects of Domestic Joint Venture Activity," Ph.D. diss., University of Florida; U.S. Department of Justice, Antitrust Division, 1981, "Antitrust Guide for Joint Research Programs," *Research Management* 24(2):30–37; Raymond S. Sczudlo, 1981, "Antitrust Aspects of Shared EFT Systems," *Journal of Retail Banking*, pp. 23–29; Brodley, "Joint Ventures and Antitrust Policy."

24. Sanford Berg, Jerome Duncan, and Philip Friedman, 1982, *Joint Venture Strategies and Corporate Innovation* (Cambridge, Mass.: Oelgeschlager, Gunn & Hain).

25. Harold L. Marquis, 1964, "Compatibility of Industrial Joint Research Ventures and Antitrust Policy," *Temple Law Quarterly* 38(1):1–37; Lawrence G. Franko, 1971, "Joint Venture Divorce in the Multinational Company," *Columbia Journal of World Business* 4(3):13–22.

26. Brian Twiss, 1974, *Managing Technological Innovation* (London: Longman Group); Philip Friedman, S. Berg, and J. Duncan, 1979, "External vs. Internal Knowledge Acquisition: An Analysis of Research and Development Intensity and Joint Ventures," *Journal of Economics and Business* 31(2):103–110; J. Peter Killing, 1982, "How to Make a Global Joint Venture Work," *Harvard Business Review* 6(3):120–127.

27. Steffan Gullander, 1976, "Joint Ventures and Corporate Strategy," *Columbia Journal of World Business* 11:104–114.

Chapter 3

1. K. R. Harrigan and W. R. Newman, 1985, "Bases of Interorganization Cooperation: Propensity, Power, Persistence," working paper, Columbia University.

2. *Ibid.*

3. "Inertia barriers" are the exit barriers that delay or completely deter firms

from taking a particular action; see R. E. Caves and M. E. Porter, 1976, "Barriers to Exit," in *Essays in Industrial Organization in Honor of Joe S. Bain,* David P. Qualls and Robert T. Masson, eds. (Cambridge, Mass.: Ballinger), chapter 3; M. E. Porter, 1976, "Please Note Location of Nearest Exit: Exit Barriers and Strategic and Organizational Planning," *California Management Review* 19(2):21–33; R. E. Caves and M. E. Porter, 1977, "From Entry Barriers to Mobility Barriers," *Quarterly Journal of Economics* 91(May):241–262; K. R. Harrigan, 1980, *Strategies for Declining Businesses* (Lexington, Mass.: Lexington Books); K. R. Harrigan, 1980, "The Effect of Exit Barriers on Strategic Flexibility," *Strategic Management Journal* 1(2):165–176; K. R. Harrigan, 1981, "Deterrents to Divestiture," *Academy of Management Journal* 24(2):306–323; K. R. Harrigan, 1985, "Exit Barriers and Vertical Integration," 28(3):686–697.

4. Harrigan and Newman, "Bases of Interorganization Cooperation."

5. *Ibid.*

6. F. M. Scherer, 1965, "Firm Size, Market Structure, Opportunity, and the Output of Patented Inventions," *American Economic Review* 55:1097–1125.

7. Harrigan, *Strategies for Declining Businesses*; K. R. Harrigan, 1983, *Strategies for Vertical Integration* (Lexington, Mass.: Lexington Books); K. R. Harrigan, 1985, *Strategic Flexibility: A Management Guide for Changing Times* (Lexington, Mass.: Lexington Books).

8. Michael E. Porter, 1976, *Interbrand Choice, Strategy, and Bilateral Market Power* (Cambridge, Mass.: Harvard University Press).

9. G. A. Akerloff, 1973, "The Market for 'Lemons': Qualitative Uncertainty and the Market Mechanism," *Quarterly Journal of Economics* 84:488–500.

10. Anders Edström, 1975, "The Stability of Joint Ventures," working paper, University of Gothenburg; Jeffrey Pfeffer and G. R. Salancik, 1978, *The External Control of Organizations* (New York: Harper & Row).

11. Lawrence G. Franko, 1971a, "Joint Venture Divorce in the Multinational Company," *Columbia Journal of World Business* 4(3):13–22; Lawrence G. Franko, 1971b, *Joint Venture Survival in Multinational Corporations* (New York: Praeger), Anders Edström, 1975, "Acquisition and Joint Venture Behavior of Swedish Manufacturing Firms," working paper, University of Gothenburg; Steffan O. O. Gullander, 1975, "An Exploratory Study of Inter-Firm Cooperation of Swedish Firms," Ph.D. diss., Columbia University; Sanford V. Berg and Philip Friedman, 1980, "Corporate Courtship and Successful Joint Ventures," *California Management Review* 22(2):85–91; Sanford V. Berg, Jerome Duncan, Jr., and Philip Friedman, 1982, *Joint Venture Strategies and Corporate Innovation* (Cambridge, Mass.: Oelgeschlager, Gunn & Hain).

12. Karen Kraus Bivens and Enid Baird Lovell, 1976, *Joint Ventures with Foreign Partners* (New York: National Industrial Conference Board); Franko, "Joint Venture Divorce in the Multinational Company"; Franko, *Joint Venture Survival in Multinational Corporations*; Edström, "Acquisition and Joint Venture Behavior of Swedish Manufacturing Firms"; Gullander, "An Exploratory Study of Inter-Firm Cooperation"; Berg and Friedman, "Corporate Courtship and Successful Joint Ventures"; Berg et al., *Joint Venture Strategies*.

Chapter 4

1. Lawrence G. Franko, 1971*a*, "Joint Venture Divorce in the Multinational Company," *Columbia Journal of World Business* 4(3): 13–22; Lawrence G. Franko, 1971*b*, *Joint Venture Survival in Multinational Corporations,* (New York: Praeger); Anders Edström, 1975, "Acquisition and Joint Venture Behavior of Swedish Manufacturing Firms," working paper, University of Gothenburg; Steffan O. O. Gullander, 1975, "An Exploratory Study of Inter-Firm Cooperation of Swedish Firms," Ph.D. diss., Columbia University; Sanford V. Berg and Philip Friedman, 1980, "Corporate Courtship and Successful Joint Ventures," *California Management Review* 22(2):85–91; Sanford V. Berg, Jerome Duncan, and Philip Friedman, 1982, *Joint Venture Strategies and Corporate Innovation* (Cambridge, Mass.: Oelgeschlager, Gunn & Hain).

2. K. R. Harrigan, 1983, *Strategies for Vertical Integration* (Lexington, Mass.: Lexington Books).

3. K. R. Harrigan, 1985, *Strategic Flexibility: A Management Guide for Changing Times* (Lexington, Mass.: Lexington Books).

4. Howard Banks, 1981, "Partners of Necessity," *Europe* 23:31–33; Karen Kraus Bivens and Enid Baird Lovell, 1966, *Joint Ventures with Foreign Partners,* (New York: National Industrial Conference Board); Business International, 1971, *European Business Strategies in the United States: Meeting the Challenge of the World's Largest Market* (Geneva: Business International); Business International, 1972, *Recent Experiences in Establishing Joint Ventures* (New York: Business International); J. Peter Killing, 1982, "How to Make a Global Joint Venture Work," *Harvard Business Review* 60(3):120–127; J. Peter Killing, 1983, *Strategies for Joint Venture Success* (New York: Praeger); William J. Reid, 1971, *Interorganizational Coordination: A Review and Critique of Current Theory* (Washington, D.C.: U.S. Department of Health, Education and Welfare); Andrew H. Van de Ven, 1976, "On the Nature, Formation and Maintenance of Relations Among Organizations," *Academy of Management Review* 1:24–36; Malcolm W. West, 1959, "The Jointly Owned Subsidiary," *Harvard Business Review,* 37(4):32–39; D. A. Wren, 1967, "Interface and Interorganizational Coordination," *Academy of Management Journal* 10:69–81.

5. Anders Edström, 1975, "The Stability of Joint Ventures," working paper, University of Gothenburg; Gullander, "An Exploratory Study of Inter-Firm Cooperation of Swedish Firms."

6. Stanley Davis, 1976, "Trends in the Organization of Multinational Corporations," *Columbia Journal of World Business,* 11(2):59–71; Robert A. Pitts and John D. Daniels, 1984, "Aftermath of the Matrix Mania," *Columbia Journal of World Business* 29(2):48–55.

7. G. Richard Young and Standish Bradford, 1977, *Joint Ventures: Planning and Action* (New York: Arthur D. Little and the Financial Executives Research Foundation).

8. Peter Killing, 1980, "Technology Acquisition: License Agreement or Joint Venture," *Columbia Journal of World Business* 15(3):38–46; Killing, "How to Make a Global Joint Venture Work"; J. Peter Killing, 1983, *Strategies for Joint Venture Success* (New York: Praeger).

Chapter 5

1. Stephan Hymer and Peter Pashigian, 1962, "Firm Size and Rate of Growth," *Journal of Political Economy* 70:556–569; Y. Ijiri and H. A. Simon, 1964, "Business Growth and Firm Size," *American Economic Review* 54:77–89; Leonard W. Weiss, 1963, "Factors in Changing Concentration," *Review of Economics and Statistics* 45:70–77; S. I. Ornstein, J. F. Weston, M. D. Intriligator, and R. E. Shrieves, "Determinants of Market Structure," *Southern Economic Journal* 39:612–625; John W. Wilson, 1975, "Market Structure and Interfirm Integration in the Petroleum Industry," *Journal of Economic Issues* 9(2):319–336; F. E. Kydland, 1977, "Equilibrium Solutions in Dynamic Dominant Player Models," *Journal of Economic Theory* 15(2):130–136; Richard E. Caves and Michael E. Porter, 1978, "Market Structure, Oligopoly, and Stability of Market Shares," *Journal of Industrial Economics* 26:289–313; Michael E. Porter and A. Michael Spence, 1982, "The Capacity Expansion Process in a Growing Oligopoly: The Case of Corn Wet Milling," in *The Economics of Information and Uncertainty*, J. J. McCall, ed. (Chicago: University of Chicago Press); F. M. Scherer, 1979, "The Causes and Consequences of Rising Industrial Concentration: A Comment," *Journal of Law and Economics* 22:191–208; Moshe Justman, 1982, "Dynamic Demand Functions: Some Implications for the Theory of Firm and Industry Organization," Ph.D. diss., Harvard University.

2. Guy B. Meeker, 1971, "Fade Out Joint Venture: Can It Work for Latin America?," *Inter-American Economic Affairs* 24:25–42.

3. Thomas Hout, Michael E. Porter, and Eileen Rudden, 1982, "How Global Companies Win Out," *Harvard Business Review* 60(5):98–108.

4. W. H. Davidson, and D. G. McFetridge, 1984, "Recent Directions in International Strategies: Product Rationalization or Portfolio Adjustment," *Columbia Journal of World Business* 19(2):95–101.

5. R. Nelson and S. Winter, 1975, "Factor Price Changes and Factor Substitution in an Evolutionary Model," *Bell Journal of Economics* 6(2):466–486; Michael E. Porter, 1979, "The Structure Within Industries and Companies' Performance," *Review of Economics and Statistics* 61:214–227; B.C. Eaton and R. G. Lipsey, 1979, "Theory of Marketing Preemption: Barriers to Entry in a Growing Spatial Market," *Economica* 46:149–158; A. Michael Spence, 1979, "Investment Strategy and Growth in a New Market," *Bell Journal of Economics* 10(1):1–19; Richard E. Caves, Michael E. Porter, and A. Michael Spence, 1980, *Competition in the Open Economy* (Cambridge: Harvard University Press); Michael L. Hergert, 1983. "The Incidence and Implications of Strategy Grouping in United States Manufacturing Industries," Ph.D. diss., Harvard University.

6. R. B. Tennant, 1950, *The American Cigarette Industry* (New Haven, Conn.: Yale University Press): J. W. McKie, 1955, "The Decline of Monopoly in the Metal Container Industry," *American Economic Review* 45:499–508; C. F. Phillips, 1963, *Competition in the Synthetic Rubber Industry* (Winston-Salem: University of North Carolina Press); Michael S. Hunt, 1972, "Competition in the Home Appliance Industry, 1960–1970," Ph.D. diss., Harvard University; H. H. Newman, 1973, "Strategic Groups and Structure-Performance Relationship: Study with Respect to the Chemical Processing Industry," Ph.D. diss., Harvard University; Michael E. Porter, 1980, *Com-*

petitive Strategy: Techniques for Analyzing Industries and Competitors (New York: Free Press); William Harley Davidson, 1980, "Corporation Experience Factors in International Investment and Licensing Activities: Study of International Business," Ph.D. diss., Harvard University; Jeffrey Allen Hunker, 1982, "Structural Change in the U.S. Automobile Industry, 1980–1995," Ph.D. diss., Harvard Business School; John Alan Stuckey, 1982, "Vertical Integration and Joint Ventures in the International Aluminum Industry," Ph.D. diss., Harvard Business School; Kathryn Rudie Harrigan, 1985, "Vertical Integration and Corporate Strategy," *Academy of Management Journal* 28(2):397–425; Michael Tushman and Elaine Romanelli, 1985, "Organizational Evolution: A Metamorphosis Model of Convergence and Reorientation," *Research in Organizational Research* (vol. 7), (Greenwich, CT: JAI Press.)

7. Charles Carter and Bruce Williams, 1957, *Industry and Technical Progress* (London: Oxford University Press); E. Mansfield, 1962, "Entry, Gibrat's Law, Innovation and the Growth of Firms," *American Economic Review* 52:1023–1051; J. A. Menge, 1962, "Style Change Costs as a Market Weapon," *Quarterly Journal of Economics* 76:632–647; F. M. Scherer, 1967, "Research and Development Resource under Rivalry," *Quarterly Journal of Economics* 81:359–394; S. G. Winter, 1971, "Satisficing Selection and the Innovating Remnant," *Quarterly Journal of Economics* 85:237–261; E. Mansfield, 1968, *Industrial Research and Technological Innovation* (New York: Norton); D. F. Greer, 1971, "Product Differentiation and Concentration in the Brewing Industry," *Journal of Industrial Economics* 19:201–219; Summer Myers and Donald G. Marquis, 1969, *Successful Industrial Innovation* (Washington, D.C.: National Science Foundation); Chester R. Wasson, 1974, *Dynamic Competitive Strategy and Product Life Cycles* (Chicago: St. Charles); Jean Jacques Lambin, 1976, *Advertising, Competition and Market Conduct in Oligopoly Over Time* (Amsterdam: North Holland); Derek F. Abell, 1978, "Strategic Marketing," *Journal of Marketing* 42(3):21–26; W. S. Comaner and T. A. Wilson, 1979, "Advertising and Competition: A Survey," *Journal of Economic Literature* 17:453–476; A. Michael Spence, 1981, "The Learning Curve and Competitor," *Bell Journal of Economics* 12(1):49–70; Pankaj Ghemawat, 1982, "The Experience Curve and Corporate Strategy," Ph.D. diss., Harvard Business School; Marvin B. Lieberman, 1983, "Capacity Expansion, Firm Strategy and Market Structure," Ph.D. diss., Harvard Business School.

8. John D. Daniels, 1971, *Recent Foreign Direct Investment into the U.S.: An Interview Study of the Decision Process* (New York: Praeger).

9. Peter P. Gabriel, 1967, *The International Transfer of Corporate Skills* (Boston: Harvard Business School, Division of Research); Malcolm Baldrige, 1983, "Testimony on Government Policies to Promote High Growth Industries Based on New Technologies and to Increase United States Competitiveness," (Washington, D.C.: Committee on Finance, United States Senate, January 19).

10. Michael E. Porter, 1976, "Please Note Location of Nearest Exit: Exit Barriers and Strategic and Organizational Planning," *California Management Review* 19(2):21–33; Kathryn Rudie Harrigan, 1980, "The Effect of Exit Barriers upon Strategic Flexibility," *Strategic Management Journal* 1(2):165–176; Kathryn Rudie Harrigan, 1982, "Exit Decisions in Mature Industries," *Academy of Management Journal* 25(4):707–732; Kathryn Rudie Harrigan, 1981, "Deterrents to Divestiture," *Academy of Management Journal* 24(2):306–323; Kathryn Rudie Harrigan, 1983, "Exit

Barriers and Vertical Integration," in *Proceedings,* Kae Chung, ed. (Dallas: National Academy of Management Conference); Kathryn Rudie Harrigan, 1985, "Exit Barriers and Vertical Integration," *Academy of Management Journal* 28(3):686–697.

11. Joe S. Bain, 1956, *Barriers to New Competition* (Cambridge, Mass.: Harvard University Press).

12. Porter, "Please Note Location of Nearest Exit: Exit Barriers and Strategic and Organizational Planning"; Harrigan, "The Effect of Exit Barriers upon Strategic Flexibility"; Harrigan, "Exit Decisions in Mature Industries"; Harrigan, "Deterrents to Divestiture"; Harrigan, "Exit Barriers and Vertical Integration."

13. J. R. Galbraith, 1971, "Matrix Organization Designs—How to Combine Functional and Project Form," *Business Horizons* 14(1):29–40.; Stanley M,. Davis, 1976, "Trends in the Organization of Multinational Organizations," *Columbia Journal of World Business* 11(2):59–71; S. Davis and P. R. Lawrence, 1978, "Problems of Matrix Organizations," *Harvard Business Review* 56(3):131–142; E. Cascino, 1979, "How One Company Adapted Matrix Management in a Crisis," *Management Review* 68(11):57–61; W. G. Egelhoff, 1980, "Matrix Strategies and Structures in Multinational Corporations," paper presented before the Academy of International Business and Management, New Orleans; S. Berg, J. Duncan, and P. Friedman, 1982, *Joint Venture Strategies and Corporate Innovation* (Cambridge, Mass.: Oelgeschlager, Gunn & Hain).

Index

About the Author

K athryn Rudie Harrigan (D.B.A., Harvard; M.B.A., Texas; B.A., Macalester) is an associate professor of strategic management at the Columbia Business School of New York City. Her research interests include industry and competitor analysis, strategic management, turnaround management, competitive dynamics, global strategies, and business-government relationships. Her books, *Strategies for Declining Businesses* (1980), *Strategies for Vertical Integration* (1983), *Strategies for Joint Ventures,* and *Strategic Flexibility: A Management Guide for Changing Times* (1985) are published by Lexington Books.

Professor Harrigan received the General Electric Award for Outstanding Research in Strategic Management, presented by the Business Policy and Planning Division of the National Academy of Management, for her research on declining businesses, and their Best Paper Award in 1983 for her research on vertical integration (or make-or-buy decisions). She also won an IBM Research Fellowship in Business Administration and a Division of Research Fellowship at Harvard Business School, during her doctoral studies.

Professor Harrigan's consulting experience includes work on competitive strategy and strategic management for both private and public organizations. She has acted as consultant to strategic consulting firms, as well. She is a founding memeber of the Strategic Management Society and appears each autumn on their international programs.

Professor Harrigan writes for and serves on the board of editors of the *Academy of Management Journal,* the *Strategic Management Journal,* and the *Journal of Business-Strategy.* She is an ad hoc reviewer for and frequent contributor to the *Academy of Management Review.* Her articles have also appeared in the *Harvard Business Review, Long Range Planning, Boardroom Reports, Executive Woman,* and the *Proceedings* of the National and Regional Meetings of the Academy of Management.